Franco

General Francisco Franco, also called the Caudillo, was the dictator of Spain from 1939 until his death in 1975. His life has been examined in many previous biographies. However, most of these have been traditional, linear biographies that focus on Franco's military and political careers, neglecting the significance of who exactly Franco was for the millions of Spaniards over whom he ruled for almost forty years.

In this new biography Antonio Cazorla Sánchez looks at Franco from a fresh perspective, emphasizing the cultural and social over the political. Cazorla Sánchez's *Franco* uses previously unknown archival sources to analyse how the dictator was portrayed by the propaganda machine, how the opposition tried to undermine his prestige, and what kind of opinions, rumours and myths people formed about him, and how all these changed over time. The author argues that the collective construction of Franco's image emerged from a context of material needs, the political traumas caused by the Spanish Civil War (1936–1939), the complex cultural workings of a society in distress, political manipulation, and the lack of any meaningful public debate. Cazorla Sánchez's *Franco* is a study of Franco's life as experienced and understood by ordinary people; by those who loved or admired him, by those who hated or disliked him, and more generally, by those who had no option but to accommodate their existence to his rule.

The book has a significance that goes well beyond Spain, as Cazorla Sánchez explores the all-too-common experience of what it is like to live under the deep shadow cast by an always officially praised, ever present, and long-lasting dictator.

Antonio Cazorla Sánchez is Professor of History at Trent University, Canada. He specializes in twentieth-century dictatorships and is author of six books on Franco's Spain, and several chapters in books and articles. His previous publications include *Fear and Progress: Ordinary Lives in Franco's Spain, 1939–1975* (2009).

Routledge Historical Biographies

Series Editor: Robert Pearce

Routledge Historical Biographies provide engaging, readable and academically credible biographies written from an explicitly historical perspective. These concise and accessible accounts will bring important historical figures to life for students and general readers alike.

In the same series:

Franco

The biography of the myth

Antonio Cazorla Sánchez

Routledge
Taylor & Francis Group

LONDON AND NEW YORK

First published 2014
by Routledge
2 Park Square, Milton Park, Abingdon, Oxon OX14 4RN

Simultaneously published in the USA and Canada
by Routledge
711 Third Avenue, New York, NY 10017

*Routledge is an imprint of the Taylor & Francis Group, an informa
business*

British Library Cataloguing in Publication Data
A catalogue record for this book is available from the British
Library

Library of Congress Cataloging in Publication Data
Antonio Cazorla Sánchez
Example of a typical title and sub-title
Contents
1. Category. 2. Category. 3. Category.
LVVPD number

ISBN: 978-0-415-47172-5 (hbk)
ISBN: 978-0-415-47173-2 (pbk)
ISBN: 978-0-203-79615-3 (ebk)

Typeset in Garamond
by Taylor and Francis Books

Printed and bound in Great Britain by
TJ International Ltd, Padstow, Cornwall

Contents

List of plates

Acknowledgements

Research for this book was made possible by a generous grant awarded by the Social Sciences and Humanities Research Council of Canada. The people at Routledge were most helpful and understanding. Robert Pierce read my early drafts and made very insightful comments and suggestions. Paulette Bak, Robie Loomer, Ryan Perks, Oscar Rodríguez Barreira, Sofía Rodríguez López, Adrian Shubert, and other dear friends worked hard to force me to be both clear and concise. María and Antonio explained Franco to me. Céline, Mélina, Yasmin and Sofía are a constant source of inspiration.

Introduction

A different type of biography

This book goes into print one hundred years after a young officer named Francisco Franco Bahamonde (1892–1975) went to war in Morocco in 1912. At the beginning of the Spanish Civil War (July 1936 to March 1939), he became the commander of the colonial Army and transferred it to mainland Spain in order to destroy the democratic Second Republic (1931–1939). During that conflict, he became the leader of the whole rebel army, and then dictator of Spain, assuming the title of Caudillo or Leader. He stayed in power until he died—in a hospital bed—in 1975. His personal and political life has since been described in detail in many excellent biographies.[1] Yet the significance of who, exactly, Franco was for the millions of Spaniards over whom he ruled still needs to be explained. Seeking to address this neglected aspect, this book is a study of the evolution of Franco's public image as experienced and understood by Spaniards; by those who loved or admired him, by those who hated or disliked him, and more generally, by those who had no option but to accommodate their existence to his rule. Put simply, the following pages will describe what was said about Franco, when it was said, by whom, how this message changed over time, and how the historical context in which this message developed shaped ordinary people's perceptions of the dictator's image.

Franco's name came to prominence, in Spain as in the rest of the world, in July 1936. From this moment to the present, it has been impossible to avoid him when talking of Spain's twentieth-century history. Politically and culturally speaking, Spain and Europe in the 1930s were very different from what they are today: Fascism ruled some countries, Fascist and authoritarian movements achieved an extended following in many others, and, in general, democracy was on the defensive. In most of Western Europe, this situation drastically changed after 1945, while the Spanish political system—which is to say the Franco dictatorship—remained basically intact. As this book will show, the contradiction between a democratic Europe and an ever-authoritarian Spain led to European (and more generally Western) uneasiness concerning the existence of the Franco dictatorship. Behind this uneasiness stood Europeans' own insecurities about the strength of their democratic values. Franco reminded Europeans of the historical skeletons that lurked— and not so deeply—in their closets.

For all his international notoriety, Franco was the Spaniards' problem. Inside Spain, the issues at stake were real, not just a matter of political opinion or historical memory. Unlike for the citizens of a free Europe, what Franco did or said made a difference in all Spaniards' lives. Moreover, the Caudillo had more power than any other political leader in recent Spanish history. This power brought with it a terrible price, beginning with the number of lives lost. Franco cannot be compared—either in scale or intentions—to Hitler, Stalin or Mao, but he was a mass killer nonetheless. Yet, as with these other dictators, many people, both inside and outside of Spain, thought (and still think) of the Caudillo as a hero: a stern man, perhaps, but essentially a good, well-meaning ruler. How is this possible? Why, when and by whom were these opinions held? Did this image change? If so, when and why? The moral implications of these questions are evident; the historical relevance, in terms of explaining both Spain's and Europe's history, should be too.

Most narrated lives share a common element: they include a key moment or reason—often several—that explain why this particular life has become extraordinary, and thus deserves to be told. Yet the fact that it is decided that a person has done something important exposes all biographers to the danger of projecting what happened in the future as a necessary, unavoidable development of the past. This, of course, can also be an indication of the author's biases. The solution to this is to try to avoid the classic, power-centred "great man" (and less often "great woman") narrative and to write a biography that matches as closely as possible the options, ideas, actions and images of the personage as he or she and their contemporaries experienced them; and also, to illuminate how these factors have been explained and re-interpreted after the fact.

This book is a combination of traditional biography, together with social as well as cultural history. It is based on the belief that historical narratives continuously change, and that biographies of historical figures are no different: for although lives are lived only once, their posthumous significance can be re-interpreted many times. These transformations imply the discovery of new purposes and roles for some figures, even discarding previously relevant interpretations for them and for their contemporaries. This is both a privilege and a duty for each new generation of historians. Revising established ideas and questioning the significance of historical personages is part of the process of discovering who we are as a society. Yet a relatively new element in this process of re-interpreting the past can be seen in the fact that historians are increasingly reluctant to present themselves as independent voices removed from any specific socio-political context. Reflecting the criticisms elaborated by feminist, post-colonial and post-modern thinkers, historians are now much more likely to let the narratives they write reflect their own background, specific interests and biases. This is a matter of intellectual honesty that, among other things, helps to explain why this biographer has decided that the present subject—the life of Francisco Franco—is worthy of analysis.

No biographer is independent of the subject he or she analyses, and it should be seen as a matter of intellectual honesty to inform—if you like, to warn—the reader of their own personal biases. I, the author of this biography of Francisco Franco, have no personal sympathy whatsoever for my subject. However, this was not always so. I am now a Spaniard teaching history in Canada, and identify myself with an anti-Fascist and anti-Communist social-democratic tradition that embraces both personal freedom and social justice as the best, most noble and rational solutions to humanity's problems. Born in 1963 to a working-class family from Almería, then a very poor province of Spain, I was twelve years old when the dictator died. At that time, I, like millions of other Spaniards, believed the Caudillo was a gentle old man who had achieved the best possible solutions to Spain's problems. In spite of having the day off from school, I still remember how sad I was on the morning of 20 November 1975. Certainly, I had been politically indoctrinated in school, as well as in the regime's youth organization, to believe in Franco's goodness.

But there were other factors that influenced my ideas, and which I consider stronger than the official institutions' indoctrination. The main factor behind my thinking at the time was a political pessimism, shared by my family and by millions of ordinary Spaniards, about my country's fitness to live in a democracy. In 1975, millions of Spaniards, probably the majority, were more concerned with preserving peace than with acquiring political liberty, and were happy enough with the idea that, thanks to Franco's peace, life had been getting better since the early 1960s, after the horrendously long and hard post-war misery. The irony of this situation is that while we respected the dictator, in my family, and in millions of others, we held the regime in contempt because we often experienced its corruption, nepotism and callousness. We also rejected violence, either from the regime or from the opposition. However, our loyalties were not frozen in time because our reality and values were changing. As I have explained, I believe, with more detail elsewhere, the years prior to Franco's passing were characterized by the increasingly common use of a language of equality and freedom.[2] This process accelerated after 1975. The fact that the younger generation to which I belonged was far better educated than our parents made a difference, in our lives as well as theirs, and, of course, in the evolution of the country. Less than two years after the Caudillo's death, my family and I clearly identified with social-democratic ideas, and our opinion of the dictator has since completely changed.

After more than twenty years of studying the Franco regime I am convinced that the Caudillo was not a particularly gifted individual. I believe he was a self-promoting opportunist; and he was, more tragically, also a cruel man whose authoritarian rule caused an enormous amount of damage to Spain. Yet, it would be disingenuous to present his dictatorship solely from the point of view of the fully democratic and, in spite of recent economic and political problems, fairly successful Spanish (and European) society of the early twenty-first century. We need also to understand how people saw things throughout the different stages of the regime. If we ignore these aspects, readers today will find it difficult to see, for example, why Franco enjoyed such a high level of popularity. However, while one of the main ideas behind this book is that no dictatorial regime can survive for four decades without some form of support, this study does not forget the other tools that make possible a dictatorship's survival: personal interest, fear, relatively hard to explain contradictions, and lies. For example, in 1939 and afterwards many people saw themselves as material winners of the war, and Franco as the main guarantor of their interests; but while they fared well, millions of Spaniards, particularly in the post-war period, suffered not just hunger but starvation. The fear imposed by the Franco dictatorship has been explained in hundreds of books already. The numbers reveal only the beginning of vast personal and collective dramas: over 150,000 executed, hundreds of thousands charged and sent to prison, tortured, raped, robbed, dispossessed, marginalized and otherwise victimized.

Only recently have studies appeared detailing perhaps the most striking contradiction of Francoist rule: that such a man and his regime could gather widespread support. Nonetheless, I suspect that the degree of support for Franco or for his regime will remain a matter of permanent speculation, if only for the basic reason that it is not easy to study the evolution of popular opinion in a dictatorship for the very simple reason that people are not free to talk and no poll can reflect the real situation. Political opinion polls and dictatorships are mutually exclusive. In spite of this, most of the available studies agree that at least by the economically prosperous 1960s the majority of Spaniards had a positive, if rather passive, opinion of the dictator. Other historians, including this author, have argued that active and passive support for the Franco regime was clearly evident, and probably in the majority, at least since the materially harsh late 1940s.

Some readers may think that Franco's popularity was just a product of propaganda, and, of course, this book does not forget that dictatorships resort to lies, and that these lies often go uncontested. However, it would be erroneous to think that propaganda is an all-powerful tool with which to manipulate people. As this book will show, official propaganda worked far better when it coincided with people's interests, their hopes and fears, than when it ran against them. In this sense, this book demonstrates the existence of a widespread tendency amongst the post-war Spanish population to see Franco as a badly informed but essentially well-meaning ruler, and that this belief helped to make the regime's otherwise ridiculous claim acceptable to many Spaniards. The traumatic experience of the Civil War, and even more the fear that the country might descend once again into a renewed period of political violence, provided the context in which this propaganda would flourish.

One of the main myths created by Francoist propaganda—and bolstered by genuine popular hope— and one which is still believed by many Spaniards and foreigners today, is that Franco's rule was responsible for Spain's post-Civil War peace and subsequent economic success. Paradoxically, this myth gained currency in the 1940s, a period when the Spanish economy was crumbling and hunger and misery were widespread. As the reader will see, Franco, ignoring this unfolding catastrophe, was the leading proponent of the idea that the country was experiencing a material—not to mention a spiritual—rebirth. He pretended that his victory in the Civil War had brought security, prosperity and unity to the country for the first time in nearly two centuries. This was a dubious claim in the 1940s and 1950s, to be sure, but these ideas became more credible as the Spanish economy experienced its "miracle" of the 1960s. Peace and progress thus became the dictator's main source of political legitimacy; they were proof that Franco had always been right.

In June 1977, less than two years after Franco's death, Spain experienced its first democratic elections since February 1936. Democracy took root in the country rather quickly and strongly, and a great number of Spaniards changed their opinions of the dictator as a result. Yet many of the myths created by the regime survived among large segments of the population. For example, in 1994, after twelve years of Socialist Party government, a comprehensive poll conducted by the Centro de Investigaciones Sociológicas (CIS), Spain's official public opinion institute, revealed that 52.6 per cent of Spaniards claimed they had a negative image of the Franco regime, while 27.8 per cent had a positive one. A total of 24.4 per cent considered him "one of the best rulers of Spain in the twentieth century"; 58.1 per cent disagreed. Some 47.4 per cent thought that he had guaranteed peace in Spain; 38.1 per cent disagreed. In total, 27.1 per cent believed that he also modernized and developed the country; 52.3 per cent disagreed. A further 30.4 per cent agreed with the idea that he saved the country from communism; 43.4 per cent disagreed. Finally, 30.5 per cent considered Franco to be "a man of good intentions" who ignored whatever wrongdoing his collaborators might have done; 41 per cent disagreed. At the same time, only 15.9 per cent of Spaniards thought that if the country had been a democracy instead of a dictatorship it would now be worse off. Basically, these numbers reveal two crucial phenomena. First, nearly two decades after the dictator's death, almost half of all Spaniards still thought that Franco had brought peace to the country, and more than a quarter thought his rule had resulted in material progress. Second, on the one hand, many Spaniards had a much better opinion of the dictator than of his regime, yet on the other hand they had a highly ambiguous sense of his legacy.[3]

There are reasons for the persistence of Franco's positive image among many Spaniards. Between 1961 and 1974, and for the first time since 1936, life in Spain became much better for the majority of the population. The economy was booming (Spain's GDP growth was surpassed during this period only by Japan), people were buying refrigerators, television sets, washing machines, scooters and, increasingly, cars. Families were sending their children to university for the first time, most popular songs were about happiness (if they weren't frivolous interpretations of sadness), fashion was becoming less and less conventional, and young people were supposedly very different from, and evidently better-off than, their elders. Nowhere were progress and change more apparent than on the beaches of the country's coastal towns. People were receiving paid holidays, and had money to spend. Sunny Spain was presented as a happy country, visited by millions of tourists every year, each year more hopeful than the last. Tourists could see and experience Spain's prosperity with great places to stay, eat and have fun—even if they were democrats and loathed Franco. Spain, the Spanish Tourism (and Propaganda) Ministry claimed, was now "different". Many visitors certainly agreed. For many Spaniards, too, it seemed as if a promise had finally been fulfilled.

The main architect of this triumphant image of life under the regime was no other than Franco himself. In his 1969 televised

Christmas speech, the aging dictator, now looking increasingly like a benevolent grandfather, provided proof of Spain's progress under his command:

> In this decade there have been built 85 out of 100 of all cars that travel our streets and roads; there have been installed 60 out of 100 of all existing telephones and 1,175,000 new homes have been built. This means that in this decade about five million Spaniards have moved into their new homes. Regarding tourism, we have gone from little more than four million people who visited us in 1959, to 21 million tourists this year. The effort realized in educational matters at all levels has also been gigantic ... [4]

However, behind this carefree, optimistic façade, the trauma of the Civil War, as always, remained. Yet the meaning of the war, and the role Franco had played in it, were now presented very differently from how they had been thirty years before. History had not changed, but its interpretation—the selection of events and their meaning—had.

What never changed was the dictatorship's official vision of the circumstances and reasons for the birth of this new happy era. The year was 1936, and the reasons were Spain's imminent ruin under a catastrophic republic impregnated with chaos and revolution. But History, instead of delivering horror, was about to give birth to redemption. It all started on July 18, the day war was declared. Francoism would later make this date an official holiday. Many things happened that day, but for the regime's official memory the main event was an aircraft ride that began in the afternoon on Las Palmas de Gran Canarias (the Canary Islands) and ended the next morning in Tetuán, then Spanish Morocco. On this trip, Franco, the peerless hero of previous African wars, once again risked both his life and his career to save Spain. It had all occurred as if by providence: Franco was meeting his destiny.[5]

Under the dictatorship, there was no lack of witnesses to Franco's glory and purpose of mind. But probably the most qualified among them was a man who, by an irony of destiny in sunny and supposedly happy Spain, had been the head of the Spanish tourism department. His name was Luis Bolín y Bidwell. In 1967 he published a book called *Spain: the Vital Years*.[6] Bolín was no ordinary bureaucrat or politician. Thanks to his flawless grasp of English, he had been Franco's feared press secretary during most of the Civil War, until February 1938, and thereafter head of the tourism department until 1952. Finally, he served as an adviser to the Spanish Embassy in Washington until 1963.[7] He died in 1968. As his name indicates, there was British (and Swedish) blood in his veins. There were other British connections in Bolín's life, too; the book's prologue was written by none other than Sir Arthur Bryan, C.B.E., the well-known British popular historian, who was also an anti-Semite and one-time admirer of the Third Reich. This was no coincidence. Bolín belonged to a particular group of *haute* bourgeoisie Spaniards from Andalusia whose names and traditions have been linked to England since the eighteenth century, when families from that country started to settle in Jerez, Cádiz and Málaga to trade in the region's famous wines. They prospered and became large landowners and rich merchants. Their children were, and still are, educated in English, either by British nannies, in British boarding schools, or both. The result was a compact, interlinked group of people with a split cultural identity: conservative gentlemen and ladies in England, ruthless aristocratic masters in Andalusia. They became Franco's staunchest supporters, among other reasons because their lands, which had been expropriated by peasant unions, were saved by the rebels' victory in the Civil War. Victory in this part of the country had been swift, but repression, nevertheless, was extremely harsh.[8]

In his 1967 book Bolín recalled a story that had already attained canonical status as an orthodox account of the beginning of the Spanish Civil War, a moment that marked Spain's pivotal moment of salvation. The importance of this account derives from the fact that Bolín was a "witness", a certifier of that promise of progress, peace and happiness made by a tired yet sleepless hero and saviour on the eve of the conflict, Francisco Franco Bahamonde, and the moment of revelation was, as it could only be, July 18, 1936. The journey toward redemption had started on July 5, when Bolín, the London correspondent for the conservative monarchist newspaper *ABC*, had been contacted to hire an aircraft to fetch a mysterious traveller somewhere in Africa: "Somehow I felt that that hour had struck"; "I knew that only force could now save my country, and that the alternative to that force was Communism and chaos".[9] The mysterious passenger was Franco, who in "the Canary Islands was a virtual prisoner of the Republicans".[10] Money for this trip that "liberated" Franco—as well as money for much of the larger revolt that "liberated" Spain—came from Spain's richest man, Juan March, a former smuggler who became a banker who was then a fugitive from justice. Later he helped the British and the Americans during World War II, and made even more money doing so. In 1955, in collaboration with the Rockefeller and the Carnegie foundations, he created his own foundation, which finances scientific and cultural research to this day.

Franco's plane took off from Las Palmas shortly after 2 pm, on July 18, 1936. The travellers proceeded with caution. That night, crew and passengers rested in Casablanca. This city, rather than Tangiers, was chosen because in the latter city there was supposedly a "group of paid assassins" waiting for them with "pistols and sub-machine guns".[11] It was neither the first nor the last time that Franco's precious life had been supposedly threatened by killers (as the reader will see in Chapter 2). That night, during a conversation, or rather a monologue, which lasted until 2 am, Franco told Bolín about his dreams for Spain. For the Francoists this conversation would be retroactively seen as the first of many visions, predictions, prophecies and promises expressed by their Caudillo, and implemented during the next thirty-nine years. As Bolín has it, Franco:

> was then forty-three years old, well-proportioned and good looking [...] He was determined to make up for the years of misery and oppression which his countrymen had suffered under Republican rule [...] His ambition was to serve. All his thoughts were for the people. He wished to improve the lot of the working man and the position of the middle classes, both of which had so many times been deceived by republican promises, to increase their living standards and provide their sons with opportunities for education and advancement. He wanted to develop housing, industry, and agriculture. Franco knew that law and order would have to be enforced with a firm hand throughout the country. But he did not think this would be difficult, after peace had been restored. Much as

Spain would have to change if the nation was to progress, he also knew that the fundamental traditions of Spain had to be upheld.[12]

Always one step ahead of potential killers, not to mention French colonial authorities, the plane that carried Franco landed at Tetuán's Sania Ramel air base, not far from the headquarters of the Spanish Army in Morocco, at 7 am the next day, July 19. A group of rebel officers were waiting for him. The base commander, Major Ricardo de la Puente Bahamonde, Franco's cousin and childhood playmate, had been arrested the day before. He had been the last officer to remain loyal to the Republic in the whole North of Africa; summarily court-martialled, he was shot on August 4.[13] He did not live to see his cousin become the official head of the new regime less than two months later, on October 1, 1936.

But let us stop the story here, at the beginning of the narrative that has Franco arriving in Africa first to save Spain, and then to make it peaceful and prosperous. This 1967 account of the arrival of the saviour is of course plagued by the same omissions and lies that have always underpinned the dictatorship's official discourse. This is the story of terror and forced forgetfulness on which the regime was based, or, put differently, the contradictory perception of Franco as the man who employed terror yet also created the uneasy peace in which the country lived. Franco's Spain did not want, and indeed was not allowed, to face the past full on. This is why people such as Major de la Puente never appeared in Bolín's or other officially approved biographies or hagiographies of Franco. The executed cousin's name was excised from Spain's official record. His case was not exceptional, and belongs to the deep well of fear and forced silence on which Franco's image as the maker of both peace and belated progress rested. Indeed, this particular omission is part of a bigger lie: Francoist accounts of the war and the post-war period would systematically ignore the fate of the regime's victims; their names would be banned from the public sphere. In the story of Spain's redemption, as told by Bolín and many others, only the victors, and their deeds, not to mention the cause's martyrs, counted. As a result, in twenty-first-century Spain, more than 100,000 bodies of Franco's victims still lie in hundreds, if not thousands, of mass, often unmarked, graves.

There are many people, including prominent ruling politicians and officials, who see no problem with this situation (see Chapter 6). Those who speak of Franco's contribution to Spain's progress often forget or downplay such terror and its legacy.[14]

Bolín's version of events, and his analysis of what they meant, is just one example of the sort of narrative the reader will find in this book, as you are taken on a journey into Spain's not so distant past. In the process, the reader will learn what Spaniards said, thought, or were told about Franco and, just as significantly, the context in which those ideas took shape. In the end, the reader will understand how it was possible that a majority of people living in a country with so much misery, so many dark secrets and lies, and with so many unpunished crimes, often loved and respected their dictator. Finally, the reader will understand why to this day Franco's legacy remains the subject of so many contradictory opinions. It is a complicated story; but it is also a fascinating one.

Notes

1 The most detailed one being Paul Preston, *Franco. A Biography*, London, HarperCollins, 1993.

2 Antonio Cazorla Sánchez, *Fear and Progress: Ordinary Lives in Franco's Spain, 1939–1975*, Oxford, Wiley-Blackwell, 2010.

3 Alberto Reig Tapia, *Franco "Caudillo": Mito y realidad*, Madrid, Tecnos, 1995, pp. 79–81.

4 Francisco Franco Bahamonde, *Mensaje de Su Excelencia el Jefe del Estado Español en la Navidad de 1969*, Madrid, Ediciones del Movimiento, 1969, pp. 8–9.

5 Ángel Viñas, *La conspiración del general Franco y otras revelaciones acerca de una guerra civil desfigurada*, Barcelona, Crítica, 2011.

6 Luis Bolín, *Spain: The Vital Years*, London, Cassell, 1967.

7 A scathing snapshot of Bolín during the war can be found in Judith Keene, *Fighting for Franco: International Volunteers in Nationalist Spain During the Spanish Civil War, 1936–39*, London and New York, Leicester University Press, 2001, p. 67.

8 A terrifying account can be found in Francisco Espinosa Maestre, *La columna de la muerte. El avance del ejército franquista de Sevilla a Badajoz*, Barcelona, Crítica, 2003.

9 Bolín, *Spain*, pp. 10, 13.

10 Ibid., p. 13.

11 Ibid., p. 46.

12 Ibid., p. 48.

13 For Ricardo de la Puente's execution, see Preston, *Franco*, pp. 7, 151, 198.

14 See Antonio Cazorla Sánchez, "Revisiting the Legacy of the Spanish Civil War", *International Journal of Iberian Studies*, 21, 3, 2008: 231–246.

1 Military hero, 1912–1936

African fortunes

Francisco Franco's public persona, the military hero that we think we know, was constructed shortly after the Spanish Civil War began in July 1936, using elements of truth, to be sure, but also elements of false recollection and outright invention. The construction of this image was part of a wider process set in motion at the time by the propaganda apparatus of the nascent rebel state. This narrative was placed in the service of contemporary political and cultural needs, and in particular to serve the burgeoning cult of the Caudillo. The double process of re-interpreting and inventing Franco's life was not limited to manipulating the past by either creating events by selecting or removing them from their context. On the contrary, it also included erasing the memory of the people who made possible his meteoric rise through the ranks of the Army. These people had no place in what was intended to be a unique career pre-ordained by Providence, which led to the supreme moment of heroism: the beginning of the Civil War. Separating truth from fiction, this chapter explains the life and times of Franco, the military officer, before the birth of the myth.

Francisco Franco Bahamonde was born in 1892 into a military family in El Ferrol, then a remote naval base located in the northern region of Galicia. He was the second of three brothers (Nicolás, the elder, and Ramón, the younger). There was also a sister (Pilar). The parents did not get along well, and when Franco was a teenager, his father, Nicolás, an officer in the Navy's administrative branch, decamped to Madrid, where he took up with his common-law wife. Franco's mother, also named Pilar, was a smart, conservative woman with a keen sense of Christian values, who confronted her painful situation with dignity. Franco always felt close to his mother and rejected by his father. As a boy he wanted to be a sailor, like his father, but it was not to be. The Naval Academy had closed after the sinking of most of the Spanish Navy during the 1898 Spanish–American War. The defeat resulted in the loss of what was left of the Spanish Empire: Cuba, Puerto Rico, the Philippines and some islands in the Pacific. Instead of joining the Navy—he would long for the sea the rest of his life—the young Franco had to settle for the Infantry, one of the less prestigious branches of the Spanish Army. At the military academy in Toledo he was a mediocre cadet, graduating in 1910, 251st out of a class of 312. He was, nonetheless, an ambitious young soldier, recognizing that if he wanted to move up through the ranks there was only one road open to him: to fight in Africa. It was dangerous, but it was the right moment for it.

Franco arrived in Morocco in 1912, where he joined the Regulares (more on this unit later in the chapter). Four years later, in 1916, he was nearly killed in a minor skirmish not far from Ceuta. This serious wound was the only one he would ever receive in action (in December 1961 he would accidentally shoot himself while on a Christmas hunting outing near his palace). Unlike hundreds of other young officers seeking fame and promotion, he survived and prospered. Moreover, this timid, mediocre student with a weak physical constitution would discover in Africa's brutal lottery of death, of minor skirmishes and major setbacks, his fortune and his public persona. In battle, he showed leadership, cold courage and tactical skill. His superiors trusted him. His soldiers, mostly Moroccan mercenaries, were said to have a blind faith in his "baraka", an Arab word that implies both blessing and good luck. Like many other young officers of his generation fighting in Morocco, Franco rapidly earned several highly prized decorations and promotions. As we shall see in this chapter, these achievements—in spite of what it will be said in the future, after Franco became the Caudillo—were not exceptional at the time. By the time Franco was reposted to the Iberian Peninsula, to a placid garrison in Asturias in 1917, the fragile and seemingly not-so-bright second lieutenant had become a twenty-four-year-old major, and a local celebrity, albeit a very minor one.

While the context in which Franco's career developed was very European, circumstances in Spain were significantly different from those of the major powers. In the late nineteenth and early twentieth centuries, Europeans—and North Americans, too—justified their military and economic hegemony by pointing to supposedly unique racial and cultural traits: it was from these traits, many argued, that certain nations derived the moral, not to mention practical, superiority with which to colonize much of the non-European world. However, there was one minor problem with this explanation: what of the European nations that failed to gain an empire? By the beginning of the twentieth century Spain had joined the ranks of these under-achievers. While it had once possessed the world's greatest empire, in the late nineteenth century it had shrank and virtually disappeared. One explanation for this decline, according to some, was that a decadent, racially mixed and intolerant Catholic Spain did not quite belong to Europe. Spain was thought of as an oriental country: inscrutable, violent, and even seductive. Indeed, Rudyard Kipling's famous poem "The White Man's Burden", was inspired by Spain's swift defeat in the 1898 war against the United States (Spaniards were not "white" people back then). Many Spaniards agreed that the nation was in fatal decline. Following the 1898 defeat, the "Disaster" as many Spaniards called it, the debate over the nation's decadence was intense, even if it did not lead to any substantial change in the country's political trajectory.

For many commentators, however, the nation's re-birth was going to begin in Morocco. There were many justifications for Spain's presence in Northern Africa in the early 1900s. In reality, however, three principal objectives determined Spain's policy in the region: securing the long-held garrison towns of Ceuta and Melilla, reversing national decline by gaining an empire, and profiting from the supposed wealth of Morocco. What eventually allowed Spain to conquer the territory was not its military might or racial strength but, paradoxically, the fact that it was a weak state. Britain was concerned with keeping its Empire's sea lines safe; it did not want France or Germany to control the Moroccan territory just across from the Gibraltar Strait. The presence there of a seemingly feeble Spain was, for the British, the lesser of several evils. For the French, conceding Spain this unruly little portion of its new colony in North Africa was a relatively small price to pay for strengthening the new rapprochement with Britain at the expense of hated Germany. The 1906 Algeciras Conference and the 1912 Treaty of Fez ratified the interests of both Great Powers and Spain's future role in Northern Morocco. As a result, Spain got 20,000 square kilometres of a territory where central authority had long collapsed and where tribes (*kabila*), bandits, and, increasingly, nationalists were restive, and generally eager to resist the unwelcomed presence of a new colonial master.

Spaniards got the first taste of their colonial "burden" in 1909 when a small army composed of untrained conscripts suffered a bloody defeat just outside the gates of Melilla. This incident not only revealed the difficulties of conquering and securing the new territory, but also illustrated how the war in North Africa was tearing Spanish society apart. The urgent call for reservists caused a revolution in Barcelona and other Catalan towns known as the Tragic Week. In general, the lower classes, democrats, and representatives of the left opposed the Moroccan adventure and how it was carried out while conservatives, business groups, most of the military, and the Crown enthusiastically supported colonial policy. A key element in this disagreement was the draft, which the upper classes were able to avoid through either social connections or payment. Being sent to Morocco thus became the poor man's destiny, which more often than not meant death by illness rather than an enemy's bullet. The draftees-to-be, however, did not necessarily accept their fate: many young men emigrated, deserted, or used other strategies to avoid being sent to North Africa. The poor's man suffering had its opposite in the colonial officers' booming careers and in the profits of those who had invested financially in the Moroccan operation. King Alfonso XIII (ruled 1902–1931) was certainly very close to most of the senior officers posted in Africa. Moreover, the left accused him and some of his ministers of personally profiting from the conquest of Morocco.

The war accentuated the nation's political problems. During the Restoration period (1875–1923) Spain was not just a parliamentary monarchy but, on paper at least, a democratic one. It had adopted universal male suffrage in 1891. In theory, the Spanish parliament was more representative than Britain's. In reality, however, *caciquismo*—electoral manipulation and political bossism—corrupted elections, and power was divided between the rather fractious Conservative and Liberal parties that succeeded each other in power. To make matters worse, King Alfonso XIII continuously meddled in the country's politics and, not unlike like "cousin" Kaiser William II in Germany, he considered the Army to be his exclusive realm. Republicans, democrats, socialists, anarchists and other sectors of political opinion were excluded from the system; and a general political cynicism among the public was exacerbated by official corruption and nepotism. However, in spite of all its shortcomings, Spain's was nonetheless a liberal political system, and there was ample room for the expression of dissent. One of the principal venues for the airing of public opinion was the press. The other was the street. Parties, unions and organizations used demonstrations, civic ceremonies, and political rallies to denounce authorities and policies they could not check in parliament. As the opposition saw the disappearance of legal venues in which it could influence the government, it began resorting to protest, often of a violent kind. In 1909 and again in 1917, Spain almost went through a revolution. Particularly after 1917, anarchist-inspired terrorism, matched by state brutality, increased the public's opinion that the parliamentary monarchical system could not cope with the new phenomenon of mass politics.

Spain had another serious problem in the making: the Army officers fighting in Morocco, usually called the Africanists. Many of these officers came to see themselves as the gatekeepers of Spain's colonial mission, and thus as a cure for the social ills behind the country's weakness. They, the monarchy, and the media that propagated their views—perhaps most significantly the pro-monarchist newspaper *ABC*—formed the core of the Morocco lobby. For the Africanists and their supporters, any criticism of the Army, the war or how it was conducted was a betrayal of the motherland. Yet, while they had the enthusiastic support and patronage of the royal palace, Africanist officers frequently complained of having their hands tied by the politicians in Madrid. They saw themselves as heroes who were misunderstood and mistreated by a society and a political regime that were indolent and ineffective. They considered themselves to be a new aristocracy in a time of confusion and mass politics. In sum, they were, so they thought, hero-victims who knew best what the country needed. At the same time, they never seriously considered the poverty of Spain's material resources, or the reasons behind their recruits' reluctance to risk their lives in Africa. In full agreement with these ideas and prejudices was the most successful of all Africanists: Francisco Franco. After years of relative anonymity, his (and other's) great opportunity would come in 1921. However, it was not caused by a feat of strength, but rather its opposite: one of the most devastating military humiliations suffered by Europeans at the hands of a native population. The desire for revenge would do the rest.

The place was Annual, near Melilla, in the eastern region of Northern Morocco, and the date was July 22, 1921. General Manuel Fernández Silvestre's forces, advancing from Melilla, had tried to connect too quickly with the forces advancing from the west in an attempt to encircle the Berber troops of the Republic of the Rif, whose president was Muhammad Abd-el-Krim al-Jattabi (1882–1963). What was supposed to be a simple pincer movement against lightly armed "barbarians" became, first a chaotic Spanish retreat, and then a succession of massacres that allowed the enemy to reach the gates of the practically defenceless and panic-stricken city of Melilla. Following this initial shock, Spanish troops continued to suffer setbacks for several weeks at a total cost of approximately 10,000—some authors say 15,000—dead or missing soldiers, several hundred prisoners, and the almost complete loss of the eastern portion of the Moroccan "protectorate". After this shocking disaster, those Spaniards who read newspapers heard for the first time the name of a young officer, Major Francisco Franco, who led one of the Foreign Legion units that hastily arrived to save Melilla.

The defeat at Annual was accompanied by many stories of the Spaniards' heroic and desperate deeds, most of which ended in failure and death. To these could be added many more shameful, cowardly and negligent acts. The defeat brought Spanish public opinion face to face with the cost of the Moroccan adventure. The debate that followed was largely predicated on a racist contempt for, and subsequent desire for vengeance against, the "Moor". The most hated among them was Abd-el-Krim, the man who had so shamefully humiliated the Spanish Army. After 1921, Abd-el-Krim's name would arouse fear, hatred, and in some cases, even, a certain sinister attraction. However, he was no barbarian. Before becoming president of the Republic of the Rif, he had studied at the University of Salamanca (his brother and right-hand man studied in Madrid) and had worked for various Spanish newspapers. Moreover, he was a modernizer, a patriot who did not hate the West, a warrior who did not target civilians, and whose behaviour was often more humane than that of his enemies. Ultimately, he had too many enemies to prevail: principally, the two colonial powers, Spain and France, and also the Sultan of Fez, from whose empire the Rif Republic had broken away. In today's Morocco, a centralist, monarchical and authoritarian state, Abd-el-Krim's memory occupies a problematic position within the nation's official history, to say the least.

Franco was one of the Spanish officers who was sent to destroy the Republic of the Rif and to punish its people in the wake of the disaster at Annual. Through a series of fortuitous coincidences he would find himself in the right place, at the right moment in time and in the right military unit to accomplish this task. As fate would have it, while in Asturias Franco courted his future wife, Carmen Polo y Martínez Valdés. Her social standing was higher than his; also, Franco's philandering father cast a shameful stigma over the prospective groom. At the time, Major Franco's career was going nowhere. However, in the interim the future Caudillo became friends with Lieutenant-Colonel José Millán Astray, whom he had met during a training course near Madrid. The two men were very different in many respects: Franco was a shy, moralistic puritan, while Millán was an outspoken womanizer. However, both were ambitious and ruthless. At the urging of Millán, Franco joined the newly founded Legion (*Tercio de Extranjeros*) on October 10, 1920, as second-in command. Until that day, Major Franco had been just another young and ambitious career soldier with combat experience in Africa—one whose future prospects were not particularly bright. The charismatic and sinister Millán was the real star, a student of bushido, the Japanese Samurai code, and a darling of the news correspondents whom he fêted and for whom he provided, by means of his almost suicidal behaviour in combat, plenty of exciting material to write about. From Millán, Franco would learn the important lesson on how to cultivate a mutually beneficial relationship with the press.

When the ineptly led Spanish Army was smashed at Annual, Franco was in Ceuta, at the other end of the colony, training the newly-created crack military unit that would be urgently called upon to save Melilla. This occasion was the beginning of Franco's climb to the higher posts of the Spanish Army. Less than five years later, in 1926, not yet thirty-four years old, he would be promoted to brigadier general. As his propagandists would later insist, only Napoleon Bonaparte, a similar man of destiny, had risen so quickly. This was nonsense: there were other, more spectacular cases in nineteenth-century Spain. (For example, Baldomero Espartero, 1793–1879, a general and politician, reached the rank of brigadier at thirty, having started as a private. Like Franco, he profited both from colonial wars abroad and civil wars at home. Unlike the reactionary Franco, he was also a liberal.)

At any rate, Melilla was crucial to Franco's fate. Today, the last existing public monument to Franco in democratic Spain still stands there, just outside the old city's walls. It was erected in 1977, two years after the dictator's death. The conservative local authorities have repeatedly refused to remove it, in spite of state laws demanding the dismantling of monuments to the perpetrators of the July 1936 coup. They argue, falsely, that it is a monument not to the dictator, but to the man who saved the city in 1921. The inscription below the statue says: "To the Legion Major Franco Bahamonde 1921–1977." In reality this monument is the product of a historical fabrication; like so many others erected under the dictatorship—and since withdrawn from public view. All formed part of the elaborate political myth that surrounded the Caudillo, and which consisted in presenting the dictator's African years as the early stirrings of a great destiny finally realized in 1936. In this way, Franco was presented as a hero whose extraordinary career was made possible thanks solely to his unique, providential personal qualities. However, Franco was not a unique hero. His exploits, real or invented, and his career blossomed in a time of hero inflation in Spain.

So many heroes

The Spanish Army in Africa was full of brave men, but not many competent commanders. In the latter category, having the right connections and luck in battle was a necessary complement to bravery. Franco had all three, but his career was also possible because of a fourth factor: optimum timing. The context for his meteoric rise appeared as he was about to graduate from the military academy in 1910. The 1909 defeat near Melilla not only gave way to the revolutionary events of Tragic Week, but also revealed the political cost, and the military limitations, of using conscript soldiers in an unpopular colonial war. The response of the Army command was to imitate policies practised by other empires: in 1911 they created a new force of "regulars" (Regulares), that is, local Moroccan mercenaries commanded by Spanish officers. The man put in charge of this force was the then Lieutenant-Colonel Dámaso Berenguer. Simultaneously, in 1910 the policy of promotion by strict seniority alone was supplemented by one of promotion by war merits, aimed at enticing officers to volunteer for Morocco and to fight bravely. This system offended many peninsula-based officers and would contribute to the near revolution that shook Spain in 1917. The use of mercenaries and the division within the Army between Africanist officers and supporters of promotion by seniority, would henceforth be a constant in Spanish military and political affairs up to the Civil War.

Berenguer, a man not without talent, became one of the King's favourites and was thus promoted rapidly. In 1918 he became Minister of War, and in 1919 High Commissioner (Governor) in Morocco. Even before that, always with the enthusiastic support of the King, he was promoting subordinates, creating in the process a vast patronage network, perhaps the most successful in modern Spanish military history. Berenguer was among the senior officers who helped to cement a tradition of granting military rewards to an underperforming yet self-congratulatory Army. For example, between 1909 and 1914, when there was no decisive victory over the Moroccans, the high command nonetheless handed out 132,925 medals and 1,587 promotions. The officers who benefitted most were those who left the academy after 1909. Such was the frenzy of promotions that there were rumours of fake skirmishes with the Moroccans, a sort of pact with the other side, to create merits. There were cases of spurious rewards: Franco's future collaborator, Agustín Muñoz Grandes, is supposed to have been promoted as a wedding present. In any case, many officers complained that promotions went to the more reckless officers rather than to the better-prepared ones. Not surprisingly, casualties among junior officers were high, since reckless courage was seen as the road to promotion. In spite of these losses, however, the majority of officers, Franco included, survived and thrived. In fact, being wounded in action was an unimpeachable reason for promotion. In 1916 Franco almost died with a bullet wound to his lower stomach; the next year, he was promoted to major. Not surprisingly, this exorbitant policy of promotions only furthered a chronic problem for the Spanish Army, which the Republic would seek to resolve in the early 1930s: an unrealistically high number of officers in proportion to other ranks. In 1921, the year of Annual, the Spanish Army had 111,435 men compared with the British Army's 374,000; 419 were colonels and 60 generals, compared with 377 and 20 for the British Army. In Spain there was an officer for every four soldiers, while in Italy and Germany the proportion was more like one for every twenty.

Fully backed by the King, Berenguer's network, particularly the officers in charge of the Regulares, Franco included, did very well. Future generals and leaders of the 1936 rebellion, such as José Sanjurjo—one of the King's new favourites after the death of General Silvestre at Annual—soon had their own networks of protégés, which included Millán Astray and Franco, who themselves were soon enjoying the King's special attention. Indeed, in all the legal proceedings conducted by the military during the period of 1922–1926 for Franco's promotions from major to general—in addition to the awarding of medals—Sanjurjo's name appears as one of, if not *the*, main champions of his career. Other officers who did well include Emilio Mola, a "deep friend" of Berenguer, Manuel Goded, Gonzalo Queipo de Llano, José Varela and Francisco Gómez-Jordana (another "personal" friend of the King). All of them pestered the monarch with petitions, claims, or requests for letters of recommendation for themselves or for somebody else. According to the King, of all the Africanists, Franco was the most frequent visitor to the Royal Palace. This may or may not be true, but what was certain was that Alfonso was delighted to have such loyal friends and heroic followers. Of course, jealousies abounded and in a world of fierce competition for the next promotion or coveted medal (the *Laureada*, Spain's equivalent to the Victoria

Cross, was always the big prize) it was only a matter of time before the inevitable falling-out occurred. Franco, for example, did not forgive Berenguer for not promoting him to division general in 1930. The rivalry between Franco and the equally ambitious Goded was notorious (and it helps to explain, in part at least, his elimination from the Francoist historical record during and after the Civil War). Even more apparent, Mola and Millán Astray hated each other. Indeed, this was a petty world of resentment and ambition, one that hardly matched the image these officers cultivated of themselves as "heroes", "caudillos" (leaders), "saviours of the race", "glorious", "Spanish gentlemen", and "conquistadors".

Franco's career was turbo-charged during the 1910s and early 1920s. But the same happened to many of his contemporaries. For example, in 1909 the man who was to be the original caudillo of the 1936 rebellion, Sanjurjo—Franco's patron during the early to mid-1920s—was stuck in a career that seemed to be going nowhere. He had been a captain for ten years; then he became a major because of war merits. In 1914 he joined the Regulares, won his first *Laureada* and ended the year as lieutenant-colonel. In 1920 he was already a brigadier general. In other words, in eleven years he went from being an obscure captain to one of the King's favourite generals. This is exactly the same amount of time it took Franco to be promoted from captain to brigadier general. The career of Mola, the man who effectively organized the 1936 rebellion, was similar. He graduated early from the academy in 1907 to profit immediately from the post-1912 promotion boom, but after joining the Regulares in 1911, his career soared. He was wounded in 1912 and promoted to captain. Fifteen years later, only forty years old, he was a brigadier general. Had he been in the Legion, he probably would have been promoted even faster.

But let us return to Melilla in the summer of 1921. It must be said that if Franco was the man who saved the city from the "Moors", people did not notice this at the time. Certainly, he was *part* of the army that saved Melilla. In contemporary accounts of the city's redemption, Franco either went unmentioned or he was relegated to a secondary role at best. The man who received the excited public's attention at this time was Millán Astray. When Franco arrived in the city, he was seconding Millán in leading the Legion's small contingent of 32 officers, 641 men, 197 mules, and a company of machine guns—hardly an impressive force, even if more reinforcements arrived the next day. In the chronicles of the time, other higher-ranking officers systematically eclipse Franco's name. These would include such figures as General Miguel Cabanellas, later the first nominal head of the 1936 rebel generals; and Lieutenant-Colonel Núñez del Prado, who in July 1936, having been promoted to general, was the loyal head of the republican Air Force. At this time he flew to Zaragoza to try to convince his "friend" Cabanellas not to rebel, only to be detained by him and executed.

Franco and his contemporaries' fame would profit from the sensational, uncritical and reactionary tone of most Spanish war correspondents. Later, when he was becoming the Caudillo, these chronicles would be reinterpreted as early demonstrations of his exceptional qualities. Most publicists of the war were imperialists who believed that with good policies in place the investment in men and material would pay off. For example, the journalist Víctor Ruiz Albéniz was very enthusiastic about Spain's mission in Morocco. He also went a little "native", as it were, adopting an Arab pseudonym, *El Tebib Arrumi* (The Christian Doctor). In 1922, he published a vivid, novelistic account, full of supposedly accurate dialogues, of the recent disaster at Annual. The significance of Albéniz's testimony is that he would later become one of Franco's main propagandists (as we will see in Chapter 2), and as such greatly contributed to the creation of the myth of the dictator's heroic destiny. In his 1922 account of the panic that had shaken Melilla the previous year, when rumours concerning the fall of Annual arrived in the city, Albéniz showed two traits that help to explain his future role during and after the Civil War. The first was contempt for civilians (especially poor ones); the second was a crude militarism.[1]

In Albéniz's writings one can see early indications of the Africanist lobby's predilection for professional units and their officers, which they would elevate to the category of heroes and martyrs, using language that would grow increasingly disconnected from the reality of the events described. Instantly, upon arrival in Melilla, the Legion became the war publicists' favourite unit. A halo of mystique surrounded it. This was helped by a number of novels and pseudo-biographies written by journalists and legionnaires.

Petty-officer Carlos Micó España wrote a book in 1922 that was the first "inside" description of the Legion's deliverance of Melilla. The work included both a prologue by the future Francoist propagandist Tomás Borrás and letters by Millán. According to Micó, when, at 2 pm on July 24, 1921, the *Ciudad de Cádiz*, the boat carrying the first Legion units, docked at Melilla, two "*caudillos*"— this is the exact word used in the original—talked to the frightened crowd; one was Lieutenant-Colonel Millán Astray, the other was General Sanjurjo:

> The saviours, the saviours! Long life to the Legion! Up with Spain! Millán Astray! The Saviors! Sanjurjo! González Tablas! Women raised their little ones as we marched and yelled: Look at the saviours! Say Long Life to the Legion!, son.[2]

Fourteen years later, in late 1936, many of the journalists who witnessed this moment would suddenly "remember" that the true saviour of Melilla was actually Major Franco.

During the summer of 1922 there were many such individuals in Melilla, not just heroes but "caudillos," ahead of the future Caudillo in the queue of History. The *ABC* newspaper, always enthusiastic about the Moroccan adventure and the army, used this word profusely. Even when reporting the death of the incompetent General Silvestre on July 24, it claimed: "He had the looks, ingenuity and unbreakable optimism of a caudillo."[3] This same paper, however, did not mention Franco at all between the crucial days of July and the end of August. Sanjurjo's name, however, was featured thirty-eight times in its pages, and Millán's fifteen times.

Not everyone agreed with the pro-Legion version of events, or with attributing the sole credit for saving Melilla to Millán and Sanjurjo. The progressive Eduardo Ortega y Gasset—brother of the famous philosopher José—reserved a prominent role for the Regulares led by the "modest and serious" Lieutenant-Colonel Santiago González-Tablas, who would be gravely wounded twice in the next months (dying after the second incident in May 1922) and was awarded the coveted *Laureada*. Gasset, however, also honoured the Legion. He specifically named Lieutenant-Colonel Millán and his "distinguished complement" the "courageous" Major Francisco Franco.[4] He, like his conservative colleagues, could not know what History had in store for them all. In 1936 Gasset became the Republic's Attorney General. He later died in exile in Venezuela. Other people who contested the official version of events, or in particular criticized the Army, would later pay for their words during the Civil War. Alfonso Sánchez Portela, the man who took the famous pictures of Abd-el-Krim after Annual, was later deported by Franco. The writer Fernando Mora, who called the soldiers of Annual "cowards", was arrested in Zaragoza by the military rebels in July 1936. After acknowledging that he was the author of the article—written fifteen years earlier—he was shot.

Franco's incipient fame was not acquired solely through fighting. He became friendly with the journalists covering the conflict, particularly those enthusiastic about the exploits of the professional troops. In this, Franco was no different from the many colonels, generals, and other high-ranking officers who became national heroes after 1921 due to their deeds in Morocco. This was a mutually beneficial relationship. Bellicose journalists needed heroes and exploits for their avid, patriotic readers. The young Major Franco greeted them, and posed for them, and gave them the stories they were looking for. One famous war correspondent was the afore-mentioned Ruiz Albéniz; another, Gregorio Corrochano, a former bullfighting critic turned war correspondent for the *ABC*, who became a friend of General José Sanjurjo and his group of protégées, Franco among them. Yet another bellicose pen was that of José María Carretero, *El Caballero Audaz*, Sanjurjo's main propagandist during the monarchy, the Republic and—by then a lonely voice from the past—during the early years of the Franco dictatorship.

Thanks to the press, the heroic actions of the Army and particu-larly the professional troops and officers were transformed into epic battles between Spain and the barbaric "Moor". Their message was a racist tale in which civilization and courage were set against, and ultimately victorious over, savage force. It was also a calculated manipulation of the truth by which minor skirmishes were ele-vated to the level of History's greatest battles. The government encouraged this rhetoric because it was interested in fomenting a patriotic frenzy that could obscure its own irresponsibility. For example, the authorities distributed postcards showing the remains of the soldiers killed at Annual. As the lost territory was re-conquered, newspapers published horrific photographs of the soldiers' remains. The response to such brutality, whether accurate or exaggerated, was more brutality, both verbal and physical. In the process, the Legionnaires, the favourite unit of the press, became the avengers of Annual. They copied their enemies' supposed practices, such as the mutilation of captured soldiers, and were sometimes even depicted by press photographers showing body parts as souvenirs.[5] While there is no doubt that the Rif rebels committed countless atrocities against surrendered Spaniards, as well as their corpses, there is also evidence to suggest that they were also capable of moderation and restraint.

The myth-making rhetoric of the pro-war press was paired with the competition by local elites to identify with and fête their particular heroes. It was normal that each town, and even village, would look for its famous "sons" fighting in Africa, whose exploits they followed in a sort of competition to see which town had the best champion. Every incident was thus reported in the local newspapers, particularly if the officer in question made sure that these papers were informed of his exploits. When he returned home he would be received in grand style by the local authorities. Bombastic speeches were given during banquets and public homages; if the local hero went to the bullfight or the theatre, the public often stood to applaud and cheer him. When Major Franco visited his hometown of El Ferrol on March 5, 1922, several ornamental arches were prepared, a caravan of cars went to the nearby town of Betanzos to escort him, and a banquet was prepared with the garrison's officers. The King and the Minister of War even sent messages of congratulations to El Ferrol's mayor for having prepared such patriotic ceremonies. After visiting El Ferrol, Franco went on to Oviedo, where he met not only his fiancée but also a devoted group of admirers waiting to make sure the hero would receive an enthusiastic welcome.

Before returning to his hometown, however, Franco went to Madrid. This visit was aimed at cementing his status as a national celebrity; he also made important new contacts with the capital's elites. The *ABC* newspaperman Corrochano helped facilitate these contacts. Between February and March 1922 he and other colleagues had published a number of articles praising Franco. In Madrid, a group of friends and admirers organized a big banquet at the Ritz for the "heroic chief". Two former government ministers attended:

the master of electoral corruption, Natalio Rivas, and Antonio Goicoechea. There was also a representative from the Radical Party, and plenty of senior officers such as General Saro, Millán Astray, and others. Several ministers, including the Prime Minister, José Sánchez Guerra, sent messages of congratulations. Franco was becoming an idol of the colonial lobby.

However, Franco's triumphant ascendency was not unique. The post-1921 period saw many heroic celebrities. Days before Franco's short peninsular tour had resulted in his new national fame, several other officers received similar adulation by local authorities in Madrid and elsewhere. A number of ceremonies were performed in General Sanjurjo's honour in Melilla, which far surpassed those in honour of Franco, or any other Spanish officer of the time. These included games, football matches and, of course, banquets. In Peninsular Spain, Lieutenant-Colonel Serrano was also rewarded with a banquet at the Madrid Ritz, and so was the recently promoted General Saro. Even lesser known officers had their moment of glory. Major José Candeira (now lost to posterity) was fêted in his hometown of Puenteareas (Galicia), where he was treated to lavish festivities and a banquet of honour. The wounded Captain Eduardo Mendicuti was fêted by his hometown of Sanlúcar (Andalusia).

However, none of these officers, perhaps with the exception of General Sanjurjo and Lieutenant-Colonel Millán Astray, showed as much skill and determination in promoting his own image as did Franco. Still only a major, he was the subject of an article published in Spain's most prominent conservative newspaper, *ABC*, where he was called "The Legion's Ace". However, the same term "ace" was widely applied to other officers of the time as well.[6] Franco made it to the front page for the first time on November 1922, when the fashionable magazine *Nuevo Mundo* (New World) published an article in which they called him one of "the men that Spain does not want to forget and should not forget".[7] The context of this article was a monographic issue, offering the novelty of photographs of the Legion, wherein the "heroic" exploits of the unit were amply described. Franco appeared in a picture while riding a horse; other images illustrated the Legion's daily military rituals.

Franco benefitted from the mystique of the Legion among the Moroccan lobby. The praise was based not only on the fabrication of epic tales, but also on the omission of inconvenient facts. Behind the bushido codes and heroic posturing stood the cult—and corresponding practice—of sheer brutality. However, the Legion's behaviour was not exceptional: even the glamorous Air Force, another corps that received plenty of attention, hid the shameful reality that they were using poison gas against the rebels. The pro-war journalists embedded among the troops were fervent propagandists and chose not to act as witnesses to any of this. Not content with merely ignoring the principles of civilized society, they helped to undermine the already weak liberal system in Spain by denouncing the internal enemy of the Africanist army—members of which they located even in the government—for not promoting their African heroes quickly enough. In January 1923, the deeply conservative Catholic newspaper *El Debate* opined: "had Franco been born in another time, he would today be a general". Moreover, times were bad for these heroes in a country where "a worker earns more than an officer". *Nuevo Mundo* explained that same month that Franco was returning to the mainland because, after the days "of panic during the shameful defeat" when they were "heroes" and "caudillos", the days of "bureaucracy" and "mediocre envy" had arrived.[8] War and warriors seemed to be the desirable, and even natural, antidote to Spanish society's malaise.

Franco not only learned to cultivate the pro-Africanist press; he also became the principal witness to his own glory. This would be one of the singular traits of his forty-year reign: that the dictator would serve as the guarantor of the authenticity of his version of the past. A few months after his triumphal 1922 tour, he published *Marruecos: Diario de una bandera* (Morocco: Diary of a Battalion); which included a prologue written by Lieutenant-Colonel Millán Astray.[9] This book was a personal account of his exploits, labours and merits as a colonial officer, and as such it cemented even more his reputation as the "Ace of the Legion". For Franco (even though some doubts have been raised about his authorship), the *Diario* probably served a further purpose—since 1912, a government decree had stipulated that to become a general, an officer had to publish works that contributed to the instruction and technical improvement of the Army. Franco would partially achieve this requirement with the *Diario*, as well as with the articles that in the next few years he would publish in the Moroccan Army's official journal, the *Revista de Tropas Coloniales* (Colonial Troops

Review). The *Revista* was created in January 1924 by another officer, and future participant in the 1936 rebellion, Gonzalo Queipo de Llano. Franco immediately began publishing articles there, mostly on technical matters, and then, the following year, became its director. In some of the forty articles he published in the *Revista*, he conducted macro-analyses of policies and possible strategies for Morocco. He also narrated the development of military operations in which he took part in two larger pieces, *La Hora de Xauen* (1924) and *Diario de Alhucemas* (1925). At the same time, he became interested in movies, particularly in filming combat, sometimes even placing himself behind the camera.

What the original *Diario*, as well as Franco's other, minor, publications reveal, is that he professed not to have any political opinions; in fact, he was quite content with the socio-political milieu of the monarchy as long as his own career progressed. In more ways than one, this would set the tone for the rest of his career, even after the arrival of the Republic in 1931: that he would comply with the law as long as it benefitted him personally. Another noteworthy aspect of his writings from this period was the fact that he never failed to present his own role in contemporary events in the best possible light. In Franco's texts he described himself and the Army, particularly the Infantry Corps, as the most heroic elite of the nation, and Africa as both the school and the testing ground of this elite.

War spoils

Franco's path to glory after Melilla was not straightforward. By late 1922, posted back to Oviedo (Asturias' capital), the hero and caudillo must have thought his career in Africa was over once again. However, good luck and good connections were on his side. In June 1923 the officer who replaced Millán Astray as commander of the Legion, Lieutenant-Colonel Rafael Valenzuela, was cut down while leading a brave but ill-conceived attack. There were homages, articles, ceremonies and orations for the fallen hero all over Spain. His body was returned to Spain and laid to rest in *El Pilar* basilica, in Zaragoza—the most patriotic temple in the country. (Having inspired its inhabitants to resist in two heroic sieges by the invading Napoleonic troops in 1808 and 1809, the

Madonna of *El Pilar* has held the rank of Captain General of the Spanish Army, since 1908). Franco replaced Valenzuela.

The personal circumstances of Franco's appointment as head of the Legion are very well known. Yet in professional terms they are rather more obscure. It was Alfonso XIII who personally chose him. But this was not all. Since the unit had to be led by a lieutenant-colonel, Franco was promoted to this rank, retroactively to 1922 (making him the youngest lieutenant-colonel in the Spanish Army), and, in addition, granted the honorific title of *Gentilhombre de cámara* of the King. The irregular promotion of a favourite was not unusual during Alfonso's reign, but we still do not know for sure why Franco was chosen. There were other candidates who already had both the rank and the experience to take over the post. At the time rumours were rife.

Alfonso's extension of royal patronage to Franco came not long before he was to marry Carmen Polo. Franco had already temporarily postponed the wedding in 1920 to join the Legion. Now he left her waiting a second time to return to Africa. It was his golden chance to rise even farther and faster. As the commander of the favourite corps of the pro-Moroccan lobby, Franco saw a chance to become a truly national figure. He finally married Carmen in October 1923. The King was the best man, although he was not present at the ceremony. The only child of the marriage, also named Carmen, would be born in 1928.

The Annual disaster created opportunities for ambitious (and lucky) officers but it also ended up derailing the fragile and corrupt political system of the Restoration. In September 1923, General Miguel Primo de Rivera, the military governor of Barcelona, staged a *coup d'état* with royal blessing, and proclaimed himself dictator of the country. Primo de Rivera quickly ended the investigation into the responsibility for the Annual disaster, conducted by General Juan Picasso (cousin to the great painter), which was clearly affecting the prestige of King Alfonso XIII. Parliament and public opinion had been focusing on the close relationship between the King and the two men seen as the main culprits of Annual: the deceased General Silvestre and his commander, High Commissioner General Berenguer; although rivals, both men were Alfonso's favourites. In his first years in power, General Primo de Rivera was to become a rather popular ruler, even among the country's liberal elites, as he appeared capable of purging the country's notoriously corrupt public administration and political culture. He was also considering options for refocusing the expensive and badly run war in Morocco, including abandoning the Protectorate. Moreover, it was known that he did not like the war merit system.

For the Africanist officers, as well as many mainstream politicians and even some businessmen, Primo de Rivera's intentions for Morocco spelled disaster. If Primo de Rivera had carried out his original plans, Franco's career, not to mention that of many other Africanist soldiers, would likely have gone nowhere. Paradoxically, the man saved by the coup, King Alfonso XIII, agreed. He had been the principal force behind the Moroccan adventure and the main patron of the colonial Army—his most loyal officers. The King would help his friends again. Primo de Rivera's coup not only stopped the investigation into Annual, but restored the affected officers to their positions. Berenguer was soon pardoned and then appointed by the King to head the military branch of his household: the grand patron was now in an even better position to assist the King in his meddling in the affairs of the Army.

Whatever his intentions, Primo de Rivera was a politically naïve individual and had little room to manoeuvre: the King and his African Army wanted to stay in Morocco. In addition, international pressures, particularly the objections of France to any withdrawal, were working against his goals. Primo de Rivera hesitated. The Africanists did not. Franco was one of the many officers who made clear his opposition to withdrawing from the colonial enterprise. Franco was a strict disciplinarian. For example, in 1925 he coldly ordered the public execution of a Legionnaire who had thrown a plate of food at an officer. And yet, in July 1924, he presided over, and perhaps contributed to, acts of indiscipline against Primo de Rivera in which his Legionnaire officers took part. This much commented-upon event (one should perhaps say "much rumoured" event, since there was severe press censorship at the time) took place at the Legion encampment of Ben Tieb. The details are contradictory, but the essence of the story is clear. When the dictator visited the Legion, Franco, his host, made it clear during the banquet and his subsequent speech that the Legion would never accept a withdrawal from Morocco. In his reply, Primo de Rivera reminded those present that nobody had exclusive claims

over patriotism. His words caused such indignation among many
officers that at least one of them reached for his sidearm. Franco,
the unit's commander, was not punished for this egregious breach
of discipline.

A few months after this incident, in the autumn of 1924,
Franco would cover himself in glory, first during the relief of the
besieged garrison at Xauen, and then in the near-catastrophic
retreat from that place, which once again cost the lives of thousands of Spanish troops as they covered the extreme rear-guard of
the retreating forces. On this occasion, he again asked for the
coveted *Laureada*, and once again, as had happened every time he
had asked for it since 1916, he was denied. Instead, the Army
rewarded him with a new promotion to the rank of colonel in
February 1925. The pro-war press also congratulated him. In an
article published in March 1925 the *Revista de Tropas Coloniales*,
the magazine he edited, he was said to have become "a Caudillo", and
his head anointed with "a double tiara of wisdom and courage".[10]
This was followed by even better news: Primo de Rivera had now
finally decided that Spain would not withdraw from Morocco,
and that a decisive effort should be undertaken to achieve a swift,
definitive victory. In addition, more and better war materiel
(including planes and chemical weapons) kept arriving.

On September 8, 1925, the Spanish Army, with French support,
staged an amphibious landing at Alhucemas Bay. The invading force
was made up of some 18,500 men. The French provided ships and
planes. The operation's main objective was to take Axdir, Abd-el-
Krim's home village, and the historic centre of his *kabila*, the
Beni-Urriaguel, thereby destroying the Rif rebellion by eliminating
its power base. It was a much-celebrated deed and widely reported,
since it represented the biggest and most decisive Spanish victory
in the war. Contemporary accounts of the landing described Franco's
role in the event—which would catapult him to the rank of brigadier general the next year—as significant but not exceptional.
Given his rank of colonel, his name and achievements were placed
far below those of other officers. The names that appear most in
contemporary chronicles are those of the then prime minister and
dictator, General Primo de Rivera (Marquis of Estella) and the
commander of the operation, General José Sanjurjo, both of whom
were awarded the *Laureada* for this operation! In one account, for

example, Franco's name appeared for the first time ... on page 42, in a footnote discussing the organization of the convoy that carried the landing forces: "The names of Sanjurjo, Saro, Fernández Pérez, Goded, Martín, Franco and Vera, are sufficient enough guarantee that the execution of the orders of the supreme chief have not been delayed even by a minute ... "[11]

The pro-Africanist lobby did not allow the occasion to pass unnoticed and resorted to distorted historical comparisons and inflated metaphors. For example, in spite of their superior technology, armament and numbers, the Spanish (and some French) forces' actions were presented as having been on par with those of the Spartan King Leonidas defending (and heroically dying for) the Pass of Thermopylae against the overwhelming might of the Persian Army in 480 BC:

> There they go, the *Kaes* [landing crafts] commanded by the Navy officers with fair names of glorious roots: each of them a Leonidas leading towards the landing place [...] advancing towards death and leaving behind both the easy life and the memory of their heroism. Perhaps a hidden enemy awaits them, protected by defences, hiding behind a bush, ready in a crest, glued to the ground, to plant death and create a hecatomb. [...] The Legionnaire knows only that he is sent either to win or to die ... [12]

However, this time King Leonidas (Sanjurjo) and the Spartans (Spaniards) were more numerous and far better armed than the Persians (Berbers). The combined French and Spanish naval force had arrived near the landing place on 7 and 8 September, but it did so in disorder (strong currents were blamed for this). High in the mountains, the Rif patriots learned in advance what was coming, but there was little they could do: it was not a surprise but an overwhelming display of military superiority. Early in the morning of the 8th, the armada and several squadrons of aircraft bombarded the area. Franco was not the only senior officer who came under fire; though according to some reporters, he and his superior, General Saro, were almost killed when a grenade landed "at their feet" but failed to explode. At the time, it was Saro who got most of the credit for these exploits, as well as for the mopping-up operations in the following weeks. However, one of the Legionnaires later claimed that Franco somehow discovered that the beach on which they were to land had been mined by the enemy, avoiding almost certain disaster. But, according to General Saro's subordinates, it was a Navy commander, not Franco, who reconnoitred the beach and, upon realizing the danger, took the landing crafts to an alternative landing site, thus saving the troops.[13]

Regardless of what the war propagandists claimed, Alhucemas was not Thermopylae: the Spaniards easily and almost bloodlessly smashed the Berbers. Once the troops set foot on land, the operation went rather smoothly—save for the lack of food and munitions, a result of Sanjurjo's poor planning. Combined shelling by the Navy and the Air Force seems to have been fairly effective at weakening the enemy. Just thirty-three minutes after landing, Franco's Legionnaires and the Moroccan Regulares of Agustín Muñoz Grandes had secured the beachhead. The battle was far from fierce. Franco told a journalist that the Legion had only six casualties (in total 206 Spaniards died). In the following days, Franco conducted himself with professionalism, asking for support from the fleet and aircraft when his troops confronted well-entrenched enemy. He showed once again that he was a competent field commander. According to one correspondent:

> We know for some time now, the great serenity, skill and good military eye of this young colonel of legionnaires; many times all the correspondents have highlighted his figure and his military talents which perfectly complement those of his generals and column chiefs, proving once again Franco's value. This is why all admire him and like this man who, in addition, is deeply modest.[14]

Franco was not alone in receiving this type of praise. In the Alhucemas operation, as in previous campaigns, plenty of officers gained recognition as "heroes". Colonel Goded, for example, was described as "a man of great military merit, who was the one who planned the landing operation ... "[15] But it was Sanjurjo, the supreme commander, who according to the Moroccan-lobby press, was the event's greatest "hero"; even if he spent the whole first morning of the operation on a torpedo boat cruising around the convoy trying to re-organize the less than perfect arrangement of the landing craft and troop transports.[16] In the following weeks, he received a number of tributes. On October 12, Day of the (Spanish) Race, Spain's most patriotic holiday, he attended a solemn "Te Deum" at the church of the Sagrado Corazón in Melilla. On this occasion two "vintner ladies" (Sanjurjo was fond of ladies of dubious reputation: the two *vinateras* in question ran mobile taverns) embraced the General. The *Diario de Barcelona* correspondent described him as a "true caudillo". Later, a Legionnaire read a collective message from the troops to the General saying: "Spain, cradle of unique warriors that in the past astonished the world with its deeds, only needs a chief like His Excellency, General Sanjurjo, to repeat the brilliant pages which are still alive in our hearts." A group of journalists also read a message congratulating Sanjurjo for his promotion to Lieutenant-General, because "Spain has found a caudillo".[17] King Alfonso agreed and made him a marquis. The new city and port built in Alhucemas Bay were named after him.

Alhucemas came to occupy a major position within Francoist mythology as the moment when Franco became a redemptive hero. The Franco regime's propagandists manipulated the real story of the landing for the Caudillo's glory (as we shall see in Chapter 2), while burying the role of the other protagonists. Franco was even credited with having conceived the idea of the landing first and later convincing both Primo de Rivera and the King of its feasibility. Other witnesses, if alive, might have disagreed. Writing in 1932, Goded, then a brigadier general, explained both the origins and the execution of the Alhucemas operation. As he and others knew, "the idea of a landing" did not appear at any "precise moment", but rather had evolved since 1909, as "we learned more about the territory's difficulties". The idea of striking at the heart of Abd-el-Krim's territory was "widely shared in the Army of Morocco", and by 1911 (one year before Franco was first posted to Africa!) there was a "landing plan" in place. Goded wrote that both the merit and "the will to execute the plan" belonged to General Primo de Rivera, because there was "widespread incredulity" even in the Army about the feasibility of such an operation. In his book, Goded praised many of his colleagues for the landing, including Franco. He also wrote that, in spite of the "harshness" of the first day of battle, the total number of casualties "did not reach one hundred".[18]

Alhucemas ended the war and cemented the reputation of a number of "heroes", many of whom would play an important role in the Civil War—Agustín Muñoz Grandes, Manuel Goded, José Enrique Varela, among others—and these "heroes", of course, gained quick promotions. Initially, nobody seemed to profit more from the operation than the dictator himself, Primo de Rivera, who became more popular than ever before (or after). To the country's relief, the dreadful Moroccan war was almost over. Soon, all Moroccan resistance ended. Had Primo de Rivera retired then, his name would probably have enjoyed a positive memory. Instead, he decided to entrench his regime, trying, but ultimately failing, to institutionalize his dictatorship. Opposition and conspiracies mounted. Several generals (and politicians) became involved in plotting a coup on the Peninsula scheduled for June 24, 1926. It failed.

Like other senior officers, Franco did very well from Alhucemas. In 1926, just a year after he became a colonel, he was promoted to brigadier general (his friend Millán Astray took over the Legion once again). The young general then moved to Madrid where he sought out new friends and patrons, regularly visiting the homes of prominent politicians and joining a variety of social clubs. These efforts included learning to play *the* networking game: golf. While the African hero was celebrated by numerous towns and institutions, it was his mercurial brother Ramón, a pilot, who ironically was the most famous military man of the time. In January 1926, Ramón and his crew had flown the hydroplane *Plus Ultra* from Spain to Argentina. The flight was hailed by the national and international (mostly Latin American) press as one of the greatest feats of aviation—even if Ramón had committed serious mistakes that endangered the operation. The dictatorship and the King rushed to cover Ramón with honours. They would come to regret this, as he would eventually become politically radicalized, joining several conspiracies against the government. Later, after a long and convoluted stint on the far left, broken marriages, and Masonic activities, he would end up fighting on his brother's side in Civil War, dying in a bombing mission in 1938.

From 1926 to the beginning of the Civil War, Franco saw no more direct military action. This, however, did not halt the acceleration of his career. It was well known that the King had taken a particular liking to him; it was said that Franco was his favourite general; his name appeared in newspapers as a candidate for several royal appointments and honours. Finally, in February 1928, he was appointed director of the newly-created General Military Academy, located in Zaragoza. This was a curious appointment for a man who lacked a General Staff diploma and had little higher military education. His new position enabled him to expand his network of friends, admirers and protégés, with the new cadets and their fathers, who were usually military officers themselves. Nepotism was rife in the selection of new admissions, as it was for the selection of professors. Zaragoza was a pleasant town where Franco was likely the most important person, after the Archbishop. He was well received by the best families of the region. A street was even named after him. There, his wife Carmen's sister, Zita, met and married a brilliant local lawyer and emerging politician, Ramón Serrano Súñer. This marriage would have important repercussions on Franco's career. The groom's witness was José Antonio Primo de Rivera, the dictator's son and the future founder, in 1933, of the Falange, Spain's truest Fascist party. Franco's physique even started to reflect the comforts of the sedentary life of a senior officer whose work was done mostly behind a desk. Short, progressively fat and balding, he cut an unimpressive figure—one that largely masked his coldness and practical intelligence.

However, Franco's state of satisfaction was increasingly threatened by politics. By the end of the 1920s, Primo de Rivera's dictatorship had become unpopular. Primo's health was also rapidly deteriorating, due in part to his heavy drinking. In January 1930, after losing the support of the King and of key senior officers, he resigned and went into exile, dying shortly afterwards. More worrisome for Franco, his foremost patron, the King, was also in trouble. After Primo de Rivera's resignation, the Africanists' primary patron and the King's long-time protégé, General Berenguer, had become the new Prime Minister (January 1930–February 1931). The monarchy was attempting to turn the clock back to September 1923, as if the dictatorship had never occurred, by re-instating the liberal system. However, Berenguer's attempt to save the monarchy by restoring the old 1876 constitution failed. Public opinion was increasingly against Alfonso, and even former monarchists were now declaring themselves republicans. Calls for reform, democracy, socialism, anarchism, and demands for autonomy for Catalonia and the Basques, among others, emanated from all quarters.

Franco, for his part, served the existing regime to the last moment. On December 12, 1930 a group of republican officers revolted in the garrison town of Jaca, in the Pyrenees. The rebellion was part of a wider conspiracy led by republican politicians, but the Jaca garrison acted too soon and alone. Several senior officers, including the exiled General Gonzalo Queipo de Llano, and Franco's own volatile brother Ramón, were involved in the plot. The rebellion caused several casualties on both sides, in addition to innocent bystanders. Franco was appalled, not only by the behaviour of his brother and his co-conspirators, but also by what he thought was the misguided and prejudicial attitude of the republican politicians, who were involving the Army in their plans. The King's favourite, a supporter of Primo de Rivera, and a darling of the pro-war lobby now claimed he resented politicians' meddling in the Army. Furthermore, he placed himself morally above the attempts by the democratic forces to overthrow the royally backed Berenguer (supposedly soft) dictatorship. In mid-December 1930, as a member of the military court that in forty minutes judged and sentenced the Jaca rebels, Franco co-signed the death warrants for two of the leaders, Captain Fermín Galán Rodríguez, a veteran of the Legion, and Captain Ángel García Hernández. When less than four months afterwards, on April 14, 1931, the Republic was proclaimed, both officers became official martyrs. By then, Franco's main patron, King Alfonso XIII, had left Spain. Hoping one day to return, he refused to abdicate. He died in Rome in 1941. The Caudillo never allowed him to see his homeland again.

Republican general

In April 1931, mass politics brought forth democracy. The new democratic government arrived with high hopes that later proved to be unfounded and contradictory. As a result, the "Beautiful Girl", as the Republic was called, would meet a terrible end. But before the dread, came the reforms. Under the Republic, the supremacy of the civilian government over the military was asserted. The advancement of the Africanists' careers slowed because now promotions were only by seniority. Morocco was calm. Manuel Azaña, the new Minister of War (April 1931–September 1933), and also the Prime Minister (from October 1931 onwards), was an admirer of the French Army (he had been a correspondent on the Western Front during World War I). He initiated a process of rationalization of military resources that included reducing the number of senior officers. Knowing that many officers, if not most, had monarchist sympathies, he offered them the possibility of early retirement with full rights and pay. Those who remained had to promise loyalty to the new democratic regime. Most of the senior Africanists decided to stay but, as a result of this reform, the number of generals was reduced in 1932 to one-third of those in the last days of the monarchy. However, among those who remained, many were unhappy, mostly because of the freezing of their rank (which in many cases the new government regarded as having been achieved in an irregular manner) until they attained sufficient seniority. Franco was now stuck at the rank of brigadier general with dozens of more senior generals ahead of him.

Later Francoist propagandists would make a lot about this supposed republican persecution of brave and efficient officers and favouritism towards incompetent, pro-republican ones. This was not true. The republican government, like any civil government in the world, sought to control the Army, and logically appointed trusted officers to sensitive positions. Moreover, there was, indeed, a policy of generosity in this matter, forgiving people's past trajectories and showing them a measure of trust. Sanjurjo, for example, King Alfonso's favourite and the most "caudillo" of all "caudillos" of the pro-war press, would be appointed to the prestigious position of High Commissioner in Morocco. Other generals who had opposed the Primo de Rivera dictatorship only at the last moment, such as Goded, were also entrusted with commands. By the end of the first year of the Republic, both men were conspiring anew to overthrow the government.

Franco's only notable public performance during this period was a speech he gave in June 1931 to the cadets at the closing of his beloved Zaragoza Military Academy. It drifted towards sedition as he criticized the government's decision to dissolve the Academy. As a result, Azaña issued a reprimand, which was registered in his military record. This incident would later be construed as part of the myth of Franco as the obedient soldier persecuted by a regime that, as was becoming increasingly clear, was destroying both the Army and Spain. The beginning of Franco's suffering was to become the symbol of Spain's painful national ordeal. As Spain marched towards its martyrdom (i.e. communism), waiting for its saviour, evil was incarnated in the person of Azaña, who was called "Warts" (mocking his facial skin condition) by the right, as the leader of a gang of criminals and buffoons.[19] The first meeting between the saviour and "Warts" took place in August 1931, when the Minister of War agreed to see the young brigadier general, who had been left without a command since the Zaragoza incident. Later versions of the meeting would present this moment as the one in which a mortal challenge started, as Azaña understood that he had met his nemesis. Upon seeing Franco, Azaña was supposed to have immediately feared the Caudillo:

> Azaña's mind is a cold exudation of his gelatinous flesh, which while crawling along the road encounters a name and in that moment recoils and shrivels like a slug. The name that freezes him, perturbs him, cuts him in two is that of General Franco.[20]

This was written not in 1931 or 1932—at which time it would have been just pure nonsense—but in 1939, the Year of Victory, by which time the past had so dramatically changed, Francisco Franco's image along with it. From the moment of the 1931 meeting, the Francoist myth goes, Azaña had sought Franco's friendship out of fear, all the while plotting the future dictator's destruction. Even today, some authors repeat this fanciful tale.

Franco hated the Republic but he was not the Caudillo-in-waiting of a Spain needing to be saved. Nor did politicians fear him, at least no more than other generals of dubious loyalty. In fact, he never openly confronted the regime until the start of the Civil War on July 18, 1936. To be sure, he tried to manipulate politicians and institutions to enhance his own goals, but this was an entirely different matter. During the five years of the democratic Republic, Franco behaved exactly as he had in the past: his main objective was to advance his career. In the eyes of the public, at least until October 1934, he was just a young general—in other words a not overly well-known, albeit in certain circles prominent, citizen of the Republic. But Franco was biding his time, calculating the risks and opportunities, all the while keeping his opinions as guarded as possible. Eventually, by late 1934, he understood that only collaboration with the rising right-wing parties could allow him to fulfil his ambitions.

The first test of his resolution (and cunning restraint) came when his former patron, Sanjurjo, attempted his coup against the Republic in August 1932. In spite of his dubious role in the fall of the monarchy—when as head of the Civil Guard he had refused to help his "friend" the King—Sanjurjo was still the right's favourite. In January of 1932, *ABC* had described him as a "caudillo and […] legendary Spanish warrior [because of] his capabilities for command, serene courage, and scientific strategy".[21] Franco, who had been invited to join the conspiracy, rightly suspected the plan to be woefully underprepared, and declined to participate. However, just in case, he asked Sanjurjo if, were the coup to succeed, he could be appointed new High Commissioner in Morocco. Sanjurjo was not amused, calling him a slippery (*cuquito*) lad. The coup, indeed, failed but Sanjurjo's fans only increased. The following year (1933), *El Caballero Audaz*, the same glorifier of the Legion in the early 1920s, published a passionate defence of Sanjurjo calling him a "caudillo", a "victim", and a "hero".[22]

In November 1933, Azaña and the left lost the general elections, and a centre-right government was formed, led by the Radical Party of Alejandro Lerroux. The real victor at the ballots had been the anti-republican CEDA party (Confederación Española de Derechas Autónomas), led by José María Gil-Robles. However, the president of the Republic, the moderate Catholic Niceto Alcalá–Zamora, did not allow Gil-Robles to form a government, fearing he intended to destroy the democratic regime. After forming a new government, Prime Minister Lerroux, a friend of Sanjurjo, amnestied him and those condemned for the attempted coup. Sanjurjo went into exile in Portugal, where he continued plotting against the Republic. In May 1934 *ABC* dedicated a front-page photograph and a sizeable report to the "caudillo" signing autographs for his admirers in the glamorous Portuguese resort of Estoril.[23] The previous March, Franco had been finally promoted to Division General.

The new Spanish democracy was not working well. There was too much instability, too much sectarianism, and too little desire for compromise. In addition, the republicans themselves were divided over what type of regime they wanted. On the left, the powerful anarchist movement Confederación Nacional del Trabajo (CNT)— which advocated revolution above all else—opposed the democratic regime because of its supposed reformism. The group organized a number of violent confrontations and doomed mini-revolts that frightened the public. More seriously, because it was a major pillar of the Republic, a growing faction of the Partido Socialista Obrero Español (PSOE), or Spanish Workers' Socialist Party, became disenchanted with the slow pace of governmental reform, and adopted an increasingly revolutionary stance. However, the Republic's most dangerous enemy was on the right, particularly CEDA, which did not hide its plans to establish a corporative state modelled on the Dollfuss dictatorship in Austria.

Finding themselves excluded from power, CEDA designed a strategy of undermining the government first by forcing successive cabinet crises, then joining the government, and finally both replacing the radicals, who suffered from serious internal division, and ending the democratic system. The plan seemed to succeed when in October 1934 it was announced that CEDA was joining the government. However, the socialists, and Catalan republicans and others anticipated the move. They prepared a revolt to prevent the destruction of democracy. They dreamed of using this opportunity to change the course of the Republic according to their increasingly radical views. Their plan was ill-coordinated, and resulted in a short-lived rebellion in Barcelona that was easily put down. Of far greater significance, however, was the general uprising that occurred in the northern mining region of Asturias. It was a very violent event. The death toll of the so-called Asturias Revolution has been estimated at 1,500, of whom just over 300 were soldiers and policemen. Atrocities were common with the government forces committing most of them. It would never be the same afterwards, as both the country's politics and political language became rapidly polarized. For example, the far-right leader José Calvo Sotelo stated publicly that the government's response was insufficient; he wanted a massacre along the lines of the reaction that met the Paris Commune in 1871 (which he estimated to be at the prophylactic level of 40,000 executed). After October 1934 the Republic was certainly badly wounded, if not in mortal danger.

Once again, Franco's career benefited from public calamity, as the October 1934 crisis made him one of the new champions of the right. The man with pretensions to power again surfaced behind the ambiguous mask of the general who claimed to abhor politics. He was in Madrid when the rebellion in Asturias broke out. The far-from-expert Minister of War, the Radical Diego Hidalgo, recruited him to coordinate the ensuing military operation. Franco did not take chances and ordered the crack units of the colonial army, the Legion and the Moroccan Regulares, to Asturias. Sending Muslim troops to Asturias, which many Spaniards saw as the cradle of the medieval Christian *Reconquista* of the country, was a move loaded with symbolic significance. The colonial troops acted as they were trained: swiftly and brutally. However, while Franco's role was amply noted and hailed in the conservative press, the principal stars at the time were the senior general in charge of the operation, Eduardo López Ochoa, and the Legion commander, Lieutenant-Colonel Juan Yagüe. A relative indicator of the public presence of those involved in the repression in Asturias can be found in the number of times their names appeared in the press. In 1934, in the Army-friendly *ABC*, López Ochoa was mentioned 170 times, Yagüe 78 times, and Franco only 57 times.[24] These first two were very different men. López Ochoa was a moderate republican and a Freemason who tried to limit the excesses of the colonial troops. Yagüe was a pro-Fascist officer who encouraged violent repression. Franco had put Yagüe in command of the troops when the man who should have been leading them, Lieutenant-Colonel Miguel López Bravo, a Freemason, expressed doubts about the morality of firing on civilians. López Ochoa and Yagüe would meet very different fates during the Civil War. The first would be lynched by a mob in republican Madrid at the beginning of the conflict. Yagüe would have a flourishing career among the rebels of 1936. He was responsible for the notorious Badajoz massacre of August 1936, in which some 4,000 republican militia members were shot.

As far as the right was concerned, Franco was clearly a man to count on after his performance in Asturias. In this regard he was not so much a walking revelation of a saviour-in-waiting as he was a needed instrument, another resource to transform—or, better still, to destroy—the hated Republic. Franco was rewarded well for his services to the government. Between February and May 1935, he was posted in Morocco as supreme military commander. During these months, he renewed his links with the restless colonial officers. This circumstance was crucial for Franco's future since these Africanist officers would form the spearhead of the July 1936 rebellion against the Republic. However, before that, in 1935 and early 1936, the man on whom the hopes of national redemption were truly pinned was not a military officer, but the right's much-lauded Gil-Robles, or, as he was called by his enthusiastic supporters, the JEFE (or Boss, always in capital letters). When Gil-Robles became Minister of War in May 1935 he promoted several Africanists. He also made Franco his most direct colla-borator as Chief of Staff of the Spanish Army. Franco's future was now clearly linked to the political fortunes of the anti-republican forces and, it seemed, the adored, lionized JEFE. His increasing prominence can again be detected by the number of times his name appeared in *ABC*. During the first four years of the Republic (1931–1935), General Franco's name appeared on 172 occasions, almost three quarters of which occurred in the years 1934 and 1935 (57 and 74 times, respectively). Other generals were mentioned more often. By far, the most commonly mentioned was Sanjurjo (611 times); but other officers also greatly surpassed Franco. These included Domingo Batet (369), Miguel Cabanellas (330), Manuel Goded (262), Eduardo López Ochoa (246), and Lieutenant-Colonel Juan Yagüe (239). It was only after 1934—and especially in 1935, because of his role in suppressing the Asturias revolt and, even more importantly, his position in the General Staff—that Franco became a true national celebrity—one with clear political, not messianic, overtones.

With political compromise came both fame and the risks that the prudent general had avoided until then. In 1936, prior to July 18, he was the second most prominently mentioned general in *ABC* (39 times), right after the Minister of War, General Carlos Masquelet (86). But other generals were also mentioned frequently in the press: López Ochoa (31), Nicolás Molero (28), Domingo Batet (25), Goded (17), and again, more often than Franco him-self, Yagüe (49). They were mentioned either because they were connected to the events in Asturias or because they were generals appointed or demoted by the new, post-February 1936 Popular

Front government to or from positions of responsibility. Essentially, Franco's prominence in the media throughout 1936 can be explained by the successive events that marked his professional life that year: rumours of him being demoted from the General Staff, his actual demotion, his presence in the official Spanish representation at King George V's funeral, and finally his transfer to the Canary Islands, where he was made military commander. Franco was known, in other words, because of the official positions he had held under successive right-wing governments, particularly under Gil-Robles, and not because of any extraordinary personal characteristics. This reality does not correspond to the heroic narrative of the persecuted saviour-in-waiting that would be retrospectively projected onto the dictator's past. In order to create the mythology of the Caudillo, the official Francoist memory of this period would be foggy, and it would make sure that his bosses during this time, and particularly his last great patron and former JEFE of the right, Gil-Robles, became forgotten outcasts. The same would happen with his former patrons the King, Berenguer, Sanjurjo and, to an extent, Millán Astray. Their presence in the official historical memory of post-Civil War Spain could have brought inconvenient recollections of who Franco truly was before becoming the Caudillo.

Plotter

This is the story of a myth—of an honest general who supposedly never plotted, yet who, when forced to become a rebel, was naturally acclaimed leader of a national uprising for the simple reason that he was, and always had been, Spain's Caudillo-in-waiting. In reality, however, on the eve of the war, in July 1936, Franco was not yet the man of destiny on whom Spain's salvation depended. He was certainly well known in Spain, but no more than that, and to the rest of the world he was virtually unknown. Before July 18, the international press only mentioned his name twice. First, right after the February 1936 elections, because of rumours of his involvement with Goded in a coup. The *New York Times* wrongly called him General José Maria Franco, and misspelled Goded's name as Godet.[25] The second time, a few days later, there was again mention of him as having been demoted from Chief of Staff because of his connection to Gil-Robles. But here again his name was mentioned next to Goded's.[26] Both generals were sent by Prime Minister Azaña (who became President of the Republic in May) to command distant garrisons, Franco to the Canary Islands, and Goded to the Balearic Islands, since they were the "two rightest generals who are most feared by the left".[27] After this, both men—who were young, energetic and ambitious—disappeared from view until the July 18 rebellion.

During the first half of 1936 Franco was a politically compromised general who was known by the government to talk from time to time with hothead colleagues; his professional situation was correspondingly shaky. It had been deteriorating since late 1935, when the CEDA's strategy of achieving power and destroying democracy failed, mostly because the President of the Republic had never conceded Gil-Robles the premiership. Instead, President Alcalá-Zamora dissolved parliament and called new elections for February 16, 1936. The right, which formed an anti-Revolutionary Bloc, was supposed to win, but the centre-left, now organized into an electoral coalition under the name of the Popular Front, won. However, while in terms of members of parliament elected the leftist victory was decisive, in numbers of votes it was very narrow. This was a construct of the electoral system, which favoured coalitions, and had worked to the right's advantage in 1933. The centrist vote had almost evaporated as a result of the country's growing political polarization. It was a political crisis that offered both serious risks for the country as well as opportunity, particularly for those who saw this moment as their last opportunity to tear down the hated Republic. Franco belonged to this group.

The demise of the political right also spelled Franco's own professional failure. This explains why he tried to use his position as Chief of the General Staff to secure the permanence of the right in power, even by means of a dictatorship. Upon learning of the results of the February elections, Franco and his competitor Goded urged the provisional Prime Minister, Manuel Portela Valladares, to disregard the results and declare martial law. Their excuse was the disturbances then taking place as crowds (or mobs) celebrated the left-wing victory. The two main leaders of the right, Gil-Robles and Calvo Sotelo, were also pushing the government to accept Franco and Goded's plans. The latter went further and tried to deploy the Madrid garrison supposedly to quell the unrest.

Goded's impulsiveness and Franco's relatively cautious attitude failed when key pro-republican generals objected and the plan came to nothing. Later, in his quest for personal security, Franco almost became a right-wing deputy for Cuenca in that province's repeated elections scheduled for early May 1936. However, the opposition of Falange leader José Antonio Primo de Rivera to the general's presence on the ballot foiled this plan. This was the beginning of a complicated relationship between both men.

The February 1936 elections would change the fate of Spain, but they would also invert the relationship between army officers and right-wing politicians. Since the civilian-led right-wing plan to destroy the Republic had failed it was now the turn of the anti-republican army officers to act. On March 8, 1936 there was a secret meeting in Madrid of army officers, mostly generals. The man who risked the most was Brigadier Emilio Mola, a former collaborator of Primo de Rivera's, who was now the "director" of the unfolding conspiracy. The nominal leader of the coup was General Sanjurjo, still living in Portugal. Franco was present at this meeting but, characteristically, he did not commit himself to anything concrete: he asked only that he be kept informed. He was about to be sent to the Canary Islands as the new commander of the archipelago. The plotters resented his elusive attitude, but they wanted him because they knew that the rebellion would triumph only if the colonial army became involved. Sanjurjo's 1932 coup had failed, partly because the government was able to mobilize the police against the weak rebel troops made up of conscripts. The Legion and Regulares would guarantee that this would not happen. There was no general in Africa involved in the conspiracy (according to the plan, the pro-republican generals there would either be killed or arrested). Franco was therefore the natural choice to lead the troops. He was held in high regard by the officers in North Africa: in addition to his fighting past service there, in early 1935 he had been, for a period of a few months, the supreme commander of the troops posted in Morocco (he left the post to serve under Gil-Robles). Furthermore, he could easily jump from the Canary Islands to the North of Africa. However, in the following months, Franco remained uncommitted and tried to avoid what was increasingly becoming inevitable. Yet the scale of the conspiracy left him no room to prevaricate. He had to decide to risk his career, and perhaps even his life.

Franco's attitude leading up to mid-July 1936 has since been presented by his supporters as one of his last attempts to remain loyal to the Republic—as long as the regime was capable of maintaining order—out of a reluctance to break military discipline. According to this interpretation, the last time he tried to avoid taking such a risk was on June 23, when he sent a carefully crafted letter to the moderate republican Prime Minister Santiago Casares Quiroga. The letter started by reiterating professional complaints regarding promotions. He linked this problem to the government's interference in Army matters through its use of political appointments for generals. This civilian interference had another unpleasant side, he wrote: the growing number of attacks and insults by the mobs. The future Caudillo ended the letter by showing his contempt for secret organizations and the lack of discipline in the Army. He asked the government to seek the help of professional, competent generals like himself. Throughout the letter, Franco declared himself a loyal subordinate to the very Prime Minister he would rebel against less than a month later.

There has been much speculation over Franco's real intentions in writing this letter. Some believe he was covering his tracks, or playing both sides. However, the main question behind most analyses of Franco's attitude in 1936 forms part of a larger historical problem: whether or not Franco, and the rest of the rebels, were reacting against a real—as opposed to inflated—threat of political revolution. Pro-Francoist authors and supporters have always claimed that during this period Spain was on the verge of a Communist revolution. The rebellion was thus justified since it was directed against a government that had already lost its legitimacy.[28] For anti-Francoists, the 1936 rebellion was just an anti-democratic uprising staged by one sector of the Army, and Franco was little more than a reactionary opportunist who eventually cast his lot with the side he thought offered more and whose political views were closer to his own.

The first pivotal moment in the creation of a narrative of terror and chaos came from Gil-Robles, Franco's former boss and now the waning idol of the right. Almost a month to the day before the start of the coup he gave a speech in parliament in which he surveyed the country's situation. Among other horrors that had taken place in the four months that had elapsed since February 16, he said, 269 people had been killed, and 1,500 injured.[29] The second pivotal moment came with the murder of one of the main opposition leaders, Calvo Sotelo, on July 13. Future, mostly pro-Francoist, interpretations of this event would portray the Republic as an illegitimate regime controlled by criminals and worthy of extermination; such an interpretation posited that the Civil War was unavoidable and that Franco was a reluctant rebel forced to act and to embrace his destiny as saviour of Spain. However, the denunciations by Gil-Robles and Calvo Sotelo, and the murder of the latter four days before the war started, served to obscure the fact that the Army-inspired coup had been in the making for some months, and that both men were deeply involved in the conspiracy. Tragically, when Gil-Robles pinned all the casualties prior to July 1936 on the government (knowing all too well that the killers were from both sides) he did not know that the war that was soon to start would kill more people every day for the next 1,000 days than those 269 in the six months of supposed anarchy in democratic in Spain.

Franco almost did not answer his providential mission. On July 8, Franco and his fellow conspirator, General Alfredo Kindelán, had a telephone conversation. Kindelán was horrified when he learned that Franco still had doubts about the plot. Luis Bolín had already been asked to rent a British aircraft in London, the famous *Dragon Rapide*, to take Franco from the Canary Islands to Spanish Morocco. In spite of this, on July 12 of that month Franco sent the infamous *"geografía poco extensa"*—meaning, with little imagination, that "the situation is not clear to me"—message to Kindelán and Mola. The latter got the message on July 14 in Pamplona, where he was the senior military commander. Mola never fully trusted Franco, before or during the uprising, which may explain why he almost completely disappeared from the official memory of the regime after his death in June 1937. Full of rage, Mola asked the Spanish pilot Juan Antonio Ansaldo to pick up Sanjurjo from his Portuguese exile and fly him to Morocco so he could take command of the African Army instead of Franco. This would have changed history, and we would likely have never heard much from Franco again. However, upon receiving the news of Calvo Sotelo's murder, Franco realized that there was no room for complacency. Only then did he decide to fully commit himself to the coup.

The future Caudillo acted very cautiously. The *Dragon Rapide* was already waiting for him in Las Palmas de Gran Canaria (Tenerife had no suitable airport). Franco arrived there from Tenerife early in the morning of July 17, with the excuse he was attending the funeral of his friend General Amado Balmes, who had died in a strange, still unexplained but certainly opportune, shooting incident (perhaps an accident) the day before. At about 4 am on July 18 the rebels in Morocco told him that they controlled the territory. Upon receiving the news of the uprising's success, Franco declared martial law in the archipelago, claiming that he was acting to defend the Republic (more in Chapter 2). That same morning, he embarked his wife and daughter on a German liner departing for France. At 2 pm Franco flew from the island.

A direct flight from Las Palmas to Tetuán on the *Dragon Rapide* should have taken seven hours. Instead, it took seventeen, with stops in Agadir and Casablanca, reaching its destination only on July 19 at 7 am. Franco was never personally at risk. He travelled with a borrowed diplomatic passport that *in extremis* could be used to avoid interception by French authorities in Morocco. More importantly, during the plane's two stops Franco kept in contact with the rebels waiting for him who confirmed that they controlled the territory of Spanish Morocco. While flying Franco did three things that could be interpreted in a variety of ways: he shaved his moustache, dressed himself as an Arab, and finally, dropped from the plane into the sea a suitcase in which he had put clothes and documents. What these documents contained has been widely speculated upon by Franco's critics. Before the plane landed in Tetuán, Franco donned his military uniform once again, but asked the pilot to circle the base, ordering him to descend only when he recognized Colonel Sáez de Buruaga, whose blond hair made him easy to identify. According to some authors, the financier Juan March had made an important deposit in a foreign bank in case the coup was to fail. There is no proof of this.

Franco's overly cautious (his enemies would call it dubious) behaviour was very different from that of General Manuel Goded, the man that the foreign press had been presenting in the spring of 1936 as the other possible candidate for a coup against the

Republic. Like Franco, he had been a brigadier general since 1926, having made a lucrative career out of his tenure in Africa. Unlike Franco, however, who had waited safely on the sidelines, Goded took part in the August 1932 Sanjurjo coup. He was subsequently arrested, and later pardoned. In 1936, while Franco was sent as commander of the Canary Islands, Goded received a similar posting in the Balearic Islands. Both men now had the same rank of divisional general.

On July 19, Goded rebelled and gained control of the islands (except for Minorca) and then, the same day, took a seaplane to Barcelona even though it was expected that the fight was going to be difficult, and probably hopeless, for the rebels. Unlike Franco's flight towards a safe destination, Goded truly risked his life when he flew to a city that was loyal to the Republic. He stood no chance. He was defeated and captured that same day, then forced to announce on radio his surrender. Condemned to death, he was executed in August. However, in spite of his extraordinary courage, the Francoists would never forgive Goded for his radio capitulation. He was thus nearly forgotten—or remembered with barely concealed contempt—by the regime's propagandists. Goded was excluded from the series of bombastic biographies *Héroes de España* (Spain's Heroes) published during the war to honour the main generals of the rebel side. Sanjurjo's name was also absent.

Seen from abroad, events in Spain after July 18, 1936 were sudden, brutal and certainly surprising. On July 16 the news of Calvo Sotelo's murder appeared in the international press. It was also reported that the right was now boycotting parliament. Then, almost out of the blue, on July 20 the terrific headline "Civil War in Spain" appeared.[30] Franco's name resurfaced on that day, never to disappear again, as news of a widespread military revolt started to reach the world. In these first moments, his name was still used on a par with General Manuel Goded's as the only two men "qualified to be dictator", unless the rebels were planning to resuscitate "General Jose Sanjurjo [the] amiable playboy who bungled the 1932 revolt".[31] What newspapermen abroad did not yet know was that Sanjurjo was already dead, burned inside the small plane that crashed as it was trying to take him from Portugal to Spain, and that Goded was a prisoner of the republicans. However, another rival, General Mola, the brains behind the conspiracy, was already racing towards

Madrid from the North, thanks to the tens of thousands of Basque and Navarrese Carlist volunteers who were flocking to his side. The rebellion did not yet have a clear leader, but while Franco was still organizing his professional troops on the southern shores of the Strait of Gibraltar, Mola's columns had the capital of the Republic in their sights.

Until July 20, 1936 Franco's ultimate personal and professional ambition seems to have been to become the High Commissioner of Spanish Morocco. For all his rapid promotions in Africa, his trajectory—like that of Goded, Sanjurjo, Mola and the other "caudillos"—could easily have come to nothing as a result of the terrible events that the July 1936 rebellion unleashed; and in future historical accounts, Franco's name and fate could have been exchanged with any of these other generals. Yet a number of accidents, the way in which the Civil War unfolded, and his crude opportunism, would, in a matter of weeks, make him *the* Caudillo. In the process, the public persona that up to July 1936 had been just General Francisco Franco gained a new meaning, and a new, exceptional past.

Notes

1 Víctor Ruiz Albéniz [El Tebib Arrumi], *Las responsabilidades del desastre. Ecce Homo. Prueba documental y aportes inéditos sobre las causas del derrumbamiento y consecuencias de él*, Madrid, Biblioteca Nueva, 1922.

2 Carlos Micó España, *Los caballeros de la Legión (El libro del Tercio de Extranjeros)*, Madrid, Sucesores de Rivadeneyra, 1922, pp. 5–6.

3 24-8-1921, "Hablando con el general Silvestre", *ABC*.

4 Eduardo Ortega y Gasset, *Annual. Relato de un soldado e impresiones de un cronista*, Madrid, Ediciones del Viento, 2008, pp. 127–130. First published in 1922.

5 Laura Zenobi, *La construcción del mito de Franco. De jefe legionario a Caudillo de España*, doctoral thesis, Universidad Autónoma de Barcelona, 2008, p. 56. A version of this Ph.D. dissertation was published as Laura Zenobi, *La construcción del mito de Franco. De jefe de la Legión a Caudillo de España*, Madrid, Cátedra, 2011.

6 Zenobi, *construcción*, p. 58.

7 Ibid., p. 51.

8 Ibid., p. 63.

9 Francisco Franco Bahamonde, *Marruecos. Diario de una bandera*, Madrid, Puedo, 1922.

10 Zenobi, *construcción*, p. 82.

11 Benito Artigas Arpón, *La epopeya de Alhucemas (Los alicates rotos)*, Madrid, J. Pérez Impresor, 1925, pp. 41–42.

12 Ibid., p. 45.
13 M. Santiago Guerrero, J.M. Troncoso and B. Quintana, *La Columna Saro en la Campaña de Alhucemas*, Barcelona, Tipografía La Académica, 1926, pp. 210–211.
14 Juan Canellas Romero, *El desembarco de Alhucemas. Crónicas periodísticas de Juan Luque, Diario de Bracelona, 1925*, Melilla, Comunidad Autónoma, 2007, p. 82.
15 Ibid.
16 Artigas, *epopeya*, p. 208.
17 Ibid., pp. 115–117.
18 General Goded, *Marruecos. Las etapas de la pacificación*, Madrid-Barcelona-Buenos Aires, Compañía Ibero-Americana de Publicaciones, 1932, pp. 136–139, 197–199.
19 Francisco Casares, *Azaña y ellos. Cincuenta semblanzas rojas*, Granada, Prieto, 1938.
20 Joaquín Arrarás, *Memorias íntimas de Azaña (con ilustraciones de Kin)*, Madrid, Ediciones Españolas, 1939, p. 307.
21 17-1-1932, "El Hombre y su caricatura: el general Sanjurjo", *ABC*.
22 José María Carretero [Caballero Audaz], *Sanjurjo, Caudillo y víctima*, Madrid, Imp. Sáez Hernández, 1932.
23 2-5-1934, "El general Sanjurjo en Estoril", *ABC*.
24 These statistics can be obtained by using the *ABC* newspaper website, section "Hemeroteca".
25 19-2-1936, "Spain is on guard against Army coup", *The New York Times*.
26 22-2-1936, "Two rightist Army chiefs demoted"; "General amnesty decreed in Spain", *The New York Times*.
27 Cited from 22-2-1936, "Spain empties prisons to curb radical riots", *Chicago Daily Tribune*.
28 Ministerio de la Gobernación, *Dictamen de la Comisión sobre ilegitimidad de poderes actuantes en 18 de Julio de 1936*, Madrid, Editora Nacional, 1939. This thesis has been recently defended in Stanley Payne, *The Collapse of the Spanish Republic, 1931–1936: Origins of the Civil War*, New Haven-London, Yale University Press, 2006.
29 16-6-1936, "Burn 36 Spanish churches in 48 hours: 65 slain. Gil-Robles bares leftists regime's terror record", *Chicago Daily Tribune*; 19-6-1936, "Spain is swept by terror", *The New York Times*.
30 16-7-1936, "Anxieties in Spain. Monarchists Withdraw from Cortes", *The Times*; 7-20-1936, "Civil War in Spain", *The Times*.
31 20-7-1936, "Civil war rages in Spain", *Chicago Daily Tribune*.

2 Saviour of Spain, 1936–1939

A traumatic war

The most salient features of Francisco Franco's public persona assumed a definitive shape during the Spanish Civil War, which lasted from July 17, 1936 to April 1, 1939. His image was, and remains, inextricably linked to that terrible ordeal as it was experienced by Spaniards of all political stripes and social groups. As such, the war constitutes a lens through which Franco's historical figure will continue to be examined. Yet, while for the vast majority of the population the war was physically and emotionally traumatic, for a significant minority the conflict also resulted in a personal and political defeat. The political values of Spaniards, both during and after the dictatorship, cannot be properly understood without considering these realities. Equally, people's opinion of Franco cannot be separated from their interpretation of the Civil War itself—its causes, its course, and its consequences. However, the lasting memory of the dictator was not solely and spontaneously generated by the evolution of wartime events. There were other elements that came to bear on the construction of his public figure. Franco's image was also created by a persistent propaganda campaign that commenced at the beginning of the war and which eventually produced a cult of personality without parallel in Spanish history. The main traits of this official, canonical interpretation of his public image and historical mission were firmly established after Franco became the official head of the emerging New State in late September 1936. This version of his biography, or rather hagiography, remained remarkably stable until the dictator's death roughly four decades later. Finally, there was a foreign component to this interpretation of Franco's image, and this cannot be separated from the differing opinions on the conflict generated abroad. These opinions reflected, and indeed continue to reflect, more the cultural and political biases existing in the West in the 1930s and 1940s than they do the reality in Spain as experienced or remembered by Spaniards.

In spite of the incendiary political discourse and violent incidents that shook the country after the February 1936 elections, most Spaniards, regardless of their political leanings, did not expect, nor want, a war. The military rebellion caught most people by surprise. The horror of war nonetheless came swiftly in the days that followed. Admittedly, volunteers flocked to both sides, and there were even public celebrations of the rising in Northern Spain, most notoriously in Carlist areas, where supporters of an absolutist Catholic monarchy existed in great numbers. But these were a minority; for the majority of the population—almost twenty-five million people—the outbreak of war was first and foremost a horrible imposition of pain and suffering. No area of the country was spared. To start with, the summer and autumn of 1936 would witness mass killing as tens of thousands of people were murdered. Bodies were dumped everywhere, every day. By the end of the war, almost 100,000 men and women had been assassinated behind rebel lines. They were mostly workers, journeymen, liberal middle-class individuals, and republican militants. Behind republican lines, close to 50,000 people suffered the same fate. They were mainly priests, landowners, and businessmen, but also individuals of modest standing who identified with religion and order. On both sides, military officers and policemen were executed, often at the hands of their own colleagues. Fear and hatred permeated Spanish society, and, of course, polarized it. People were forced to take sides. Men, regardless of whom they had voted for a few months before, or what they thought about fighting, were thrown into uniform and sent to the various fronts. Political repression, bombardments, material scarcity, displacement, in addition to extensive human and material losses, tore the fabric of Spanish society asunder. Countless lives were ruined. Very soon, Spaniards, regardless of political opinion, were mourning the tens of thousands of men who had died either at the front or behind the lines. While the rear-guard killings greatly diminished by the end of 1936, the misery of war, not to mention military and civilian "collateral damage", did not. As a result, most Spaniards hated the war and just wanted it to end, with increasingly little regard for who the victor might be. This feeling worked in Franco's favour, since by early 1937 his troops were clearly winning.

All of this had been unthinkable just a few months before. To begin with, no one expected the military uprising to become a long civil war; not even the plotters of the coup. Had the conspiracy gone well and triumphed in a few days, or even weeks, Franco would probably have never been more than a prominent member of the ruling junta. But chance and the relatively successful republican resistance changed history, and Franco's fate as well. It was mostly the death of the other senior generals that left him as the sole candidate to lead the rebels. If things had gone according to Mola's plan, General Sanjurjo would have been appointed the nominal head of the movement, whose aim was to establish a republican dictatorship. It was to Franco's benefit that Sanjurjo died in a plane crash on July 20, 1936, thus allowing him to take command of the 47,000 members of the colonial army, by far the best trained and most heavily armed of all Spanish troops.

But there is another, often overlooked, side of Franco's rise to power, one that the official Francoist memory of the conflict never mentions. The emergence of the Caudillo was not solely the product of a military rebellion against civilian, democratic government; it was also the result of the split in the Army, the very institution that had made his professional success possible. Under Franco, the official account of the war would present the July uprising as a national movement to save Spain undertaken by the whole Army and led by the Caudillo—a twisted caricature of the truth, to be sure. To start with, the Army was divided regarding the rebellion, with one group, the rebels, active in the uprising, and the rest remaining mostly passive. The backbone of resistance to the rebellion came mostly from the police forces at first, and soon thereafter from armed workers' militias. In total, of the approximately over 200,000 members of the Spanish Army, fewer than 120,000 rebelled and fewer than 90,000 remained loyal. The beneficial positions occupied by the victorious officers after 1939 obscured the memories of their former murdered or purged colleagues who had occupied these positions before them. The Army that emerged from the war was very different from the pluralistic institution of the 1930s. Not surprisingly, loyalty towards the Caudillo was fierce among medium and lower-ranking officers.

However, the dictatorship's propaganda machine projected Civil War dynamics onto the past. Journalists, many of whom came from the old pro-Moroccan war lobby, were integral to this operation. For these journalists, the Army of Africa was the true Spanish Army. These were the same men who for years in Morocco had created, under the monarchy, the myth of the victorious colonial army; the same men who had been creating "caudillos", "heroes" and, let's not forget their Manichean foes, the "Moors". Moreover, there was a delicious irony at play here in that these "Moors" were now fighting on Franco's side as his mercenaries against fellow Spaniards.

General Mola had expected a brief and bloody resistance, followed by a swift and ruthless elimination of officers loyal to the Republic and, of course, of left-wing and labour leaders. He predicted that some big cities, such as Madrid and Barcelona, would be hard to control. However, whatever resistance the government could mount, it would, according to Mola's plan, be overcome by the rebel columns marching on Madrid from the periphery of the country. The two main forces in those columns were, from the North, the Carlist volunteers and regular soldiers under Mola's command in Pamplona (Navarre) and, from the South, the Army of Africa led by Franco.

In the first days of the rebellion Mola's plan enjoyed some lucky successes, but also several serious setbacks. Some garrisons hesitated, and others were overpowered by the combined forces of loyal troops, policemen and hastily armed workers' militias. By far the most successful operations occurred in the northern half of the country, which except for an isolated republican pocket that comprised most of the Cantabrian coast (the provinces of Guipúzcoa, Biscay, Santander and most of Asturias) was quickly and fully controlled by the rebels, who soon would start calling themselves the Nationals. As a result, within days of the rebellion, Mola's forces were attacking the mountain passes just north of Madrid, which they hoped—and the international press expected they would be able—to force in late July or early August at the latest. However, Mola did not have enough forces to achieve this.

Even more crucially, the second pillar of the plan to guarantee the rapid victory for the rebels failed when the columns that were supposed to take Madrid from the south never materialized. This was because of the inability of the rebel leaders to transport the colonial army to mainland Spain. Although the rebels controlled key southern ports such as Algeciras, Cádiz and Sevilla, most of the Air Force and, particularly the Navy, remained loyal to the Republic. In the case of the Navy, crews overpowered, and later assassinated, their officers, the majority of whom sympathized with the uprising. The result was that the government was able to maintain control of the skies and the seas in the Strait of Gibraltar and the Mediterranean Sea, thus blocking the transfer of the rebel army to mainland Spain. In July 1936, most of Franco's feared colonial troops remained stranded in Morocco. However, a few thousand of these men and some materiel were finally flown in by plane, especially after Italian aircraft started to operate at the end of the month. In early August, German aircraft joined them.

Initially, the Nationals' situation appeared bleak, but this proved to be Franco's fortune. His emissaries contacted Mussolini and Hitler—both men had also been approached by representatives of Mola—who decided to support the uprising and also to channel most of their assistance through Franco. Franco was thus granted the double advantage of having the best-trained troops and also controlling the informal channels of communication with the new Italian and German allies. Spanish and Italian planes helped to disperse the republican fleet, allowing the first significant transport of troops from Africa to Algeciras by sea on August 5. Rebel propaganda immediately labelled this operation "Victory Convoy": this was a misnomer, since only about 1,600 troops were landed— far fewer than those already transported by air—but as we shall see later in this chapter, the Caudillo's hagiographers greatly exaggerated the value of the operation. What's more, they attributed its success solely to Franco, forgetting the crucial role of both foreign forces and his own advisers.

Paradoxically, the late arrival of the Army of Africa would benefit Franco's public standing. Mola's, as well as several other generals', early conquest of most of the North had come too easily to boost their own reputations. After the first two weeks of the war, the victories of Mola's forces (with the exception of the conquest of the key cities of Irún and San Sebastián in the province of Guipúzcoa in the first half of September) were few and far between. As a result, while the most remarkable early heroes of the revolt would be the Carlist volunteers, in the murderous and emotionally charged months from August to November it would be the Legionnaires and the Regulares—Franco's troops—that would galvanize the hopes of the rebellion's supporters. Indeed, between August and early November these professional soldiers would be responsible for most of the major rebel successes. This helped to create the prestige that would attach itself to Franco's name, thus making possible his dizzyingly fast, unexpected, political ascendency. Having been a reluctant conspirator until just days before the rebellion was launched, he suddenly found himself the supreme commander of the rebel armies on September 21, just two months later. After further negotiations, his colleagues made him head of their emerging New State on September 28 (officially, his appointment would begin on October 1). Many of his fellow generals assumed this would be a temporary arrangement until the war was over and a more final political formula could be adopted. Most of these generals were monarchists, while the remainder were in favour of a republican dictatorship, either military or civilian run. Franco, Alfonso XIII's former protégée, was known not to have an opinion on this question.

The unexpected length of the war made Franco's political rise possible. Although, when his troops besieged Madrid in early November 1936, he was already the Generalissimo, he was not yet the dictator. Had he taken the capital then, it was still far from certain that he would have been able to achieve total power. But he failed at this several times in the following months. The rebels' hopes of quickly taking the capital and winning the war were dashed by two developments: one was foreign intervention; the other was the new Generalissimo's own strategic blunders. After Italy and Germany started to help Franco, the Soviet Union decided, rather belatedly, to send military aid to the Republic. Soviet materiel (planes and tanks) arrived just in time to save Madrid. The republican government had already tried to purchase weapons from its traditional suppliers, Britain and France, but the Conservative-led British government was hostile to the Spanish Popular Front. Ignoring international law, Britain decided to establish an arms embargo, forcing France and most minor powers to join. In addition, there was strong domestic political opposition in France to any military intervention to help the Republic. British, and to a lesser extent American, "malevolent neutrality", plus French passivity, thus dictated the course of the war.

The keystone of this false neutrality was a Non-Intervention Committee that was set up outside the League of Nations and had its first meeting in London in early September. In addition to France and Britain, Germany, Italy, and the Soviet Union sat on it. The foxes were thus put in charge of the henhouse. The role played by the Committee can be fairly described as a sanctimonious farce, one that allowed Franco to get all the weapons he needed while not only preventing the legal Spanish government from doing the same, but also forcing it to seek assistance from the always dangerous hands of Stalin.

But Stalin's weapons alone did not save Madrid; Franco himself contributed to his troops' failure to take the city. In September, instead of attacking the demoralized and largely defenceless capital, he had diverted his army towards Toledo. Taking a detour, his troops went to rescue a small garrison of civil guards and some soldiers and cadet officers besieged at the fortress called the *Alcázar*. The siege became a myth of the rebel zone (about which a movie would be made in 1940, in Fascist Italy). Franco's troops arrived in Toledo on September 27, just hours before their commander was about to be appointed leader of the New State. It was a great propaganda coup for Franco, one that certainly reinforced the Generalissimo's prestige and gave him time to consolidate his power, though it may well have cost his side two-and-a-half more years of war.

The last key moment in Franco's political rise occurred in April 1937, when he forced the merger of all pro-rebel political forces into a single party, under his leadership. In name, at least, the party was a reflection of the Carlists and the pro-Fascist Falange; in fact, it was a mass party in which an amorphous group of individuals of different right-wing backgrounds could pursue their interests. The new organization was awkwardly named the Falange Española Tradicionalista y de las Juntas de Ofensivas Nacional Sindicalistas (FET-JONS). Significantly, the name of both the party and of the political boss Franco had served with such devotion in 1935—the CEDA and Gil-Robles, respectively—were absent from this political project, erased from the new official historical record.

During 1937, thanks to massive Italian and German support in both arms and men, Franco and his allies continued to advance, even if they repeatedly failed to take Madrid. After conquering Málaga in February 1937, the Italians suffered an embarrassing defeat at Guadalajara in March, as they tried once again to take the capital. Mussolini's response was to send even more reinforcements. Combined with German assistance, this allowed Franco to regain the initiative and conquer the remaining republican pocket in Northern Spain that summer. Then Franco's luck shone once again. As providence had removed Sanjurjo from his march to glory in July 1936, now, on June 3, 1937 Mola met a similar fate, perishing in another aviation accident, thus removing the Generalissimo's last competitor for power. (Immediately after his death, Mola's office safe was broken open by Franco's agents, and the contents removed, never to be seen again.)

Moreover, by mid-1937, Stalin had stopped sending any significant help to the loyalists. The Republic had been paying for the Soviet dictator's military deliveries in gold; these reserves, among the largest in the world at the time, were now completely depleted, and the government could not buy the weapons it needed to win the war. By contrast, the rebels remained well supplied throughout the war. The Nazis, and especially the Italians, provided more men and arms, delivered them on schedule, and this was all available to Franco on credit. In spite of some temporary setbacks, victory was clearly in sight for the Caudillo.

Throughout the following year, the Republic was barely able to put up any effective resistance to the rebel onslaught. Its only hopes of survival were some sort of international settlement, but this, of course, never arrived—1938 represented the climax of the Western policy of appeasement, in which Hitler received from Britain and France the green light to devour Austria and Czechoslovakia. In any case, Neville Chamberlain's convictions were very far from what the republican leaders hoped for. Both his anti-Communism and his desire to gain time for British rearmament were far stronger than his revulsion of right-wing dictatorships. The Republic was running out of time. The loss of Catalonia in January 1939 signalled that the end of the war was imminent. After a brief inter-republican civil war in March, the last republican defences collapsed at the end of the month, and Franco's troops advanced almost unopposed. The Caudillo was able to declare an official end to the conflict on April 1, 1939. Five months later, Britain and France would be embroiled in their own war against Nazi Germany.

Constructing a myth

While Spaniards had been enduring nearly three years of fratricidal war, the New State's propaganda machine was busy creating Franco's new, enduring public image. In the first months of the war this was not a uniform or centralized process. The information provided by the press on the rebel side concerning the role of various generals and, less frequently, political leaders, varied significantly depending on the area in which a paper was published or a radio speech broadcast. Local realities—which general or militia controlled a given area—determined what information was fed to the people. In very broad terms, the dynamics of this process played out differently in the northern and southern parts of the rebel zone (which were linked only after the conquest of Badajoz in mid-August 1936). This divergence would gradually disappear as the propaganda organs of the New State were established in the late summer and early fall of 1936, with the information provided across the whole rebel zone becoming consistent by December of that year.

Franco's name appeared far less often during the first weeks of the war in the northern zone than in the southern zone. Carlist newspapers in the north, such as the *Pensamiento Alavés*, reflected mostly local concerns and local heroes, and paid scant attention to Franco's glories in the south. The leader of the northern armies, General Mola, was the officer most often mentioned. Also frequently mentioned was Miguel Cabanellas, initially the nominal head of the collective of rebel generals. (On July 24, he was appointed by his peers to the figurehead position of President of the Junta for National Defence. No fan of Franco, he later opposed his appointment as Generalissimo.) But the main concern in *Pensamiento Alavés* was the fate of the Carlist volunteers, whose exploits were amply reported as they advanced towards Madrid.[1]

News from the south was also reported, especially after the taking of Badajoz, but these stories were mostly rather impersonal, descriptive dispatches—a stark contrast to the personalized, euphoric accounts of the Basque fighters described in chronicles from the Madrid and Guipúzcoa fronts.

The first southern military figure to receive ample individual reporting in the Alava-Carlist press was not Franco but Millán Astray, who visited Vitoria on August 23, 1936. According to photographs of the event, Millán's colourful figure and rhetoric attracted a great number of onlookers and admirers. The march past that day of a Legion unit (another sign of a converging reality between north and south) seemed also to have attracted a lot of local attention. One remarkable aspect of Millán's speech—if one considers the seminal role played by the general in later fostering a personality cult around Franco—was that when he showered glory on the causes dearest to the rebel side he mentioned Spain, victory, labour, love, and death, but he did not once name the person who he would later (and not much later) claim to have always been the natural leader of the military rising: Franco.[2] For the rest of the summer, Franco's name appeared in the pages of *Pensamiento Alavés* as merely *one* of the generals fighting for the salvation of the motherland. Even on September 30, the day that this same paper reported Franco's appointment as Head of the Government of the Spanish State (a designation which Franco would hence change into the Head of the Government *and of* the Spanish State), this news was trumped by an even bigger headline, which informed fellow Carlists of something far more important to them: the death (in a traffic accident in Vienna) of their movement's "glorious caudillo", the eighty-seven-year-old Alfonso Carlos de Borbón. In the smaller headline devoted to the new leader of rebel Spain, Franco is merely referred to as the "Illustrious general".[3]

The Carlist view of events was in many ways unique, but it nonetheless shared many traits with other newspapers published in the northern zone. Among other things, it reflected the fact that in the first months of the war no one knew who would ultimately rule rebel Spain, what kind of political regime would be established, or how long it would last. More than anything, what is obvious in the coverage of the northern papers is that Franco was not *the* expected saviour. Vigo's (Galicia) *El Pueblo Gallego* provides another example. The newspaper had been the crown of the republican Galician press under the Republic; its owner was the former Prime Minister, Manuel Portela Valladares, the same man who opposed Franco, Goded and Gil-Robles' attempt to cancel the electoral results of February 16. On July 19, 1936, upon hearing of a military uprising in Morocco, the paper expressed its support for the democratic government. It was then seized by the military authorities, and shut down.[4] It reappeared on August 1, but now as a pro-rebel mouthpiece. By this time, the most relevant headline news was the advance of "General Franco's" troops from the south, and the landing of more colonial troops in Andalusia.[5] Franco's name, sometimes accompanied by the epithet "illustrious caudillo", was profusely cited in its pages, but so were the names of other generals, such as Mola (who was also called "caudillo").[6] The first hint that Franco's image was gaining ground on the other generals appeared in *El Pueblo Gallego* in mid-August 1936, when the paper reported how Franco's presence in the north of the country was being met by cheering crowds. This tendency became more marked in early September as Franco's mounting victories allowed him to increasingly present himself as the leader of the national movement.

The growth of Franco's political power and prestige was not solely a result of his Army's successes. Specific political manoeuvres were being undertaken by other generals, as well as German and Italian advisers, who wanted him to be appointed supreme commander of the rebel armies. At the same time, Franco also played a direct role in bolstering his own reputation as he embarked upon a blatantly self-aggrandizing propaganda project. Shortly after the beginning of the July rebellion, *ad hoc* propaganda offices had been set up in an attempt to promote various local generals' images. Later, on August 5, the Junta for National Defence created a press office in the city of Burgos. A number of former war correspondents from the Moroccan war joined this press corp. These propagandists would apply the very same language and interpretation that they had used in their coverage of the Moroccan campaign in the early 1920s to the Civil War. The two main journalists in charge of this propaganda office were Juan Pujol and Joaquín Arrarás. Pujol, a former correspondent for *ABC* and *El Imparcial*, as well as a former right-wing Member of Parliament during the Republic, had written the manifesto for Sanjurjo's failed August 1932 *coup d'état*. Arrarás, who would be the first biographer (or hagiographer) of the Caudillo, had been a correspondent in Morocco for *El Debate* (the Catholic newspaper which under the Republic was closely linked to the CEDA and Gil-Robles, and which Franco would never allow to re-open), as well as for *ABC*. When the Republic arrived, he became a very active enemy of the democratic regime. In five years, he was sued for defamation twenty-eight times, mostly for slurs against republican supporters and politicians.

In the south, the same men linked to *ABC* who had aided Franco in his journey from the Canary Islands to Tetuán, were crucial in the emergence of his image as the conquering hero and the principal nemesis of the beleaguered Republic. In July, Franco dispatched the journalist Luis Bolín (the man who had hired the *Dragon Rapide*) and his boss, the owner of *ABC*, Luis Ignacio Luca de Tena, to Rome to solicit military assistance from Mussolini. Bolín and Luca de Tena were ultimately successful, but they did even more for Franco. The *ABC*'s Sevilla edition (the paper was also printed simultaneously in Madrid, but with a pro-republican editorial line), and a number of seasoned journalists who converged there, became the future Caudillo's main propagandists, tailoring a new image of the General that recycled old myths and clichés for the hero's new needs. Thanks to these individuals, the Legionnaire perspective of the war (Bolín himself was an honorary captain of the Legion) would march north from Sevilla, both physically and mentally, towards Madrid and absolute power. Bolín thereafter remained attached to Franco's headquarters, where he served as his press secretary. In this capacity he commanded a number of military press officers whose task, among other things, was to keep an eye on the foreign correspondents who flocked to the war. Another press officer attached to Franco's headquarters was an old acquaintance from his Moroccan days: Víctor Ruiz Albéniz (*Tebib Arrumi*). As we shall see, in addition to his war chronicles, which Franco liked very much, Ruiz Albéniz would very soon glorify the General in a number of popular books for both adults and children.

That Franco's public prestige had surpassed that of the other rebel leaders was clear by early September. When the "heroic general" and "caudillo" Millán Astray visited Galicia that month, he delivered the usual passionate, rambling speech, full of violent metaphors. On September 6, he published a short article in *El Pueblo Gallego* in which he claimed:

> We have unbreakable faith in victory. God protects us. We have at the head of the Army the best general in today's world: GENERAL FRANCO. Our troops are the bravest and most heroic. We defend the fatherland, honour and our Religion.[7]

However, in spite of this and other allusions to Franco, most Spaniards probably did not expect the extraordinary news that began appearing around September 30, when it was officially announced that "the illustrious caudillo general Franco" had been appointed by the Junta for National Defence Head of the Spanish State and Commander and Chief of the Army.[8] It was only then that journalists started to talk about Franco as clearly being above the rest of the generals. The regime's new, centralized propaganda office, now in Salamanca, the provisional capital of the rebels, would make sure that Franco's personality cult would intensify. The director of this organization was none other than his old friend and protector Millán.

The men of *ABC-Sevilla* had been crucial in creating the first myths of Franco the Saviour of Spain. However, this paper's reporting of the first months of the war reveals how Franco's journey from well-known general to national Caudillo was less obvious than official accounts would later claim. It also reveals many initial hesitations and deceptions.

Mention of Franco, the rebel general, first appeared in *ABC* on July 22, 1936. By then, Sevilla was under the control of General Gonzalo Queipo de Llano, who was already carrying out a bloody repression of local republican sympathizers (approximately 8,000 people would be shot in the province during the war). The Franco who appears that day was a defender of the Republic. He would always say, and his hagiographers would reinforce the claim, that he never lauded the hated democratic regime. However, in *ABC* that day he ended his message from Tetuán with a "Cheer to Spain and the Republic!"[9] In an earlier radio message from the Canary Islands, in which he declared himself a rebel and which was later printed by *ABC* in its July 23 edition, Franco not only claimed he had joined the rebellion to defend the constitution from those who were "violating it", but also included a call to have true "Fraternity, Liberty, and Equality" (in this order) for the first time in Spain.[10] Another note by Franco lauding the Republic was published the same day.[11] In this he was not exceptional: other generals, such as Queipo and Miguel Cabanellas (Zaragoza) also praised the Republic while at the same time shooting republicans. However, as the rebellion took hold, Franco's public messages increasingly concluded with references to "Spain", "Great and Honest Spain" or to the "Honest Spanish People", eventually dropping any mention of the Republic after July 24. From this point on, moreover, he would unambiguously present himself as an anti-republican general.

Franco was called "caudillo" for the first time in the July 26, 1936 edition of *ABC*, but the noun—which was also used for other generals—went almost unnoticed since the real news at this time were the victories in the north, where Mola's soldiers were approaching Madrid, as well as the arrival of the first airlifted troops from Africa.[12] It was only in August that *ABC* would begin applying the word "caudillo" regularly to Franco. This press campaign, launched by the General's own propaganda office, culminated on August 23 when *ABC* labelled Franco—on its front page no less—"Chief of the Movement for the Salvation of the Fatherland".[13] This was false, since such a position did not exist at the time, but it indicated that now Franco was boldly asserting his pretensions to power.

In October, with Franco's appointment as head of the New State came control of all the propaganda organs the rebels then had at their disposal. The clique of journalists that accompanied the Caudillo from the south merged with other colleagues originally from Mola's circle. From this point on they worked together in fomenting a nation-wide cult of the Caudillo. This project began immediately. On October 4 Millán Astray published an article in *Faro de Vigo* under the title "Franco, conductor of Spain", in which he claimed his friend had been "sent by God, as a Conductor for the liberation and greatness of Spain". In this article, Millán went further than anyone in praising Franco, going so far as to claim that the Generalissimo, because of his previous conduct, had been since *the early 1920s* the indisputable leader of the army and the country, thus fabricating a direct, unbroken line between the wars in Morocco and the present situation:

Franco has been the inspiration of all Generals in Chief [*sic*] during the Morocco campaigns, of the re-conquests [*sic*] of Melilla, the Xauen withdrawal, the taking of Alhucemas. Franco was the man who saved the situation during the republican rebellion at Jaca. Franco was the inspiration and director of the suffocation of the Asturias revolt. Franco is the General and Chief of the Army in today's liberation of Spain. FRANCO, AS SOLDIER—he is the number one strategist of this century: he reads the map and decides with genial clarity [...] he never commits a mistake (I have been observing him since 1921 in Melilla, and up to today, during the battle for Toledo).[14]

A few weeks later, a campaign was launched, modelled on Italian and German propaganda techniques, including cementing Franco's role by using a typically totalitarian motto: "A Fatherland, a State, a Caudillo".[15] Showing the strict control of Franco's propaganda office *Diario de Navarra*, previously Mola's exclusive turf, published two articles on December 8 and 10, which had as a title two mantras that highlighted the need to rally under the indisputable leadership of the Caudillo: "A Faith, a State, a Caudillo" and "A Fatherland, a State, a Caudillo. A Fatherland; Spain. A Caudillo; Franco".[16] At the same time, thousands of photographs and posters of the always-smiling Generalissimo were being distributed.

Paradoxically, as Franco stubbornly tried and repeatedly failed to encircle and take Madrid, and the fronts stabilized in late 1936, the Generalissimo's power and personality cult actually increased. In January 1937, Millán compared Franco to other Fascist dictators, because, like them, God himself had anointed the great leader. In his rambling narrative he said:

In Italy, the land of the Caesars [...] was born Mussolini, Il Duce. He is the son of the people, who felt hunger, pain, unemployment [...] Also by God's finger, emerged the Führer. He breaks the chains that wanted to imprison the warring people from which he was born [...] Spain is today the chosen place, with most perfidious hatred, by the Soviet Jewish-Communists [...] And you, leading us, raise your victorious sword, looking towards the Orient, and will salute the Duce and the Führer, because you are the Caudillo.[17]

At the same time, having grown increasingly confidant and assertive, Franco was no longer content to limit himself to using the voices of journalists and writers. He wanted to control the transformation of himself from a mere *object* of political propaganda into the main guardian and interpreter of the newly emergent cult of his personality. In this process, his voice became the most author- itative testament to his own glory. He would now make his own appearances in the media to explain, and indeed re-make, both the present and the past.

Franco's decisive role in the evolution of his own image is demonstrated by a selection of his speeches from the period between July 1936 and March 1939.[18] The first speech included in this selection was originally made public on July 18, 1936. At this point he was still a hesitant general. The original hurrahs to the Republic were removed from this edited/doctored historical docu- ment, but the justification for his treason—that the Republic was not democratic—was maintained. He repeated several times that the government had violated the constitution, and that the impartiality of the courts had disappeared. In place of this fraud, the Nationals offered "Peace and love among Spaniards; freedom and fraternity free from licence and tyranny". The offer was repeated at the end of the document, promising again, and in this order, the trilogy: "fraternity, freedom and equality".[19] A good republican, a Freemason even, would not have spoken much differently. How- ever, very quickly these ambiguities and insecurities disappeared from official discourse, and were substituted with Franco's true ideas and ambitions.

In a speech on October 1, 1936 when he formally accepted his position as newly elected leader of the nascent rebel state, Franco presented a very different interpretation of what he thought Spaniards should expect from him. In this speech to the residents of Burgos, broadcast by *Radio Castilla*, he declared that "Non-organic popular suffrage" (by which he meant direct universal suffrage) had lost its prestige and from now on "the nation will express itself opportunely through those technical organs and cor- porations that, rooted in the entrails of the country, represent in an authentic way its ideals and its needs".[20] From self-appointed defender of an abused constitution and a supposedly moribund democracy in mid-July, Franco had become, in just two-and-a-half months, the resolute advocate of a Fascist-style system. Yet this Franco still presented himself as a member of a political collective; the themes he elaborated on included vague calls for a national rebirth, with hints of anti-capitalist rhetoric and, even more vaguely, the need for distance between Church and state. In sum, he was acting neither like the "Caudillo" nor an outright "reactionary". This was confirmed, for example, in an interview with a correspondent of the Argentinean newspaper *La Nación* on October 12, 1936—the occasion being the anniversary of Columbus' arrival in the New World in 1492. Franco talked mostly about Spain's near-death experience under the Republic and how the army that he now commanded, the spirit of which "even impresses our enemies", had saved the nation by restoring the country to the status of a great power. Significantly, in spite of the significance of the date, which traditionally marked the beginning of the Catholic evangelization of the New World, he barely mentioned the Church.[21]

However, even before becoming a dictator, Franco was already doing what he would do for the rest of his life—namely, justifying his mistakes. In this case he rationalized his inability to take Madrid, with self-pitying excuses if not outright lies. This is how, in an interview given at the end of November 1936 to *Il Popolo d'Italia*, he explained why the capital had not fallen:

> In Madrid, our conquest would be faster if the Nationals had not imposed on themselves the duty of saving the city from destruction and saving lives amongst the population. Naturally, the peripheral areas, having become zones of resistance and military bases for the defence, must suffer the effects of the attack, but outside those areas, the neutral population will find secure shelter in the inner neighbourhoods marked as off-limits [to bombardment]. The streets, from the south until Levant, will be exempted from bombardment, to leave free passage for the enemy's withdrawal.[22]

This was a blatant lie. Having failed, against the Nationals' and most foreign press correspondents' expectations, to take Madrid in early November, Franco's artillery was at that very moment pounding the city's poorer neighbourhoods, while avoiding the upper-class areas of the city centre. Madrid was his obsession, and in explaining his failure there Franco would also reveal a trait that would remain a constant feature of his rule: his tendency to blame foreign forces, and indeed whole nations, for Spain's ills. Conspiracies, unholy alliances, dirty money, and nefarious intentions dominated his accounts of his enemies. On December 10, during a demonstration of "sympathy with Portugal" that took place in Salamanca, he said: "Madrid is no longer defended by the Spanish reds, but by Russians, Europe's trash, that sack our temples and our homes".[23] On December 31, he told Lisbon's *Diario de Noticias* how the International Brigades facing his troops were not volunteers but mercenaries "paid with many millions" by the "red" government. He also explained again why Madrid had not "yet" been taken: "this is fully justifiable in military terms". Madrid is in reality "an open city" whose gates, the towns around the capital, were reached in "resounding victories" by the Nationals. "From a strict military point of view", he continued, the capital was in his army's hands in November 1936. But the Nationals decided to "commit a military mistake on purpose", in order to divert troops and take Toledo instead, "an invincible strongpoint" of the republicans because this was "a matter of honour". The "reds" took advantage of this and made every home in Madrid a trench. Now, in military terms, they could easily "annihilate Madrid" by bombing the city, but they did not want that "because it is not in our interest as Spaniards to conquer a city in ruins". "The generalissimo Franco adds this, notably saddened: It is enough with its moral ruin, close to a million good Spaniards sacrificed during the long months of misdeeds, assaults and atrocious crimes by the Marxist hordes." Later in the interview, the Caudillo blamed England, France and other countries for their military support of the criminal republicans. He explained again how the Nationals were composed entirely of "Spanish soldiers", while "mercenaries" filled the ranks of the enemy.[24]

In fact, most foreign troops in the Spanish Civil War fought for Franco, the ratio being at least three to one in his favour. On the republican side, there were about 40,000 volunteers of the International Brigades and about 2,000 Soviet instructors and technicians.[25] Fighting against the Republic were over 70,000 Italian soldiers, 50,000 Moroccan mercenaries (some authors double this figure), about 18,000 Germans troops, perhaps 10,000 Portuguese, and about 2,000 volunteers from other nationalities enrolled in different units, mostly in the Legion. That history has paid far more attention to the role of the relatively tiny International Brigades than that of the far more numerous, and better-armed, Axis forces can be attributed in part to the left's passion for self-congratulatory myth. Yet it is also a result of the success of Francoist propaganda, which managed to hide, especially after 1945, the fact that the rebels' "national" troops were far less national then those of the internationalist republicans, and that without Hitler and Mussolini the victory of the "true Spain" (as the rebels often called themselves) would have been much less likely.

In the following months, Franco increasingly demanded an authoritarian, centralized political system, and began to talk of himself as the sole interpreter of both History's and God's designs for the country. On the night of April 18, 1937, the Caudillo gave a speech in Salamanca, which was broadcast by *Radio Nacional*, in which he justified the unification of all the rebel political forces into a single party under his direction.[26] This Unification Decree (Decree 255) was, moreover, written in the first person: "This unification, I demand, in the name of Spain and in the sacred name of those—heroes and martyrs—who fell for her".[27] A mere eight months after joining the movement, at the very last minute, Franco had thoroughly appropriated not just the rebels' but also Spain's voice.

In mid-1937, shortly after the unification of the rebel side happened, the Soviets cut-off their aid to the Republic. The Caudillo's victory was only a matter of time—time that he used to consolidate his regime. In January 1938, he formed his first regular government. By then the Republic had lost its northern territories and, in spite of some brief successes (the Battle for Teruel, for example), the democratic government was incapable of taking the strategic military initiative. Still his power was not yet absolute because, although Mola had died the previous June, there were still many influential generals on Franco's side who disagreed over the nature of the new regime. To dissuade his (increasingly muted) critics, the Caudillo started to claim that fighting the reds was the same as fighting internal dissent, and pointed out that both were part of the same conspiracy. The Caudillo was now the unquestionable "truth-maker" and also an open reactionary. His new, self-appointed role can be seen in an April 1938 speech that marked the first anniversary of the political unification:

> After the International Brigades were defeated, in spite of their accumulation of tanks and war materiel of all kinds, they put their eyes on our rear-guard and tried to divide it because this was its last resource for salvation. To that effect, instructions were sent to our zone and some people were taken from prison, at the price of treason, allowing them to enter our side with the promise to agitate this rear-guard [...] It was attempted to undermine the prestige of our highest hierarchies, exploiting small ambitions [...] Those predicting fantastic and demagogic reforms [...]; those who hypocritically lie attributing to us coldness in matters of religion [...] and those who undermine the rear-guard, are, I repeat, Spain's worst enemies.[28]

And he did not hide what these enemies could expect in the way of repression. In this sense, at least, Franco had been brutally honest from the very first days of the rebellion. For example, on July 27, 1936 the journalist Jay Allen heard Franco say, in an interview later published in the *News Chronicle*, that he would save Spain from "Marxism at whatever the cost". When Allen asked if that meant shooting "half of Spain", Franco repeated "at whatever the cost".[29] More than two years later, in a November 1938 interview with a *United Press* correspondent, Franco gave further indication of the repression he had in mind: "We have index cards on 2,000,000 individuals with proofs of their crimes, names and witnesses."[30]

And so, just as the war was about to end, Franco's program for a ruthless, reactionary, clerical dictatorship with Fascist trappings was evident for the whole world to see. So, too, was his now absolute power.

Hagiographies

The divinely chosen hero of Spain needed an appropriate biography, or rather, what may perhaps be more accurately described as a hagiography. The already well known journalist-publicists from the old Moroccan lobby Joaquin Arrarás and Víctor Ruiz Albéniz, past and present witnesses of Franco's glory, were ready for the task. As employees of the newly established propaganda office, they had already put together providential interpretations, based in part on their own exaggerated memoirs of their African experiences, to compose the official, or canonical, interpretation of the Caudillo's life. However, strictly speaking they were not the first authors to comment on Franco's life; other, lesser-known journalists also contributed to this project, providing "information" that would be recycled by the above-mentioned authors. For example, a group of journalists from the Canary Islands led by Víctor Zurita—a man who had a republican past he needed to discard—hastily composed a series of articles, published in January 1937 and later incorporated into a pamphlet, which presented a revised version of the beginnings of the July 1936 rebellion. As the work's introduction, "a faithful account of the events", explained, it was Franco who "started the re-conquest of Spain, freeing it from Marxist domination".[31] This text is important because it severely warped the historical record, placing Franco at the centre of action during the crucial months that preceded the rebellion. Moreover, in this account, Franco was presented as the obvious, indeed fated, saviour of Spain.

Zurita's team explained that Franco was the "natural caudillo" of the uprising.[32] This designation, one colonel explained to the journalists, was "etched in the minds" of the whole garrison of the Canary Islands long before the Movement started. In fact, during this time all officers' "hearts [had] beat at the same pace" hoping for Franco to lead them.[33] The same officer explained that the General's arrival in the islands meant that "the Spanish nation was not going to be sold to the Russian Soviet", as was the intention of that "Jewish merchant" Azaña.[34] This is why Franco was "condemned to death by Moscow". (Calvo Sotelo was on the same death list.) Members of an unnamed "terrorist organization" had tried to kill the Caudillo several times since they knew he was the main obstacle to their plan to deliver Spain to its enemies. They even assaulted his official residence one night—all part of a plot in which the local Popular Front authorities were involved. The article's authors, amazingly, were even able to reproduce the dialogues between the assassins.[35]

This text is also interesting in that it includes a hint of the fate of Sanjurjo's memory in the newly emergent regime. According to the above-mentioned but anonymous colonel, Franco had said to him that Sanjurjo should not have accepted a pardon following his failed coup in 1932. In fact, he should have asked to be executed since "his prestige and Spain's well-being demanded it". The Caudillo is supposed to have added: "he has risked his life a hundred times [...] it would have mattered little to lose it then." Sanjurjo's selfish, even cowardly, decision not to ask to be shot was cast as the opposite of Franco's, a man who, readers were told, said upon embarking for Tetuán and the unknown: "I know that if I fail in my attempt to save Spain, I will pay with my life; but this is little when compared to such a high ideal."[36]

The first complete life of the Caudillo appeared in the biography of Franco written by Joaquín Arrarás and published in 1937.[37] Arrarás was appointed director general of the New State press office that year. He would later publish, among other works, a multi-volume *History of the Crusade*, and a partial, manipulated version of President Manuel Azaña's diaries, which had been stolen during the war. For his seminal biography, Arrarás used none other than the Caudillo as his main informant. Thus the reader was informed by Arrarás (Franco) that the Caudillo came from a family that was both noble and had rendered great services to the nation. (The fact that his father had abandoned the family went unmentioned.) The reader was further informed that, upon arriving in Africa, Franco immediately started demonstrating his exceptional qualities. Two examples, to which there were no witnesses save for Franco himself, were reported. In May 1912, Colonel Berenguer noticed a young lieutenant leading a daring uphill attack against the Moors. He asked the name of the officer and was told "Franquito": it was the young officer's first mission in Africa.[38] Three years later, a bullet passed through Franco's fingers, hitting the cap of his thermos as he was about to take a drink: "Aim better!" he was supposed to have said to the sniper, acting as if nothing had happened.[39] In this text, Arrarás (Franco) included a line of argument, which the Caudillo would systematically apply to politics in general, and international politics in particular: conspiracy. According to this biography, during the heroic African days, unnamed "enemy" fellow officers successfully conspired several times to prevent Franco from gaining the recognition his exploits deserved, denying him medals (namely, the *Laureada*) and promotions because of jealousy. Nevertheless, the hero prevailed and soon he became a celebrity among true Spaniards. For example, when posted in 1917 to Oviedo, as the young major entered coffee shops and clubs, people immediately lowered their voices and made admiring comments about him.[40]

Further evidence of Franco as the Caudillo-in-the-making and Saviour of Spain came with the founding of the Legion, which, according to Arrarás (or his informant), had a fearsome reputation even before its first battle.[41] Confirmation of this view came when Franco saved Melilla in July 1921. In this new version of events, Major Franco was mentioned far more often than his commanding officers at the time, Sanjurjo and Millán Astray. The same happened with the narration of another key moment in the revelation of Franco's exceptionality: the 1925 Alhucemas landing. This operation was now supposed to have been both a product of his brilliant mind and of his unparalleled courage.[42] Not surprisingly, having returned from the war in Africa, Franco now moved on to become an internationally recognized strategist. For example, during a 1930 course at Versailles, he supposedly astonished his European counterparts with a brilliant response to a tactical problem written on a blackboard that no one else was able to solve.[43]

In spite of his internationally acclaimed genius, when the Republic arrived Franco had to deal with many attacks and affronts, most notoriously from Azaña. The Minister of War's reform plans were seen as a plot against the Army in general and Franco in particular.[44] In spite of this, Franco remained loyal to the despised Republic until he had to confront the utter misery of the 1936 elections and subsequent chaos. According to Arrarás, the right won the general elections of February, but the left manipulated the results. Not content with committing electoral fraud, the left concocted a plan to spark a revolution and assassinate the country's army officers. Franco himself suffered several attempts against his life in the Canary Islands.[45] While Mola was barely mentioned in the book, Franco was presented both as a prophet, one who knew what lay ahead—i.e., that the war would be long and bloody—and as Spain's only hope.[46] He was the man who had organized the crossing of the Gibraltar Strait by the colonial army, followed by the advances through Extremadura towards Madrid. That he had failed to take the capital was not mentioned. The last chapter of the book is aimed at presenting the human face of the Caudillo. The title is "Franco's smile". It is, as one passage points out:

> a smile that is a greeting to life, ignores adversity, smells of optimism, and is a signature of victory. A smile that all of Spain, the free one and the red, knows. That has transcended to the world, and is universal like the steely and fearsome one of Mussolini or Hitler's grimace [...] Franco's smile illuminates in its new path the rebirth of Spain, martyr and glorious.[47]

Arrarás would publish several editions of this biography. Every new edition reflected the cult of personality that came increasingly to surround the Caudillo. They also included some of the changes that were taking place both in the war and in the socio-political structure of the New Spain. For example, the 1938 edition was even more class-prejudiced than it had been the year before. When describing "red" Madrid as it was in the summer of 1936, Arrarás now added:

> Suffocating nights, nervous, boiling and eternal in that Madrid of July 1936 [...] Madrid is not anymore everybody's capital, happy and welcoming [...] The construction worker, the printer, tacky people and the office worker have ceased to be the people in love on their way to a street party. Now one is a leader in a Communist group, another instructs pioneers, the third one belongs to the militias of the Socialist Club [casa del pueblo], the fourth one is a neighbourhood chief for Marxist Unification. They have a gun and spend the night patrolling.[48]

The text had not only become more anti-worker but also, significantly, even more devoted than the previous edition to the aggrandizement of the Caudillo's public image. New lines and often whole new paragraphs were added to further glorify the hero. For example, one paragraph describing the arrival of Franco at Tetuán's air base now included the following sentence as it was supposedly uttered by Lieutenant-Colonel Juan Yagüe: "Here they are [the Legionnaires]— exclaimed Yagüe—. You, who so many times led them to victory, lead them now again to triumph, for Spain's honour."[49] The Saviour had arrived, and his necessary instrument, the Army, was ready to serve him in his mission to rescue Spain from her enemies. However, perhaps the most significant addition came when Ararrás described the newly designated Chief of State:

> He is not moved by small ambitions, of any kind, General Franco, when he starts a new enterprise. He is not looking for power, something that he dislikes, or human vanities, for which he has contempt, or material advantages, in which he is not interested. In his youth he reached the summits that very occasionally prestigious men reach at the end of a glorious military career. Requested with insistence by political parties for positions of popularity [*sic*] and shining, he rejects the suggestion. He can be a personage in the middle of blinding stenography, but he declines. Generalissimo of the Armies and Chief of State, he only accepts a salary of brigadier plus the corresponding extras for the crosses won in Morocco: just 2,000 pesetas per month, less than half of what Don Manuel Azaña takes every day for unmaking the nation.[50]

No human vanities tarnished the Saviour. Other authors would also use the figure of 2,000 pesetas as a glaring example of the Caudillo's modesty. If true at the time, this austerity vanished soon. Recently, it was discovered that Franco accumulated two salaries—Army officer and Head of State—plus the assignment to both his Civil Household and the Head of State Household. According to calculations, in 1975, Franco's monthly after-tax income—and it must be remembered, he was free of any living expenses—was 600,000 pesetas (a sales director of a multinational company made about 90,000 at the time).[51]

Ararrás' 1938 edition also added new "facts" for the increasingly pro-Fascist rebels, painting a darker picture of the neutrals, Britain and France. While in the 1937 edition France was considered a potential friend unfortunately ruled by the hostile Popular Front, in the new version Spain's northern neighbour was not mentioned at all, while Germany and Italy were added as friends.[52]

Ararrás' biography served as the basis for other hagiographies of Franco, including some written specifically for children. Following the pattern established by the first hagiographer, these books, often written in the style of traditional religious catechism manuals, presented Franco as the indisputable hero of Africa, one who was elected head of the Legion by a "unanimous voice", who was prevented from rising higher because he was too young, and whose name finally, on July 18, was called "by Spain" as saviour. Franco was even compared with Christ resurrecting Lazarus, when he asked democracy-stricken Spain: "Do you really want to be saved? Then rise from your bed; and walk ... "[53]

Besides Arrarás, nobody did more to assist Franco in the creation of his new image than another veteran propagandist of the African wars, Víctor Ruiz Albéniz (*Tebib Arrumi*), who wrote for both adults and children. First, during the war he published a series of books entitled "Heroes of Spain: Biographical Drafts of the Most Outstanding Figures of the Saviour Movement". Naturally, the first issue was dedicated to the glorification of the emerging dictator, a partial biography of the Caudillo.[54] The first edition was written in December 1936 "the year of salvation". To start with, the book explained how the New Spain was better than the decadent country ruled by the Republic since in the new nation "nothing is accidental, there are no careerists, there are almost no new values, because each of the military leaders [has] a glorious past" that they have been prodding along since the colonial wars.[55]

In *Arrumi*'s biography, Franco's family record was further sanitized, advancing some of the fantasies that the dictator himself would later express when, for example, in a moment of creativity, he would write a film script replete with pseudo-biographical overtones (see Chapter 3). In this new version of the dictator's family tree, Franco's father, the carefree philanderer Don Nicolás, became the number one ranking officer of the Navy administrative service (*Intendente General de la Armada*). Franco's mother was a "saint", but not because of the dignity with which she endured her husband's many personal affronts, which went unmentioned, but rather because she gave birth to three "sons of temper and appearance". Franco's eldest brother, Nicolás, at the time his main collaborator, was presented as "the best naval engineer" in Spain. Finally, his younger brother Ramón's many political and personal sins were forgotten, but not his glory as an aviator. Curiously, the temperamental Pilar, Franco's only sister, does not warrant even a mention. As part of this idealized past, Franco's poor academic performance at the military academy became "marks of an exceptionally endowed young man that highlighted his future personality". *Arrumi* explained that when Franco graduated from the infantry academy, he continued to study hard, frequently lecturing his astonished fellow officers about his readings, since "technicians of the Military Art do not hesitate to assure that this tendency towards studying [war] is a sort of Divine gift".[56]

A witness to the Moroccan wars, Ruiz Albéniz, like Arrarás, now re-arranged his account of these years to cast the young Franco as the self-evident forthcoming Saviour. For example, in his original 1922 account of the last-minute salvation of Melilla from Abd-el-Krim's troops (discussed in Chapter 1), the main "heroes" to be celebrated are the Foreign Legion's founder Millán Astray, and General Sanjurjo. Fourteen years later, Franco was now the one remembered as the main "hero" and saviour of the city in 1921.[57] The same happened with the 1925 Alhucemas landing. According to Ruiz Albéniz, even if the nominal commander of the 1925 operation at Alhucemas was Sanjurjo, Franco was the man who had truly directed the landing. When, in 1926, he was promoted to brigadier general, this meant that "Franco was already the indisputable and unquestioned CAUDILLO of Spain".[58]

In April 1931 the Republic arrived and shortly afterwards it shut down the General Military Academy. Evil people, led by Manuel Azaña, ridiculed the "exquisite sensibility of this genial, brave General who knows how to cry and who cries and cries, who feels his eyes full of tears when he talks about Spain's greatness". During this time of darkness, the hero was sent into exile, where he was appointed Commander of the Balearic Islands, living apart from the politicking of the time, studying, and preparing one of those "patriotic and perfect" plans—in this case for the defence of the islands—which once again revealed his strategic genius.[59] For a while, there was illusory hope: the centre-right won the November 1933 elections, and in May 1935, Franco was promoted by Gil-Robles, the Minister of War, to the position of Chief of the Army General Central Staff. Since Gil-Robles was a semi-pariah among the 1936 rebels when the book was written, Franco's intense and intimate collaboration with him, and his overall conduct during 1935 and early 1936, was described as a product not of the incoming Caudillo's political ambition, but rather of his "military discipline"—essentially his duty to serve Spain in whatever position he was asked to fill.[60] This may explain why Franco cried the day that both he and Gil-Robles departed from their respective jobs: "an emotive scene which those of dry spirit and limited intellect pretended to ridicule". However, during his time as Chief of the General Staff Franco managed to foil Azaña's plans to "triturate" the army. He acquired, among other things, the modern batteries and the planes with which he would lead the miraculous "Salvation Movement" of July 18.[61]

His Popular Front enemies, who were the enemies of the army and of Spain, sent the Caudillo into exile once again; this time to a very dangerous place, the Canary Islands, where he was made Military Governor by the republican government and, the author explains, a virtual prisoner: "he had his private correspondence intercepted, he could not wire or use the radio, and he could not even receive visitors in his Palace-Prison".[62] To be sure, it would get worse in future versions. But what is important about the present version is that it is from this supposedly total isolation that Franco not only "jointly with Yagüe, Mola, Varela, Orgaz and Queipo, traced the plans for Spain's re-conquest"—it is also where he gave the final call for revolt and made clear his faith in the final victory. Here Juan March's money, Sanjurjo, and the hesitations regarding Franco's potentially pusillanimous character, the sarcasm expressed by fellow generals about the wait-and-see attitude of "Miss Canary Islands 1936", are completely ignored: none of this would be incorporated into the canonical image of the dictator.[63]

A similar story, but with new and very significant variations, was told by the same *Tebib Arrumi* in late 1939: but this time for children.[64] In this text, Franco came from a happy and smart family, a sort of Holy Family. He was a brave, outstanding cadet at the Military Academy, where he got very good marks "without much effort because of his very clear intelligence which saved him from mental torture".[65] In 1921 he saved Melilla when Abd-el-Krim's rebels, who had received help from the other countries that wanted to start a world war (?) and "particularly Russia" (!), got to the city's limits. The logic of such a narrative was to create a precedent in which 1921 would henceforth be seen as only the *first* time that the colonial army had saved Spain from Communism, the next time, of course, being the July 18 revolt. As in 1936, in the weeks following the miracle at Melilla, Franco became an idol of the masses.[66]

According to Ruiz Albéniz, the rotten Spain of 1936—populated by the same mobs who would later commit so many crimes in Red Spain—could already be found in Melilla in 1921: the workers, "fat people, without spirit" who were prone to panic: "they see enemies even in their own fingers". Another proof of their cowardly and debauched nature could be seen in the fact that, unlike the selfless heroes of the army, in 1921 the moral of the people who lived in the outer neighbourhoods of Melilla succumbed to fear just because some "Moors" managed to sneak out at night and shoot at them.[67] The not-so-subtle implication was that in a few years, encouraged by the Republic, this rabble would not only fail to rise to the needs of the moment; it would try to kill the hero (Franco), as well as hundreds of thousands of good Spaniards. A body of post-1939 literature would explain all of this in gory detail and flattering language.

In the meantime, Franco married, and won medals and promotions. However, the person who had been best man at his wedding and who had nurtured his career, King Alfonso XIII, did not appear in this story. Instead we hear how Franco travelled Europe, to France and Germany, to "study in depth modern military science".[68] Of course in October 1934, he single-handedly saved Spain from revolution in Asturias. Then came his appointment under Gil-Robles, by which he tried to save the Army from the treacherous Azaña; and the extraordinary moment of his departure from the War Ministry after the 1936 elections, where everybody saw him crying because he "saw the last hope for Spain's salvation" disappearing the moment he was dismissed.[69] And he went to the Canary Islands where, with his "soul torn apart", he had to prepare, with "a bunch of loyal friends", the country's deliverance. Franco "was ready to risk everything—career, life, honour—when the moment to cry out Up with Spain! Arrived".[70] Sadly, the author ended his account here.

Soon after the end of the war, the *Tebib Arrumi* fulfilled the promise he had made to his readers by telling them the rest of the story. He started with Franco's days in Tenerife. Not only had the government and local Marxists tried to find a reason to punish him there, but, dispirited by their failure to prove any wrongdoing on the part of the general, they even tried to murder him. In spite of these assassination attempts, not to mention various other affronts, Franco remained a loyal officer. At the same time, however, the flame of national rebirth was rising in Morocco, particularly in the garrison towns of Ceuta and Melilla, where the true patriots' situation was becoming increasingly unbearable since "those cities were infested by Freemasons, Jews, Bolsheviks, Communists, Socialists and Republicans". Furthermore, the local High Command, appointed by the republican government, was infested with "Freemasons, who encouraged the spread of the Lodges among the Army ranks". It was thus no surprise that posters began appearing in the streets announcing the imminent sale of "Legionnaires' flesh at three cents the kilo" and of "Regulares' livers".[71]

Since Jewish-Marxist mobs were planning the assassination of the entire colonial army it was obvious that the time to act had arrived. Fortunately, the incompetent local authorities made this easy. The government decided to organize a large military exercise, scheduled for July 5 to 13, 1936 near Ketama, which ended with a parade and a grand banquet at the nearby Yellow Plain (*Llano Amarillo*). These festivities were presided over by the High Commissioner, "a certain Buylla, and the supreme Commander of the troops in Morocco, Gómez Morato".[72] *Tebib Arrumi* knew perfectly well that Arturo Álvarez-Buylla, the last republican High Commissioner of Morocco, had been executed in 1937. He also knew that General Agustín Gómez Morato had barely escaped with his life, and had been subsequently demoted by the rebels and condemned to prison. But his story was not about the tragic fate soon awaiting both men, but rather about the (rather macabre) joke that the plotting officers had played on these men when they sang a song about giving coffee to a beautiful girl. The girl was the "Republic" (*La Niña Bonita*) and coffee—in Spanish, *café*—was the acronym for *Camaradas Arriba Falange Española* (Comrades: Up with Spanish Falange!). The unsuspecting officials were supposed to have clapped and celebrated with these soon-to-be traitors in the merry atmosphere that concluded the military exercise. One of the ring leaders, the Legion Commander Yagüe, is supposed to have said "take coffee" several times to Gómez Morato, while joyfully winking.[73]

Finally, the loyal Franco was forced to act. On July 13, news of Calvo Sotleo's murder—"a crime committed by the Government"—arrived. Franco then proceeded to make good use of his "collaborator" on the peninsula, General Mola. This is how the now dead Mola, "The Director", became, according to the official record, one of the Caudillo's "collaborators", thus joining the ranks of Queipo de Llano in Sevilla, Dávila in Burgos, Saliquet in Valladolid, Goded in Mallorca, Fanjul in Madrid, Yagüe in Africa, etc., etc.[74] Sanjurjo was not even included in this list. Of course, neither were the names of the generals and officers who had remained loyal to the government. Not that these men had any reason to be afraid. Albéniz-*Arrumi*, explained to his readers that when republican officers surrendered they were told by their captors: "The officers of the Spanish Army are not assassins: resign your command and nothing will happen to you."[75] Albéniz certainly knew about Major Ricardo de la Puente, Franco's murdered cousin, and many others victims of summary execution.

Franco's true relationship to his former protectors, bosses and even equals, such as King Alfonso, General Berenguer, Millán Astray, Sanjurjo, Primo de Rivera, Gil-Robles, Goded, and Mola, was either systematically distorted or blatantly ignored in the new canonical biography of the dictator. Instead, they became mere bricks in the foundation of an exceptional, pre-ordained life. Providence, which had saved Franco's life so many times when fighting the Moors or the reds, was preparing this "modest" and brave man with the "tender smile", for his ultimate destiny: to save Spain from the diabolical forces of democracy, Judaism, Masonry, and Communism. The past now made sense: the almost fatal bullet in 1916, Abd-el-Krim in 1921, Azaña in 1931, the assassins in 1936 ... all were part of the same divine narrative. From these episodes of turbulence and struggle came the light. In 1938, the former *avant-garde* writer Ernesto Giménez Caballero, now employed by the propaganda office of the New State, summarized the divine emergence of the Caudillo in the following terms:

> And this is why, during the tragic reaping of our best men, God [...] with his providential hand saved the ONE, the man that Spain acclaims today with a single name, which is all encompassing: FRANCO.[76]

God seemed to agree. On April 1, 1939, Victory Day, Pope Pius XII sent Franco a congratulatory telegram. A few days later, in a longer message, His Holiness explained that "Spain, God's chosen nation [...] will be guided by Him [Franco] on a safe route of traditional Catholic greatness".[77] Franco had always been the man chosen by God and Spain. Even innocent children had to know this unquestionable truth. Thus a book for their political education explained in 1940: "At the head of the [Spanish state] there is a Caudillo, a guide, and we all must obey him [because] the Caudillo is always the best citizen, the most select one, superior and indisputable".[78]

Seen from abroad

News of the beginning of the Civil War appeared suddenly in the international press on July 20, and for several weeks it would be the major international event—that is until it became routinized, competing with developments elsewhere to capture the press's fickle attention. In military terms, three themes dominated the news during the war's first weeks. One of them was the fight around the Strait of Gibraltar, where the Republic's Air Force and fleet were trying to prevent Franco's troops from crossing to the peninsula. Following their success, Franco's and Queipo's advances were amply documented.[79] The other major focus of attention was centred on the mountain passes just north of Madrid, where Mola's troops were eventually stopped by a combination of republican rag-tag military forces and left-wing militias.[80] But the main theme was carnage, the killing then widespread throughout the country, and how it should be interpreted. The main concern for the British—and other English-language media—was not what was happening to hapless Spaniards, but rather what was happening to their nationals and how to get them out of the country. Most world powers sent fleets that solved this matter in a few weeks. At the same time, the rescue of refugees became an occasion to explore the meaning of both the war and the wider political violence then unfolding in Spain. The refugees' stories reflected the lens through which Spain, the Republic and the Nationals were being analysed from abroad. For example, on July 21, as *The Globe and Mail*, Toronto's conservative newspaper, speculated on how Britons, Americans and others trapped in Spain were going to be rescued. It published an article on "Enigmatic Spain": "Nowhere is there more spectacular illustration of the strange contradictions in national character than in present-day Spain. [The average Spaniard] blows hot and cold with utter abandon."[81]

This pathetic racist prejudice may explain why, also on July 21, 1936, as tragedy engulfed the lives of millions of Spaniards, *The Globe and Mail* offered witty jokes on the Spanish condition: "Riots and revolutions seem to be becoming just an old Spanish custom", and "In the lingo of the pugilists, Spain appears to be countering with its Left".[82] The next day, it added: "Spain seems to be suffering from too many of the Don Quixote type. She needs a few more Sancho Panzas."[83] *The Globe and Mail* was far from unique in its flippant attitude: much snobbery and insensitivity can be seen in this type of reporting on the war, and much racism and parochialism, too. The Spanish Civil War was interpreted—and not only by the right—mostly on the basis of ignorance and cliché and through the lens of local circumstance. Nowhere were these interpretations more decisive for the fate of the Republic than in Britain. Ruled since 1931 by the Conservative-dominated national government, this country's policy exerted a decisive influence on the Spanish situation. In addition to economic, ideological and strategic reasons, British policy was also influenced by a barely concealed yet extensive contempt among diplomats and policy-makers for Spaniards and their culture, which in this period was expressed in terms of a "national character" assumed by many to be violent, irrational, and unsuited to democracy. It was a very convenient argument, to be sure, for both conservative Britain and for Franco, and as we will see this thesis would reappear during the Cold War.

People with so much passion in their veins needed order and a strong leader. The conservative-oriented press was crucial in guiding democratic public opinion towards a pro-rebel position, often under the guise of neutrality. This was done by publishing a mix of intoxicating news, opinionated articles and letters to the editor, which were often printed with scant attention to truth. For example, on July 21, the London *Daily Telegraph* printed a letter, which was soon reprinted as a pamphlet, questioning the Popular Front's victory in the past elections, thus implying the illegitimacy of the republican government. The libel ended up in parliament, where some Conservative MPs used it to press the Baldwin administration to break diplomatic relations with Madrid.[84] Another favourite argument of the rebels' friends in Britain was that the July uprising had foiled an imminent Communist plot. Names as prestigious as Major-General J.F.C. Fuller, the well-known war theorist (who met Franco in April 1937), and the *Sunday Times* gave credence to these views; the same accusation reappeared as late as May 1938 in that newspaper.[85] However, no other argument generated more sympathy for Franco's side than the stories, some true but others imagined, concerning the crimes committed behind republican lines. The net effect of these dramatic, horrific stories, published by British newspapers (*Daily Express*, *Daily Mail*, *Daily Sketch*, *Evening News*, *Daily Telegraph*, *Sunday Times*, *The Times*, etc.) was that the majority of British public opinion came to support non-intervention, a policy that was as convenient for Franco as it was deadly for the Republic.

What had much more impact than newspaper reports, were the newsreels that provided many graphic images of the carnage, and even "explained" how to interpret them. The coming of the Spanish Civil War coincided with the golden age of newsreels. Before World War II cinema going was one of the most popular leisure activities amongst the general population, and perhaps the most common of paid entertainments for the working and lower-middle classes. The names of *Gaumont*, *Movietone*, and *Pathé*—which mean little to consumers today —and *Universal*, which still exists, were immensely popular in the 1930s and 40s. They brought to people's attention images of faraway events. The comments that accompanied these images were normally authoritative, leaving the viewer little option than to accept the "truth" as documented by these glimpses of "reality". The newsreels' general orientation was usually conservative, nationalistic, and jingoistic. Ownership does much to explain this: Lord Rothermere, for example—one-time friend to the infamous British Fascist Oswald Mosley—was *Movietone*'s proprietor.

On July 27, 1936 *Gaumont* released the first newsreels from Spain to be shown in British cinemas. These were called "Spanish Revolution" and centred on events taking place on the Spanish mainland, completely ignoring the Moroccan revolt. While they did not explain the origin of the conflict, they did encourage the public to feel sympathy for the plight of the Spanish people.[86] However, in these and other newsreels a dichotomy was presented between "them", the foreign Spaniards, and "us", the democratic, stable viewing public. A *Pathé* newsreel from August 3, for example, concluded its narrations as follows: "And while we watch this grim struggle let us be thankful that we live in a country where men are free to express their political opinions without being shot, where internal strife is a thing unknown."[87] Reports about the arrival of refugees to the British territory of Gibraltar, civilization itself, reinforced this idea.[88]

British and American newsreels often conveyed both racist and anti-republican messages veiled in accounts of Communist and revolutionary atrocities. In this regard, the most famous story of the first months of the war was the safely concluded odyssey through the republican zone of the fair-skinned, delicate British Miss Williams, "The Blonde Amazon". Issued on August 13 by *Gaumont*, the account by this refugee was all about "red" and "revolutionary" terror, mostly about events that she had heard second-hand. She was very happy to be back in civilized England, she said, while images of armed reds going around Spanish cities with clenched fists, and the burning of Catholic churches illustrated her "testimony". On the one hand, and in stark contrast to the chaos to be found in the republican rear-guard, newsreels emphasized the order and military discipline of the rebel zone, replete with footage of Mola's forces accompanying enormous religious processions. The hidden aspect of this "peace", such as the frequent massacre of "reds", was neatly avoided. The most blatant case was the conquest of Badajoz by Yagüe's troops on August 14. There, Legionnaires and Moroccan "regular" troops perpetrated one of the larger massacres of the war, shooting 4,000 militiamen who had surrendered. The massacre was widely reported by several international newspapers, including the *Chicago Daily Tribune*. A *Pathé* cameraman filmed the bodies, but the footage was never shown in cinemas.

Newsreels helped to make Franco's image and voice world famous. A *Movietone* newsreel from September 14, 1936, for example, explained that: "If the Rebels win, General Franco will become a world figure, so whatever your sympathies this little talk from him should be of interest".[89] Newsreels also sanitized Franco's cause by downplaying Nazi and Fascist intervention in the war.[90] Newsreels, finally, also tried to obscure the war itself. As stiff republican resistance led to a more protracted conflict, images and footage from Spain grew increasingly scarce; the Spanish conflict thus became normalized, just one of many bad things then taking place in more unfortunate, and luckily distant, lands.

In spite of this flawed reporting, there was an intense debate in Britain throughout the duration of the Spanish Civil War, a sort of rhetorical battle for Spain in which both elites and common people participated. Their arguments, honest and impassioned as they often were, demonstrated both a limited knowledge of reality and a tendency to project local issues onto Spain's struggle. By late 1937, no fewer than 148 books had been published in the country about the Spanish war; five were pro-rebel, and 127 unequivocally pro-republican.[91] In just one week in 1938, ordinary Britons bought an astonishing 100,000 copies of the Unionist politician, and yet pro-republican, Duchess of Atholl's *Searchlight on Spain*. This was twice as many as the best-selling pro-Franco book, William Foss and Cecil Gerahty's *The Spanish Arena* (also published in 1938). At the same time, luminaries such as Winston Churchill and Captain Basil Liddell Hart publicly decried Franco and what he stood for.

Nonetheless Franco's cause had numerous, and very powerful, British friends, particularly on the right of the Conservative Party. One of the more easily recognized groups clustered around The Right Book Club, the publisher of *The Spanish Arena* (albeit the first book edited by the club lionizing Franco was Harold Cardozo's *March of a Nation*). Launched in 1937, and with a readership of between 10,000 and 25,000 subscribers, the club counted among its membership influential politicians such as Lord Halifax and Leo Amery, reputed writers such as Siegfried Sassoon and Clive Bell, and popular historians such as Arthur Bryant (mentioned in the introduction to this book). Many of these people viewed the Spanish Civil War as "their war", and Franco their idol. As Foss and Geraghty explained in *The Spanish Arena*:

> Two years ago Spain was of little concern [and] Francisco Franco was a name little known except to his professional associates. Today Spain's tragedy has become linked with international complications, and the name of Franco, in too many countries,

especially in England, stands, quite erroneously, for a hated or feared "Dictator" [...] This is a "civil war", but it is no ordinary war [...] Spain has been the unfortunate land chosen as the latest battlefield [...] This war was due to an attempt to impose a foreign yoke upon Spain [...] Franco is blissfully unconscious of what people think about him. To himself, he is just an ordinary soldier doing his job. Personal ambition, he has none; as reward for himself he has asked nothing [...] Here, one feels, is a man incapable of doing a mean, a selfish or an underhand action [...] There is no sign of personal vanity or personal consideration [...] His main attraction in life (after his country) is his devotion to his wife and daughter.[92]

In these authors' minds, the truth for Britons should be obvious:

We accuse the Soviet Government and those who assisted their plans of being premeditated investigators of every major misfortune which had occurred in Spain since 1925 [...] Three of the chief republican leaders [...], Indalecio Prieto, Caballero and, perhaps in a less conspicuous manner, Azaña, were the emissaries of the Comintern [...] The news machine is vast, and there were contributory causes. For example, there is a considerable volume of Jewish influence in our Press, partly direct and partly exercised through Gentiles, and there are many Jewish or partly Jewish journalists and employees of various grades.[93]

In addition to his Conservative, often anti-Semite sympathizers, Franco would find his strongest supporters in the Catholic Church. However, Catholicism was not monolithic. For example, when the American historian and priest, Joseph B. Code, reviewed the first English edition of Arrarás' book on Franco in 1938 for *The Catholic Historical Review*, an academic journal, he explained to his readers that this was not "an adequate biography of the military genius who perhaps more than anybody else has saved Spain from anarchy—and incidentally has accorded the entire civilized world a service too enormous to be sufficiently appreciated just now". At the same time, he found it "deplorable that even Catholics, for one reason or another" considered Franco "a Fascist monster".[94] The French writer Georges Bernanos belonged to this minority of anti-Franco Catholics. He described in *Les grands cimetières sous la lune* the reign of terror and senseless murders that took place in rebel-held (and Italian) Majorca during the first months of the war. Published in 1938, the first edition sold-out in barely two weeks. An English version appeared shortly afterwards.[95]

In essence, the battle for public opinion outside Spain depended to a large extent on local constraints and anxieties. In the United States, for example, propagandists for both sides had a difficult time since isolationism was the predominant philosophy amongst the population. Interest in international events was limited and easily diverted. A Gallup poll—it is important to remember that polling was then in its infancy, and thus not as accurate as it is today—conducted in January 1937 showed that the Loyalists (republicans) had the support of 22 per cent of the American population while the Nationals had 12 per cent, yet people who were either neutral or had no opinion amounted to a staggering 66 per cent.[96] By the end of 1937, when asked what had been the most interesting events of that year, floods in Ohio, the Sino-Japanese War, disputes on the Supreme Court, the Windsor marriage, the disappearance of Amelia Earhart, to name only a few newsworthy events, easily surpassed the war in Spain. Indeed, the Spanish conflict was a concern for only a tiny minority.[97] This started to change, however, in 1938. Events such as the Nazi annexations of Austria and the Sudetenland, plus the anti-Jewish pogrom of November (the Night of Broken Glass) helped to awaken a still largely non-interventionist American public. In December 1938, though a majority of Americans still supported isolation, only 33 per cent claimed to hold no opinion on events in Spain; of those with an opinion, three-quarters supported the (by then almost defeated) Republic, and one-quarter Franco. However, only 21 per cent of Americans wanted their government to offer direct military aid to the beleaguered Republic.[98]

In Britain the situation was very different. In spite of widespread popular pacifism and the conservative press's portrayal of events, a majority of Britons were simultaneously more aware of the war and more sympathetic to the Republic than their American counterparts. In March 1938, 57 per cent of Britons supported the Republic and 7 per cent Franco. This tendency increased as the situation in Europe deteriorated. In October of that year—that is, immediately after the Munich Agreement—one poll showed that support for the Republic had grown to 71 per cent, while sympathy for Franco's side stood at a mere 10 per cent. This increase in sympathy for the democratic government of Spain surged even among national government voters; in January 1939, 64 per cent of them declared their preference for the Republic.[99] By then the legal Spanish government was widely seen as a symbol of the looming struggle between democracy and totalitarianism. The irony was that while the British government's policies caused irreparable damage to the republican cause, the Spaniards' fight for their freedom was decisive in transforming British public sentiment from one of pacifism, so prevalent in the early-to-mid 1930s, to a more militant stance *vis-à-vis* Fascism. The Spanish tragedy led to a growing British determination to resist Hitler's burgeoning war machine. Yet by the time World War II had actually begun, it was too late for democratic Spain. Not only had Franco won his war: he was already the Caudillo—the myth and the absolute ruler—and he intended to stay that way for the duration of his life.

Notes

1 22-7-1936, "Álava por España. El movimiento sigue el camino del triunfo. Centenares de jóvenes siguen alistándose en las filas de voluntarios para ir al lado del Ejército", *Pensamiento Alavés*; 27-7-1936, "Con la columna alavesa en marcha hacia Madrid", *Pensamiento Alavés*; 29-7-1936, "En el frente de Somosierra, con las tropas que combaten al servicio de España", *Pensamiento Alavés*.

2 24-8-1936, "Vitoria, en un magnífico alarde de patriotismo, se entregó ayer por entero a España. Una muchedumbre imponente recibió al heróico general Millán Astray y aclamó a los legionarios que pasaron por nuestra ciudad", *Pensamiento Alavés*.

3 30-9-1936, "Dolores y alegrías de la nueva España. Ha muerto en Austria el glorioso caudillo de la Comunión Tradicionalista. El Ilustre general don Francisco Franco, Jefe del Estado español", *Pensamiento Alavés*.

4 19-7-1936, " Se inició un levantamiento en Ceuta y Melilla. No será declarado el estado de guerra", *El Pueblo Gallego*.

5 5-8-1936, "Se confirma que el Ejército del General Franco avanza sobre Madrid", *El Pueblo Gallego*; 7-8-1936, "Llerena (Badajoz) y Ronda (Málaga) han caido en poder del Ejército. El General Franco describe, en mensajes a los Jefes Navales de Marín y el Ferrol, la brillante operación del desembarco de tropas en San Roque", *El Pueblo Gallego*; 9-8-1936, "El Alto Mando del

Ejército Libertador ha trasladado su Cuartel General a Sevilla, donde se
encuentra, desde ayer, el General Franco", *El Pueblo Gallego.*

6 14-8-1936, "El Cuartel General de Burgos confirma el hundimiento del
acorazado Jaime I. Los Generales Franco y Mola estudiaron ayer, en Sevilla,
un plan para el más rápido aplastamiento del marxismo", *El Pueblo Gallego.*

7 6-9-1936, "Consejos al ciudadano. Habla Millán Astray", *El Pueblo Gallego.*

8 30-9-1936, "El General Franco, Jefe del Estado Español", *El Pueblo Gallego*;
1-10-1936, "El General Franco, Jefe del Gobierno del Estado Español", *El
Pueblo Gallego.*

9 22-7-1936, "Una nota del general Franco", *ABC-Sevilla.*

10 23-7-1936, "La patriótica alocución del general Franco al inciar el
movimiento", *ABC-Sevilla.*

11 23-7-1936, "Nota official del general Franco. Se declara asegurado del triunfo de los patriotas", *ABC-Sevilla.*

12 26-7-1936, "La patriótica alocución del caudillo" and "Las columnas españolas
as las puertas de Madrid", *ABC-Sevilla.*

13 23-8-1936, "Primeras figuras militares", *ABC-Sevilla.*

14 Reproduced in General Millán Astray, *Franco El Caudillo*, Salamanca,
M. Quero y Simón Editor, 1939, pp. 41–42.

15 29-11-1936, "Una Patria, Un Estado, Un Caudillo", *ABC-Sevilla.*

16 Luis E. Togores, *Millán Astray. Legionario*, Barcelona, Planeta, 2003, p. 357.

17 Millán, *Franco*, pp. 55–58.

18 Francisco Franco Bahamonde, *Habla el Caudillo*, Madrid, Editora Nacional,
1939, p. 2.

19 Ibid., pp. 6–7.

20 Ibid., p. 15.

21 Ibid., pp. 80–83.

22 Ibid., p. 86.

23 José Emilio-Díez, *General Franco. Sus escritos y palabras*, Sevilla, Tip. M.
Carmona, 1937, p. 89.

24 Ibid., pp. 91–113.

25 Daniel Kowalsky, "The Soviet Union and the International Brigades",
Journal of Slavic Military Studies, 19 (2006): 681–704.

26 Franco, *Habla*, p. 22.

27 Ibid., p. 25.

28 Francisco Franco Bahamonde, *Discurso de Franco en la Fiesta de la Unificación,
19 de abril de 1938*, Granada, Delegación Provincial de Prensa y Propaganda
de FET de las JONS, 1938, pp. 3–4, 7.

29 Quoted in Paul Preston, *Franco. A Biography*, London, HarperCollins, 1993,
p. 153.

30 Quoted in Herbert L. Matthews, "Franco's Problems", *Foreign Affairs*, 17, 4
(Jul. 1939): 723–731.

31 Victor Surita, *En Tenerife planeó Franco el Movimiento nacionalista (Anécdotas y
escenas de la estancia del Generalísimo en Canarias y su salida para Tetuán)*,
Santa Cruz de Tenerife, Imprenta El Productor, 1937, s.p.

32 Ibid., p. 7.

33 Ibid., pp. 15–16.
34 Ibid., p. 18.
35 Ibid., pp. 21–28.
36 Ibid., p. 31–32.
37 Joaquín Arrarás, *Franco*, San Sebastián, Librería Internacional, 1937.
38 Ibid., p. 27.
39 Ibid., pp. 31–32.
40 Ibid., p. 35.
41 Ibid., p. 41.
42 Ibid., pp. 51–57, 67, 107–108, 123–137.
43 Ibid., pp. 149, 165–166.
44 Ibid., pp. 169–177.
45 Ibid., pp. 212–222, 259–261.
46 Ibid., pp. 262–264.
47 Ibid., p. 316.
48 Joaquín Arrarás, *Franco*, Burgos, Imprenta Aldecoa, 1938, p. 220. Sixth edition.
49 Ibid., p. 268.
50 Ibid., pp. 301–302.
51 28-3-2011, "La última nómina de Franco", *ABC*.
52 Arrarás, *Franco*, pp. 272, 309–310.
53 The citation has been taken from a chidren's book based on Arrarás' work: L. Quintana, *Franco. Al muchacho español*, Barcelona, Librería Religiosa, 1940, pp. 22–24, 103.
54 Víctor Ruiz Albéniz [El Tebib Arrumi], *Héroes de España. Siluetas biográficas de las figuras más destacadas del Movimiento Salvador: El Caudillo. S.E.D. Francisco Franco Bahamonde. Generalísimo del Ejército y Jefe del Estado Español*, Ávila, Imprenta Católica, 1937.
55 Ibid., p. 4.
56 Ibid., pp. 6–11.
57 Ibid., p. 13
58 Ibid., pp. 19–21. For the digressions on Franco's "modesty" see pp. 22–24.
59 Ibid., pp. 24–25.
60 For an official repudiation (and manipulative re-making) of Franco's past relationship with Gil-Robles, see, 11-4-1937, "A propósito de Gil Robles", *ABC*.
61 Albéniz, *Héroes*, pp. 27–29.
62 Ibid., pp. 30–31.
63 Ibid., p. 42.
64 Víctor Ruiz Albéniz [El Tebib Arrumi], *Biblioteca Infantil. La reconquista de España. La Historia de El Caudillo Salvador de España*, Madrid, Ediciones España, 1939, pp. 3–4.
65 Ibid., p. 12.
66 Ibid., pp. 20–23.
67 Ibid., p. 26.
68 Ibid., pp. 51–52.
69 Ibid., pp. 58–59.

70 Ibid., pp. 62–63.

71 Víctor Ruiz Albéniz [El Tebib Arrumi], *Así empezó el Movimiento salvador*, Madrid, Ed. España, 1940, pp. 11–12.

72 Ibid., p. 13.

73 Ibid., p. 15.

74 Ibid., p. 22.

75 Ibid., p. 28.

76 Ernesto Giménez Caballero, *España y Franco*, s.l., Ediciones Los Combatientes, 1938, p. 11.

77 Reproduced in Saturnino Rodríguez, *NO-DO. Catecismo social de una época*, Madrid, Complutense, 1999, pp. 30–32.

78 *Así quiero ser (El niño en el Nuevo Estado)*, Burgos, Hijos de Santiago Rodríguez, 1940, p. 11.

79 7-21-1936, "Spain checks rebels' drive", *Chicago Daily Tribune*. The journalist Jay Allen accompanied Franco's troops, witnessing both their advances and massacres.

80 7-24-1936, "Madrid's fall seen by Saturday", *The Globe and Mail*.

81 7-21-1936, "Enigmatic Spain", *The Globe and Mail*.

82 7-21-1936, "Notes and comments", *The Globe and Mail*.

83 7-22-1936, "Notes and comments", *The Globe and Mail*.

84 Hugo García, *The Truth about Spain! Mobilizing British Public Opinion, 1936–1939*, Brighton, Sussex Academic Press, 2010, pp. 107–108.

85 Ibid., pp. 110–112.

86 Anthony Aldagate, *Cinema and History. British Newsreels and the Spanish Civil War*, London, Scolar Press, 1979, pp. 105–106.

87 Ibid., p. 107.

88 K. W. Watkins, *Britain Divided. The Effect of the Spanish Civil War on British Political Opinion*, Westport, Greenwood, 1976, pp. 63–70.

89 Aldagate, *Cinema*, p. 127.

90 Ibid., pp. 129, 135, 142, 160.

91 Richard Overy, "Parting with Pacifism", *History Today*, 59, 8 (2009): 23–29.

92 William Foss and Cecil Geraghty, *Spanish Arena*, London, The Right Book Club, 1938, pp. 15–16, 60, 62.

93 Ibid., pp. 95–96, 435.

94 Joseph B. Code, review of "Francisco Franco by Joaquin Arrarás; translated by J. Manuel Espinosa", *The Catholic Historical Review*, 24, 2 (Jul. 1938): 203.

95 Georges Bernanos, *Les grands cimetières sous la lune*, Paris, Plon, 1938.

96 George H. Gallup, *The Gallup Poll. Public Opinion 1935–1971. Volume One, 1935–1948*, New York, Random House, 1972, p. 49.

97 Ibid., p. 80.

98 Ibid., p. 138.

99 Tom Buchanan, *Britain and the Spanish Civil War*, Cambridge, Cambridge University Press, 1977, pp. 23–24.

3 Man of peace, 1939–1947

The meanings of victory

On May 19, 1939 Generalissimo Franco, escorted by Moroccan
Regulares, arrived at Madrid's Castellana Avenue where, shortly
thereafter, he was publicly awarded the long-coveted *Laureada*.
General José Enrique Valera, himself a two-time recipient of the
medal, had the honour of pinning it on the chest of Spain's
"Supreme Hero".[1] The ceremony was followed by a six-hour victory
parade in which, in addition to Spanish soldiers and Moroccan
mercenaries, German, Italian and Portuguese troops were to march
past the Caudillo's tribune. The next day, at Madrid's Santa Barbara
Church, a massive and spectacular political/religious ceremony was
held. Here, holding closer to medieval concepts of divine power
than to post-Enlightenment principles, the heads of the Spanish
Church, as well as Vatican representatives, blessed the Caudillo in
the name of God. During the service, Franco offered the Church
his sword of Victory. The Creator and Spain were now firmly
behind him.

Depending on whether they were viewed from inside or outside the
country, the celebrations briefly described above could be interpreted
very differently. This is because Franco's victory in the Spanish
Civil War marked a sharp split in how foreigners and a majority
of Spaniards viewed the dictator—a split that would last for the
duration of the regime. Henceforth, outside observers tended to
interpret the Caudillo in accord with the interests of their own
countries, their own local ideological conflicts and, last but not
least, preconceived notions (and prejudices) regarding the so-called

Spanish "character". Very broadly speaking, foreign conservatives, and Catholics in general, would be more lenient if not downright positive towards Franco and his regime as long as it did not threaten their countries' national interests and security. Predictably, progressives everywhere would be radically opposed to the Spanish dictator.

Spaniards, too, analysed the Caudillo through both their own ideological lenses and recent historical experiences and, accordingly, their interpretation of reality was very different than that of foreigners. Spaniards had failed to maintain a free and peaceful coexistence, and this failure created a widespread sense of collective guilt, frustration, and fear. The memories of the horrendous killing and destruction perpetrated during the Civil War consumed Spanish society, whose main political value was now echoed in a phrase commonly heard during this period: "never again". This sentiment benefited the war's principal victor—Franco—because everybody understood that the removal of the Caudillo would almost certainly result in another violent confrontation between his supporters and his enemies. However, this sense of collective failure was not the sole reason for the support the Caudillo enjoyed. While for the majority of Spaniards Franco's assumption of power meant stability and some sort of peace, for many others it also brought or secured material wellbeing. These were the people who profited from, or were not deeply affected by, the terrible scarcity and widespread social misery that arrived with Franco's peace.

After the war, there was increasing mass starvation in the country, which hit workers and landless peasants the hardest. The poorly designed rationing system was crippled by incompetence and corruption. Starvation and malnutrition contributed to the spread of illnesses such as tuberculosis and typhus. Starvation and disease killed close to 200,000 people between 1939 and 1945. Paradoxically, this misery reinforced the dictatorship because, while it affected relatively few of the regime's supporters, it succeeded in distracting popular opinion from political matters. During the long post-war period, ordinary Spaniards were busy struggling to feed themselves and their families, and while deeply resentful of this situation—and by no means unaware of the negative impact of local officials and authorities—they had little time or energy for dangerous opposition politics, which could bring only harsh persecution. Grumbling thus became the most common form of protest. To survive, poor Spaniards often devoted what remained of their strength to participation in petty corruption and black-market schemes. In sum, while it was a brutal, callous and deeply unfair period, widespread social misery led most people to want normalcy above all else.

As if hunger was not enough, the losers in the war had to endure an additional major problem: state violence. People, if they did not support the regime, were often too afraid to speak out, as firing squads and prisons consumed the lives of hundreds of thousands of their compatriots. Between 1939 and 1942, close to 50,000 Spaniards were shot and dumped in mass graves. Still in early 1943 approximately 90,000 Spaniards were held in prison for political crimes. Many more had been sentenced, fined, purged from their jobs or were on parole. They were part of a broader group of people living in fear, traumatized because they were survivors of beatings, robberies, insults and humiliation at the hands of the victors; and they all were officially stigmatized for being associated with the "red" "criminal hordes". To be a "red", or even a relative of one, in Franco's Spain was to live in a country in which only your side had committed crimes and in which your killed or missing loved ones did not officially exist. If they were remembered at all, it was only to have their alleged crimes thrown in your face and be insulted. In addition, existing resources, from public jobs to social assistance—which could make the difference between survival and death—were denied to the losers of the war. Moreover, quite often the "reds" and their families lived more or less isolated in their own communities; while non-compromised people kept themselves away from politics of any kind, and often even avoided "political" types. Experience and daily reality had shown that they were very dangerous to be around. In sum, the regime's violence, massive in the immediate post-war years, imposed social conformity and kept both dissenters and neutrals quiet.

As we will see later in this chapter, there was another phenomenon that helped to cement Franco's regime, and, in this case, the dictator's public prestige. In this impoverished, deeply traumatized, divided and terrorized society, there was a widespread fear that Spain would get involved in World War II. This fear came perilously close to reality twice during the war: first on the fall of France in June 1940, and then twelve months later on the Nazi invasion of the Soviet Union. These are only the most obvious examples, because many more times throughout the war Franco's often imprudent and bellicose words caused anxiety amongst the people, and foreign governments, that Spain might join the Nazis. Luckily for the dictator, his words failed to result in Spain joining the Axis powers. On the contrary, they resulted in something else called the myth of "Franco's Peace". This was a powerful and complex political and cultural phenomenon in Spain—almost completely misunderstood in post-war Europe after 1945—that, linking the horrible experience of the Civil War to the false Spanish neutrality during World War II, constituted the principal myth behind the Caudillo's prestige among Spaniards to the day of his death three decades later.

Finally, another factor that contributed to the acceptance of Franco's rule and his high personal prestige was the belief among large segments of the Spanish population, which in some ways survives to this day, that the Caudillo "did not know" about the abuses, corruption and violence that his regime, and in particular local authorities, practised. This is the old myth—probably as old as politics itself—of the good ruler who is misled by deceiving courtiers because of the breadth of the territory he governs, and the sheer amount of work that keeps him from seeing the truth and thus imposing justice. In reality, this belief is basically a mechanism for powerless people to reconcile their miserable reality with their natural desire for justice: by hoping that the dictator is as good as the propaganda makes him out to be. In the case of the Caudillo—and the present author does not subscribe to any alternative interpretation to any other dictator or absolute ruler—this type of wishful thinking was just that, wishful thinking. Franco was very well informed of the daily reality of Spaniards, constantly receiving a fairly accurate picture of events and circumstances from even the remotest corners of the country. In addition to what ministers, courtiers, profiteers and others may have told him, both his police and the security services of the Falange provided him with detailed, weekly reports detailing problems, conflicts, people's opinions, and daily living conditions.

Many of these reports are preserved in the Francisco Franco Foundation's archive (for the Franco Foundation, see Chapter 6), and they often contain underlined passages, and sometimes even annotations, penned by the Caudillo himself (however, the passages that Franco most often underlined were those dealing with threats to his power rather than those that addressed social conditions). For example, in a typical police report, dated January 1941, popular opinion was described as "honestly unfavourable and pessimistic" because of high prices and the "extremely limited purchasing power" of workers, who also felt cheated by recent announcements about improvements in the rationing of bread never being implemented. It also described how "Unemployment grows continuously and begging increases at alarming rates. It is sad to see poor children going around with no control because their parents cannot afford to pay for their schooling [...] those children are starving". On the other hand, employers, especially large companies, had few complaints, mainly because they were enjoying excellent profits.[2]

Franco clearly knew most of what he needed and wanted to know, and based on this information he acted to preserve his power and to punish or reward those around him. What he certainly chose not to do was to change the socio-economic system that was failing to restore the country's economy and, more importantly, to feed, clothe and educate millions of poor Spaniards. In fact, it was worse than that: Franco himself made the political decision to keep salaries low, which, as he knew perfectly well, caused extensive misery and hunger. He also knew about widespread injustice and privilege. For example, the Barcelona police told him in late 1941 that while exhausted workers often fell to the factory floors, they also reported that "some companies have had fabulous profits".[3] The Caudillo also was repeatedly informed that the children of the New Spain were suffering. A few months later, in August 1942, a similar report informed Franco of the situation in another industrialized region, Asturias: "in the industrial areas the social problem gets worse because of the insufficiency of salaries to acquire the necessary food, which causes" the widespread presence of children begging in the streets.[4] And, finally, he was perfectly aware of the corruption and impunity of certain privileged members of society. For example, in November 1941 the Ministry of Justice sent the Caudillo a memorandum on the very lenient sentences imposed on a number of big black marketers in the province of Barcelona. Those implicated were part of a network of industrialists and merchants. Of the 188 people indicted only 69 were found guilty. All but 10 of these individuals received a sentence of house arrest, and those unlucky 10 received only the briefest of jail times.[5] In the same year, the anti-black market court (*Fiscalía de Tasas*) sentenced close to 5,000 people, most of them of modest financial condition. As the head of the Francoist unions recognized in an internal memo written in mid-1942, "the big sharks always get away with very lenient punishments".[6]

In spite of the regime's incompetence, corruption and blatant injustices, Franco's power was safe, not only because of the combination of popular exhaustion, fear, and myth-making but because he controlled Spain's real political force at the time: the Army, which was the fiercely loyal backbone of his dictatorship throughout its existence. There were a number of intertwined material and ideological reasons behind the Army's loyalty towards Franco. The war and the elimination of republican officers opened the ranks of rebel soldiers to rapid promotions. Officers and non-commissioned officers were blind followers of the man who led them to victory, never losing, they liked to believe, a single battle along the way, and then gave them material rewards and a social prominence unparalleled in Spanish history. Up to 1945, more than one-third of all senior positions in the state administration, including nearly half of all ministers, were held by Army officers. Individual officers, from the Caudillo down, directly benefited from their privileged status by holding positions in public and private institutions and companies—a privilege that their relatives often enjoyed too. Officers also participated in extending the impunity that well-connected black marketers enjoyed during the hunger years of the 1940s. These social and political privileges more than compensated for the meagre salaries and abysmal situation of the armed forces, which, in spite of the New State's leaders' professed intentions, remained chronically under-equipped and ill-trained for the entirety of the dictatorship. Moreover, given its ideology, mission and deployment, the Army acted more as an army of internal occupation than as a credible deterrent against a foreign enemy.

The Army's omnipresence also meant that a culture of militaristic values (mixed with Fascist and Catholic ones) would become officially prevalent in society. For example, in the Spanish cinema of the 1940s, officers were presented as attractive, honourable and courageous characters, while civilians usually lagged far behind in all of these attributes. The logic was simple: they were the saviours of

Spain and the keepers of the nation's recovered greatness. Few documents reflect this vision more than *Historia de Jaime de Andrade*, a film script that Franco himself wrote, and which was subsequently made into the 1941 film *Raza* [Race].[7] Drawing freely from his own family past, but not without significant alterations (for example, in the film Franco's philandering father is made into a dead war hero, and his roots are made to look more aristocratic than they really were) the Caudillo presents a stand-in for himself in the character of José, an Army captain who survived a republican firing squad in Madrid and went on to become a hero. At the same time, his brother Pedro—who shares many traits with Franco's real-life brother Ramón—is presented as a materialistic republican politician who ends up paying with his life for his moral failures: having repented at the last moment, he is nonetheless killed by his former republican friends (in reality, Ramón died when his plane crashed while trying to bomb republican Valencia during the war). After many unbelievable adventures, as well as the portrayal of several republican crimes, *Raza* ends with the victory parade of 1939, which represents, in the words of one female character, the "Spirit of the [Spanish] Race".[8]

Franco's political prejudices against civilian government, which he developed as an Africanist soldier, were widely shared by his subordinates. These prejudices included the centrality of Castile as the physical heartland of Spain (and an accompanying contempt for other regions), a so-called "organic" vision of the nation, the role of a predestined saviour (the Caudillo, of course), and the concept of race, which was understood as the intrinsic identification of Spanishness with Catholicism. Officers saw themselves as a new aristocracy that had replaced the old, decadent elites. They also looked at the other possible competitor for power, the Falange, as little more than a necessary tool to achieve their control over the masses; that is, as an instrument to deal with the working class and social misery. The Army dreamed of transplanting its values onto the organization of both state and society. It also embraced the ideas of economic autarky, which were designed to create a powerful industrial nation capable of sustaining at least two million men in arms. In this chimera, each branch of the armed forces had its own dream. The Air Force was to get thousands if not tens of thousands of planes, the Navy dozens of battleships, etc.

Spaniards paid a terrible price for these unrealistic plans. The policy of autarky (self-sufficiency) brought ruin and starvation to post-war Spain, as the country sunk into a Franco and Army-made Great Depression from which it only started to emerge in the early 1950s. The Franco regime's dreams created the famine that tormented and killed so many people. The sheer callousness of the Caudillo, his Army, and the other elites in the face of the catastrophic results of the regime's economic policies during the early 1940s can be explained in two ways. First, the regime's failure did not affect the calorie intake of the regime's leaders, Army officers, high civil servants and those who produced food, or had capital or employees they could exploit. Misery was the problem of workers, landless peasants and the lower-middle classes—in sum, the strata to which the "reds" belonged. The second factor was ideology: the belief that the economic model of autarky, that had made Germany so powerful in just a few years (and, they assumed, Italy too) was going to lift Spain to the rank of a world superpower again, while the decadent, plutocratic, "Jewish-infected" democratic nations would slip into decline. Whatever sacrifices people were enduring at the time were justified as the necessary and temporary cost of a great empire to be acquired sooner rather than later. Only this fanaticism can explain reports like the one that reached the Caudillo in September 1940. Higinio París Eguilaz, his main economic adviser during the first two decades of the regime, wrote it. According to this courtier, whatever problems the Spanish economy may have been experiencing at the time were mostly due to the "effects of the Liberal-capitalistic policies" of the past. There was no doubt in his mind that the future was certainly going to be brighter, and the present not as bad as some people claimed. In his report, París Eguilaz argued that "we cannot say that there is hunger in Spain, despite all the difficulties generated by our war and the international war".[9] In Franco's Spain problems, if acknowledged, always came either from the past or from abroad, and were suffered by those who dared not speak out.

A precarious peace

In a freer, less traumatized society, the mass starvation and the widespread corruption and ineptitude of the government would likely have resulted in some sort of change. Yet in Spain this was not the case: ironically, governmental failures in many cases actually contributed to the Caudillo's prestige. People decided to have hope: problems were blamed on his underlings. In this sense the dictator's popular standing existed in inverse proportion to that of the other members of his regime and closest collaborators. No one highlighted this negative relationship more than Franco's brother-in-law—the two men's wives were sisters—and *de facto* right-hand-man until September 1942, Ramón Serrano Súñer (1901–2003). A shrewd and ambitious political operator, he had been next to Franco since early 1937. During his tenure Serrano was seen (and still is according to some conservative historians) as the man behind the regime's most radical, pro-Fascist economic and social policies, and an ardent advocate of joining the Axis powers during the war. Both policies—the move towards Fascism and pro-Axis intervention—backfired, however, when autarky led to an economic stagnation and Germany lost the war. But Serrano took the blame for Franco's faults. When he was finally dismissed, his enemies, some of whom had been his protégés in the Falange, would blame him for the country's recent failures. In addition, the timing of his departure, which was caused by purely internal factors, would also later be presented by the Caudillo's sycophants as further proof of their leader's genius: another sign of Franco's wisdom and foresight, redirecting foreign policy towards neutrality just before the war turned against Germany. Serrano therefore passed into the official record of the dictatorship—and to an extent into the historical memory of ordinary Spaniards—as the man who caused the hunger of the 1940s, and as an ambitious pro-Nazi who wanted Spain to join the European war in 1940. His failures were contrasted with the wisdom of the supposed prudent ruler, the Caudillo, who preserved peace and brought progress to the country. Of course, the real story had been a rather more complicated, and altogether more sordid, affair.

At the end of the Civil War, the Vatican, the Germans, and the Italians, invited Franco on an international tour to celebrate his triumph and to be lauded by the masses of the Fascist countries. The trip never took place. During his more than three-and-a-half decades in power the Caudillo took very few trips abroad, and most of these were to Portugal, to visit his fellow dictator Antònio de Oliveira Salazar. There were two other trips abroad, but not very far: one, a few kilometres across the French border, was to meet Hitler (Hendaye, October 1940); the second, to Italy to visit Mussolini (Bordighera, February 1941), stopping along the way for an encounter with Marshal Pétain in Montpellier. The main purpose for the trips was territorial ambition, or, to put it differently, to expand Franco's victory in the Civil War into the creation of a new Spanish Empire at the expense of the much-hated French and British. Like a lucky poker player on a magical night, he was convinced throughout 1940 that all his recent successes were a result of his own superior talent. However, less than four years later, once the World War was clearly going to end in a way less favourable to the infallible Caudillo than it had begun, and the magic of the night had dissipated into a bad hangover, he saw no problem with drastically altering his recollections of those frenzied previous years.

The big lie started with the doctored account of the most important meeting of them all: the Franco–Hitler encounter at Hendaye, inside a recently defeated France, in October 1940. Franco's propagandists would later insist, and indeed some historians still echo the claim, that the Caudillo resisted—and he was the only man daring enough ever to do so—Hitler's demand that Spain enter the war. First, a shrewd Franco was said (after 1945) to have driven Hitler mad by arriving late to the meeting point, the Hendaye's train station. In reality, it was Franco who was mortified and embarrassed by his own late arrival, caused by the fact that Spanish trains were a wreck at the time. Next, as the fairy tale goes, the Caudillo ignored Foreign Affairs Minister Serrano's reckless advice to join the war. With sly cunning, he deliberately asked for too much and offered too little, and this in such vague terms, that the Führer, upset and out of patience with Franco, cut short the meeting, never wanting to see him again. In sum, Franco's performance was supposed to have been a carefully planned and masterly executed plan to keep Spain out of the war.

This claim is nonsense. In reality, the Caudillo went to Hendaye overconfident of his usefulness to Hitler and he showed up with a long shopping list, little to offer in exchange and very unreal expectations about the duration of the war. He wanted all of Morocco and Algeria's Oran region, then part of the French Empire, a request with which Hitler could not comply—first because, at least temporarily, he preferred to appease Vichy France, a far more useful ally, as much as possible; second, perhaps because he wanted those territories for Germany once the war was over. In fact, what happened at Hendaye was basically a tragi-comic display of inflated self-importance by the Caudillo: he wanted to capture an empire but could afford only a very short war, and this only if was completely financed by Germany. This is exactly what he told Serrano, the key man in the negotiations, in a letter dated September 24, 1940.[10] In this letter he even contemplated the possibility of a longer war, but only if Germany first built-up Spain's military industries.[11] Hitler could not afford to finance and rebuild Spain just to obtain Gibraltar. He believed that England would sue soon for peace anyway, and, furthermore, he was already planning his invasion of Russia. If he needed Gibraltar later, he could take it with or without Franco's consent.

The path to the fantastic narrative that the regime adopted after 1945, the Caudillo as the man of peace and a secret enemy of Hitler during World War II, was neither direct nor coherent. It could not be otherwise as the evidence was fully against it. In 1940 and afterwards, there were plenty of public signs of Franco's bellicose ambitions. First, when France fell, in a move that matched Mussolini's prior to Italy's entry in the war, he declared Spain a "Non-Belligerent" power. Everyone understood that the move implied that neutrality could be abandoned at any time.

This was followed by the Caudillo's vociferously anti-Allies speeches, his barely concealed logistical support for the Germans, and his decision in the summer of 1941 to send the Spanish Blue Division (close to 50,000 supposed volunteers) to fight for Hitler on the Eastern Front. There were plenty of other more or less serious misdeeds, including the ludicrous running of a Japanese spy network by the Spanish embassy in Washington after Pearl Harbor.[12] The Caudillo was lucky. When he was behaving at his worst, between the critical years of 1940 and 1942, keeping Gibraltar secure and out of Axis hands was more important for Britain than punishing a pro-German, but fundamentally weak, Spain. For both the British and the Americans, tightening the maritime supply of wheat and petrol to Spain (they restricted the number of navigation permits, or *navicerts*, available to Spanish boats) guaranteed enough control over the behaviour of the reluctantly non-belligerent and starving country for the entirety of the war. Also luckily for Franco, an overwhelmed Stalin did not declare war on Spain in the summer of 1941 when Spanish troops joined the invasion of the Soviet Union.

However, the Caudillo was not the only lucky dictator; his colleague Salazar also enjoyed the blessings of fortune. Throughout all of these convoluted and fortuitous circumstances, Portugal was the lucky third party because, as a recently discovered document shows, Franco planned to invade the country as soon as the British were defeated.[13] It would be the Caudillo's way of repaying Salazar for all the help received during the Civil War. However, on the surface, both countries were, like their respective dictators, friends. In one of their first encounters (March 1939) Franco and Salazar produced a Friendship and Non-Aggression Treaty, validated in July 1940, and further enhanced by the creation, during their encounter in Sevilla, of an Iberian Bloc (February 1942). In October 1949, the University of Coimbra, Salazar's Alma Mater, made the Caudillo *Doctor Honoris Causa*.

Franco was also fortunate because, in their arrogance and contempt (Hitler often complained about those talkative Latinos), the Nazis kept him in the dark about their operations and plans so that, even if he had wanted to, he could not join them on time. In effect, Franco's representatives in Berlin knew little more than the average German of what was going on. This, in the end, helped the regime to claim innocence after the war. It is a pity that, in spite of the little trust he inspired among the Nazis, the Caudillo kept saying the wrong things, and proclaiming them very loudly. For example, in December 1942, as the German 6th Army stood hopelessly surrounded at Stalingrad, after the Afrika Corps had retreated across North Africa following its defeat at El Alamein, and with Allied troops advancing in Morocco and Algeria as part of Operation Torch, Franco was still proclaiming the death of democracy in his speeches. In a much-publicized talk given that month in front of the Falange's National Council, the clear-sighted Caudillo explained how:

> The liberal world is succumbing, victim of the cancer of its own mistakes, and with it crumbles commercial imperialism, financial capitalism and its millions of unemployed [...] The

genius of Mussolini channels Fascist solutions to everything
fair and humane that existed in the Italian people's rebellion
[...] Later it is Germany which with National-Socialism
gives a new solution to popular needs [...] They lie to
themselves, those who dream about establishing in Western
Europe a democratic-liberal system next to Communism [...]
The World goes by a very different path.[14]

These are statements from a manipulative and opportunistic,
anti-democratic politician, now conveniently pro-Fascist (and they
could not be blamed on Serrano, who was by now already out of
office), but they also reflect a dangerous fanaticism. Because, even
conceding Franco's cunning and adaptability to circumstances, in
the years of the World War and afterwards the Caudillo also continuously showed a deeply paranoid vision of reality and history.
In the following speech, delivered at the opening of the new
rubber stamp parliament, the *Cortes*, in May 1943, we see a prime
example of both Franco's cynicism and his concept of history as
one long line of conspiracies (to make it worse, it was officially
translated into English):

The present War is planned [by Masons and Bolsheviks] for a
long time. The strength of the opponent is great and impossible
to calculate through the ups and downs that battle may offer.
But the presence of Russia on the one side gives to the European
struggle the meaning of a contest for life or death.[15]

However, as the war neared its end, and regardless of Franco's
desires and prejudices, the regime had to prepare itself for a future
that it hated. Fascism was about to be defeated but the regime's
paranoia did not wane; on the contrary, it only grew. The strategic
thought (and the obsession with conspiracies) behind Franco's
actions in the last stages of World War II was illustrated by a
November 1944 report by his new right-hand man, the Navy
officer Luis Carrero Blanco (1904–1973). Carrero considered the war
lost for Germany. While he was correct in observing that the
conflict would result in the decline of Europe and the primacy of the
USA and the USSR, he blamed Britain for committing the fatal
mistake—"England fought the wrong enemy," he claimed—of not

agreeing to a peace treaty with Hitler. According to Carrero, the British had fulfilled what he called the Soviets' "Lenin Plan" for conquering the continent. World War II was only the latest development in the unfolding of that plan. Before that, the formation of Popular Fronts, the 1938 Czechoslovak crisis, and the invasion of Poland had all been Soviet strokes. As a desperate solution, Carrero suggested an alliance of all remaining Western powers with the Nazis to attack the Soviets and fight the Japanese at the same time. Only this would preserve both Western civilization and the control of the "white race" over colonized peoples.[16] This would be Goebbels' and Hitler's fantasy until the moment of their suicides, trapped in their infamous Berlin bunker. Almost to the last, both Nazi and Francoist leaders shared the same strategic delusions. But unlike Hitler, Franco still had an exit strategy: to change the past by repeating his lies again and again … for the next thirty years.

Although the Francoist press had been projecting a more balanced tone since the end of 1943, the year in which hopes for a German victory seemed to evaporate, the dictatorship commenced its campaign of changing foreign public opinion *vis-à-vis* Spain's role in the war only in February 1945.[17] In the last months of World War II, the regime's propaganda machine bombarded an anxious Spanish population with this new version of the past. As Germany faced complete defeat and occupation in the spring of 1945, the *Arriba* newspaper explained that "For Spain the reestablishment of peace will be the dawn of a great day [.] Spain maintained its neutrality most scrupulously. For this great feat time will heap the highest praise on Franco."[18] Another article in the same daily noted that "at every moment Spain proclaimed, through the voice of Franco, that it disapproved of war between Christian, European and American peoples". This statement contained a grain of truth, and several falsehoods. Six years before, the same newspaper had blamed a Christian, indeed Catholic, country, Poland, for starting the war. The sycophantic Manuel Aznar (more on him in Chapter 5), the rising star of Spanish journalism, had even suggested that Poland should surrender as soon as possible to eliminate the possibility of Soviet intervention.[19]

During 1945, newspapers of all colours—Falangist, Catholic, monarchist— carried the same message: not only had Franco been a man of peace during the whole of World War II; he was the *only* man who could guarantee peace in Spain. The alternative was foreign intervention and/or another civil war. Misinformed, repressed, fearful of more violence, and with no other reasonable options, and having witnessed the horrific toll of World War II, Spaniards had to agree. In May, when the war in Europe had only just ended, the monarchist *ABC* appended the following headline to a front-page picture of the Caudillo: "He appears to have been chosen by the benevolence of God". *Arriba*'s headline, though more sober, was only slightly less fantastic: "The Caudillo of neutrality".[20] If Franco meant peace—even God said that—anybody who opposed him represented war.

Franco could explain everything and even convince fearful Spaniards of his foresight, but he could neither change the outcome of the war, nor what citizens of the now victorious democratic nations had read of his words. He tried, nevertheless. A typical (reinvented) summary of the regime's peaceful intentions and tolerance for other nations' political systems, and in particular for liberal-democratic ones, was published in 1947.[21] Its purpose was to connect Spain's (i.e. Franco's) supposedly neutral stance during World War II with post-war material reconstruction, in which the regime should play, it was argued, a significant role given its achievement of internal stability. The Caudillo was the crucial leader for Europe's future. The official account repeated the claim that, when the war started in September 1939, Franco had decreed neutrality—but not only that: the following day, using "the authority of having carried for three years the burden of the liberation of our Fatherland" he had asked the contending parties to avoid "the pains and tragedies that Spaniards had suffered" and seek alternatives to the war.[22] The man who led the barbarous Army of Africa in the summer of 1936 was now depicted as regretting the horrors that took place during the Civil War. Next, the book demonstrated Franco's moderation once again with its insistence that the Caudillo, though he could have acted very differently, had behaved like the Christian gentleman he was during the world conflict:

> ... when in June 1940 the German armies reached the Spanish border, occupying France, and the country was left completely disarmed, Spain, instead of taking advantage of the circumstances and stabbing her [France] in her back, something that

does not belong to its [Spain's] traditions because it is incompatible with its nobility [*hidalguía*], had made generous gestures towards the neighbouring country.[23]

It must be remembered that this—an attack on an almost defeated France—is precisely what Mussolini opportunistically did in June 1940, only to be defeated by the broken French army—and Italy's army was far stronger than Spain's. Unfazed by inconvenient realities, this revision of the past also offered as proof of the regime's essential decency in 1940–1941 the fact that England had enjoyed free passage in the Mediterranean during the war. What the pitiful Spanish Navy and the depleted Air Force could have done against the Royal Navy is a question altogether ignored in the text. What this book did not say is that Spain and Germany had actually jointly prepared an operation to storm Gibraltar, and that Spain allowed German and Italian spies in the vicinity of Gibraltar full freedom to collect information on British convoys en route to Malta, with dreadful consequences for the British Navy. In fact, the Germans ran a complete network of spies, radio stations, logistics and other installations and services more or less openly in Spain, and were regularly helped by Spanish authorities, the police and the armed forces in their operations.

The 1947 whitewash attempt included one real bomb. What the Anglo-American public did not know, the book argued, is that the Spanish nation, under Franco, had not only showed restraint and charity during World War II; it also had been a potential *victim* of the Germans during that conflict. Moreover, Franco was also a victim of the Germans ... because, since 1936, the Nazis had undermined the Caudillo's war efforts to achieve victory in the Civil War! Supposedly, documents newly discovered by the Allies proved that, Franco said and his propaganda machine repeated, "during our War of Liberation the German interest and intention was to extend our war and that I should not obtain a complete victory".[24]

Curiously, perhaps naïvely, the 1947 book included the propaganda instructions given by the regime to the press in August 1945. The intention of reproducing these "orientations", as the book called them, was to show Spain's goodwill towards the Western Allies. However, this only proved that what the press had been saying all along during the war was merely what Franco wanted it to say, thus making credible the claim that the previous five years of strident pro-Axis headlines were also "oriented" by these same sources. Now, the "orientations" had to stress "Spain's solidarity with the world people's at this moment of peace". This was specified in a number of talking points: "The satisfaction of the Spanish people because of the end of the world conflict"; highlighting "the efforts by the United States and England to achieve victory over Japan, and how this victory favoured Western Christian culture"; the beginning of the "era of world peace", to which Spain had contributed its work and enthusiasm. This led to the last point: respect for Spain's internal political system, which had enabled the country to recover its moral and material strength.[25] Effectively, the book demanded respect for the Caudillo.

The Caudillo's fanciful tales failed to impress the West but not most Spaniards, and this was what mattered most. The fear and uncertainty that attended the closing of World War II rendered this opportunistic myth of Franco's Peace not just plausible, but necessary in the minds of many ordinary Spaniards. What mattered to them most was that the Caudillo had not joined the war; that while Europe lay in ruins and social and political turmoil, Spain was living in a situation of semi-normalcy, even if for millions of them this normalcy was marked by misery. Capitalizing on this fear, the Caudillo emerged in the popular imagination as a peace-loving man, not the ruthless imperialist who his enemies claimed had risked another long war. In sum, the regime's manipulations, combined with Spaniards' all-too-real anxieties, cemented a powerful, legitimizing political myth: Franco's Peace. The Caudillo was widely believed to be a wise, prudent ruler who preserved a peaceful oasis in the middle of a Europe hell-bent on destruction. This official recreation and fabrication of the past worked well because it coincided both with the expectations of people, as well as with their ignorance of the dictator's real intentions and actions.

The victory of the anti-Fascist coalition in 1945 brought hope to the minority of Spaniards who firmly opposed the regime; but for the majority it was a year of renewed fears. What would happen if the Allied armies crossed the Pyrenees or if Spain was blockaded? Thus, if 1945 was for most Western Europeans the year of liberation and a shift to democracy and hope, for most Spaniards it was the opposite: it was the year that threatened another war or at least more suffering. This fear placed Spaniards' future more firmly even than before in Franco's hands. The splintered perceptions of Franco, inside and outside Spain, reached their climax during 1945 and 1946. For the Allies and liberated Europeans, the Caudillo was a reminder of their recent tragedy (and shameful ambiguities); for most Spaniards, he was the least bad option because so long as he remained in power there was not going to be a second round of the Civil War.

Many qualified foreign observers realized what was happening to Spanish popular opinion. The American ambassador, Norman Armour, wrote to Washington in October 1945, just prior to his departure from Spain:

> No single factor in the present political scene exercises such influence as the war-wariness of the people. It is a state of mind described not merely in terms of lethargy or exhaustion: it is an active and affirmative conviction that further civil strife cannot be endured and must not be allowed.[26]

This was true enough; but he also went along with the benign interpretation of Franco's conduct during the war. In spite of Spain's earlier wartime transition from neutrality to non-belligerency, as well as the general impression that the Franco regime had helped the Axis powers more than the Allies, Armour reported in November 1945 that "From the record as known to this Embassy emerges that at least during the period of American belligerency the Allies received far greater aid and far more important facilities from Spain to their war effort than did the Axis."[27]

Franco was internationally isolated and had very few other options beyond waiting for better times; but he knew which role he had to play: the lier. A few days after writing the reports cited above, Ambassador Armour had his farewell meeting with the Caudillo. He asked Franco about the (lack of) evolution of the regime. In response the Caudillo embarked upon a "long harangue" concerning the dangers of Communism that the ambassador managed to interrupt only when Franco "paused for breath", 20 minutes later. When Armour told him how disappointed he was with the lack of democratization in post-war Spain, "Franco expressed surprise at this and insisted that real progress had been made. He said that his regime had no intention of staying on any longer than was necessary, but that they must complete their work" and stated that progress had been made "particularly in the social field, in which he had a very real interest".[28] A few days before, the Caudillo had confided to the soon-to-depart American military attaché, Lieutenant-Colonel Albert Ebricht, that while the United States had a great democracy, in:

> Europe, and in Spain particularly things were different, he said the minute one has been given the seat of authority everyone tries to oust him instead of being with him, and he is not able to do the work he should because he is continually hanging onto his chair to keep it from being thrown out.[29]

The Americans could certainly see the two Francos: the potentially useful ally with a supposedly moderate past, and the cynical and narcissistic dictator. In the future, they could choose to see the one that was more convenient to them at any given moment.

There was, finally, yet another sinister side to Franco's policies during World War II, one that was first concealed and then selectively altered—quite successfully, it should be noted—after 1945, and that is both the regime's role in the Holocaust and the role that it *almost* played in this dark chapter. After the war Franco would pretend that his government, unlike the Nazi and Fascist regimes and even some democracies, had a humane policy *vis-à-vis* the persecuted Jewish people. This claim was plausible only insofar as his polices in this matter were highly ambiguous and often contradictory. On the one hand, tens of thousands of Jewish refugees survived the Final Solution by crossing the Pyrenees into Spain in 1940, at which point they were forced to continue farther afield, or, if they had no place to go, to face internment in Spain. On the other hand tens of thousands of European Jews were also turned back at the Spanish border, and thus were ultimately sent to their deaths. In addition, in the last months of the war, the actions of a few brave and honourable Spanish diplomats in Eastern Europe saved the lives of thousands of Jews through the granting of visas and/or diplomatic protection. These individuals acted as exactly that—individuals—and often behaved in direct contravention of orders from Madrid. However, things could have been much different had the course of the war gone in the opposite direction. During the early years of German military success in Europe, Franco's security apparatus was making arrangements to collaborate with the Nazis in carrying out their policies towards the Jews by giving them the names of all 6,000 Jews living in Spain. To prepare for this, in May 1941 local authorities were ordered to compile a census of Spanish Jews, which became the so-called Jewish Archive. The results were passed on to the Nazis, who added them to the list of Europeans Jews to be exterminated as decided during the infamous January 1942 Wannsee Conference. Towards the end of 1945, the Jewish Archive was destroyed, and nothing else was said about it. It was only in 1997 that several incriminating documents were discovered.[30]

A post-war oddity

Franco's need for a new, more convenient past coincided with the Western Allies' post-war weakness and insecurity. The regime knew that, with a bit of luck, it could resist until it could exploit both the diverging strategic interests and prejudices of the war's victors. There were already precedents that supported this hope. During World War II, Winston Churchill, that symbol of defiance in the face of Nazism, had been sending mixed signals, both in private and in public, mostly when speaking in parliament, to Franco's Spain. The underlying message was "behave well and we will correspond". As the war drew to a close, Churchill was mostly concerned with two problems related to Spain: how to preserve British economic interests from American competition, and how to prevent Communism from spreading into the Iberian Peninsula. When, in late 1944, his ambassador to Madrid, Sir Samuel Hoare—a former champion of appeasement who had undergone a rather radical political transformation during the war—persuaded Foreign Secretary Anthony Eden to ask Churchill for some sort of action that might bring about a liberal monarchy in Spain, Churchill's response was blunt: "What you are proposing to do is little less than stirring a revolution in Spain". Although Churchill preferred the restoration of the monarchy, the British premier's policies were, in practice, fully aligned with the main discourse of the regime's propaganda: it was either peace and Franco or war and Communism.[31]

While still a very important international player, Britain—with a bankrupt and rapidly declining Empire in the wake of World War II—was the minor partner amongst the post-war Western Allies. The United States, on the contrary, had power, money, and an increasing number of interests to protect and foster in Europe. These interests, and burdens, included Spain's strategic position at the gates of the Mediterranean. In this regard, there was a serious problem for Franco because under Roosevelt, and initially under Truman, the United States was officially, and avowedly, an anti-Fascist power.

However, history and time both worked in favour of the Caudillo. Long before the articulation of a strategic argument in favour of normalizing diplomatic relations, and even before the end of World War II, a moral bridge between American wartime anti-Fascism and Cold War realism towards Spain had been built on cultural (and even racial) prejudices. For example, in March 1945, as the war neared its end, the military attaché in Spain explained in an intelligence report that among the reasons "for the continuance of the present regime" was "Spanish individualism and lack of responsibility". Elaborating, the attaché said that "the racial heritage and the individualism imparted by almost 800 years of Moorish domination and the lack of responsibility in all but a few individuals make Spaniards as a group incapable of establishing and operating a democracy".[32] Ambassador Armour's temporary replacement, counsellor William W. Butterworth, was even more openly anti-Communist, and less appreciative of Spaniards' wisdom, than his predecessor. In February 1946, just as international condemnations of the Franco regime were mounting, he sent the State Department a report on the Communist threat in the country. He linked this threat to Spaniards' idiosyncrasy, stating that:

> Communism as such conflicts harshly with the Spanish national character, with its marked anarchistic tendencies and rugged individualism. But it is that same intense individualism which cripples most open political parties, thereby leaving Communist discipline and organisation a wide open political field in any time of violent crises.[33]

In many ways a realist, Butterworth told his masters in Washington in his annual overview of the country that Franco was "firmly in control" and, while making some "occasional concessions to democratic opinion", was "confidently gambling on a break between Soviet Russia and the Western allies" that "would transform his uncompromising enmity with the former into an asset which would guarantee Spain's acceptance into an anti-Russian western bloc of nations".[34] He was correct, but before success came a number of crises that, on the surface, looked fatal to the Franco dictatorship.

As Butterworth was writing, the first serious international problems for the regime were appearing. In February 1946, France closed its border with Spain. In March, a tripartite American-Anglo-French declaration repudiated Francoism and expressed the desire for a return to democracy in Spain. However, as the Western powers soon discovered, international pressure served to further consolidate Franco's internal standing, as a combination of nationalism and fear of another civil war moved many Spaniards to support a regime whose policies they had often rejected.[35] American representatives observed this ambiguity in the dictator's trips to several provinces in 1946: Murcia and Alicante in April, Asturias in May, the city of San Sebastián in August. They noticed that "while not an extremely popular figure, [Franco] still was not the object of unanimous detestation among Spaniards that many people affected or wanted to believe".[36] Medium-sized crowds, admittedly organized by the Falange and the unions, turned out to greet him. But they also did so out of a genuine admiration for Franco, as well as a mixture of anxiety and fear for the future.

The Caudillo's cause was also aided by the cynicism, the inaccurate claims, and the outright lies of many of his enemies, particularly, though not exclusively, the emerging Eastern European Communist Bloc. Franco used the wolf of Communism to scare his moderate supporters, as well as those Spaniards who could see the clears signs of another confrontation emerging from beyond the Iron Curtain. The exiled opposition and Stalin's minions were often quite happy to fulfil people's fears. According to some Spanish exiles, between 100,000 and 500,000 exiled Nazis, including 6,000 feared scientists and technicians, had received shelter in Spain by 1946. More modestly, the French Communist leader André Marty put the tally at 100,000. The domestically unpopular Polish Communist government took this information, reworked it, and, at Moscow's behest, led the charge with a sensational revelation: there was, it claimed, a nuclear plant being built in Ocaña, near Madrid, watched over by some 600,000 to 700,000 soldiers. The Polish delegate to the United Nations, the remarkable economist and diplomat Oscar R. Lange, declared Spain a "threat to world peace".[37]

Filtered through the official propaganda machine, such declarations put Spaniards in the difficult situation of having to decide whether to laugh or cry. Although ridiculous, these words, uttered in no less a venue than the United Nations, were clearly a harbinger of trouble. Evidently, thousands of Nazis, Fascists, and other war criminals had escaped to Spain—at times with the Vatican's help—often en route to Latin America. But in Ocaña there was nothing more than a brick factory and a distillery. In reality, most Spaniards were painfully aware of the low level of technological development in the country, sharing ironic jokes at its expense. But laughter is not always an anti-authoritarian weapon: sometimes it can help dictators too, especially when the laughter is of the nervous kind.

What was said at the newly created United Nations reflected, at least in part, public opinion in the Free World. After the war there was a deep antipathy among the American and British public towards the Caudillo. In a Gallup poll conducted in April 1946, ordinary Americans cited the following reasons to cut diplomatic relations with the Franco regime: Spain harboured Nazi scientists (false: the USA, not Spain, did); the Franco government was a Fascist government (true enough); Spain aided the Axis powers during the war (certainly true); Spain was a menace to world peace (hardly). At the same time, there was a strong desire amongst the public for peace and cooperation between nations, and many did not see any real advantage, only risks, in breaking off relations with Spain. The result was that opinion was equally divided on this issue, with 43 per cent in favour of breaking relations with Spain, 43 per cent against it, and 14 per cent undecided. However, only 53 per cent of the American population was said to know who Franco was, or even where Spain was located.[38]

The international calls for the Caudillo's removal were never more intense than in December 1946, when the outcry over the dictatorship reached something of a crescendo at the United Nations. On December 2, for example, Senator Tom Connally of Texas, representing the American delegation, proposed barring Spain from all United Nations specialized organizations and called upon Franco to "surrender the powers of government to a provisional government broadly representative of the Spanish people". If they wanted to join the UN, the Spanish people would first have to get rid of Franco.[39] Since the Spaniards did not overthrow their Caudillo, on December 12, 1946, the United Nations excluded "Fascist" Spain from all its organs and advised its members to withdraw their ambassadors from Madrid. The Vatican, Portugal, Ireland, Argentina and some other minor countries refused to comply. In response to the UN resolution (the usual declaration of good intentions minus the teeth) the regime organized massive demonstrations in support of Franco. However, help for the Caudillo was on its way, and it would start arriving just three months later. In March 1947, the so-called Truman Doctrine—which stated that the US would help any government facing the Communist threat—was elaborated in response to the Greek Civil War. Many consider this the official beginning of the Cold War.

One of the Caudillo's responses to the international affronts to his regime was to organize a referendum. Held on July 6, 1947, the vote was Franco's attempt to gain legitimacy through "democratic" means. The Spanish people were asked to approve a law that would make Franco regent for life of a monarchy without a king. The referendum was, of course, rigged. As the American consul in Málaga noted, pro-Franco propaganda was ubiquitous, mixing exhortations to vote for the Caudillo with reminders of the horrors of the Civil War. Spaniards had to walk to the polling stations with their votes in their pockets, as there were no closed booths in which to mark their ballots. In a country where many people were still starving, the rumour—which was based on truth for once —that rationing cards would be stamped at the booth, with failure to show the stamp resulting in one's card being annulled, exerted a significant influence on the proceedings.[40] However, what very few people—including foreign diplomats—knew, was that the presidents of the polling stations were given secret instructions to produce pre-determined results. What indeed was widely understood by Spaniards was that the only guarantee of peace in the country was for Franco to remain in command. He and his supporters would never relinquish power peacefully. In any case, the Caudillo probably could have won even without resorting to fraud.

Having achieved another source of legitimacy, in addition to military victory and God's support, all Franco had to do now was wait. He already knew that the voices of international condemnation towards his regime would not be followed by any firm or coordinated actions aimed at removing him from power.

From the last days of World War II until well into 1947 there had been a lot of wavering amongst American policy makers over what to do with Franco—a conversation that occurred largely unbeknownst to the American public. American democratic idealism was at this time experiencing a confrontation with its new international responsibilities as one of the world's two superpowers, as well as an increasing mistrust towards its main global competitor, the Soviet Union. The eventual outcome was the adoption of anti-Communism, the emergence of the Cold War, and, luckily for the Spanish Generalissimo, an increased interest by the United States government in the strategic possibilities of Spain.[41] This resulted, first, in a growing tolerance towards Franco's dictatorship, and later, an open, if unequal, friendship. The Caudillo and his closest collaborators had anticipated this shift, and not just because they could predict the future; rather there was no other source of hope for them. They had waited patiently for this change in policy to take place, unmoved by the enormous cost to Spain's economy and social welfare.

And true enough, in 1947 anti-Communism became more important to the Americans than their anti-Fascist reservations, a change in which cynicism definitely came into play. In late December of that year, Paul Culbertson, the American Chargé d'Affaires at the embassy in Madrid, could report to the State Department his disdain for Spaniards, and their unsuitability for democracy—after more than 50,000 people had been shot in the previous eight years of Franco's Peace. Commenting on the groups in opposition to the regime, Culbertson wrote:

> The opposition elements inside and outside of Spain have been living in the false expectation that we and other powers will unseat Franco and place them in control. None of these elements has ever seemed to figure out the mechanics of this change. In fact, they never tried.[42]

This gentleman neglected in his report to do a little comparative history and political science. Up to 1945 very few people in

Germany, Italy, and even in France or the Low Countries, had tried very hard to recover democracy, and yet they were now part of the Free World.

Spain was now on a very different trajectory from that of its northern European neighbours. Under Franco's peculiar "peace", the country's evolution contrasted with that of most of Western Europe after 1945. While most states (with the exception of Portugal and to some extent Greece) became democracies, Franco's regime remained staunchly authoritarian. While most Western European citizens lived in freedom, Spaniards lived under a repressive state. And unlike the rapid process of economic development that followed the end of World War II, the so-called Golden Age of European (and North American) economic growth, Spain remained a chronic underperformer until the early 1960s. The two factors—dictatorship and poverty—not only seemed to put Spain on a different path but, more importantly, had direct and dire effects on ordinary Spaniards' lives. In any case, Spain's reality under Francoism, observed by those who enjoyed both freedom and increasing progress, seemed to confirm some of the prejudices and misconceptions about the country that had been in circulation since the sixteenth century. The idea of the essential "otherness" of Spain, fundamentally a reactionary one, was shared, from a different perspective and with very different intentions, even by a left-wing sector of European public opinion. This opinion maintained a romantic attitude about the country and particularly towards the nature of the Spanish Civil War, as the great, noble cause of the century. Spain was different because old Europe and Cold War America seemed so disappointingly the same.

This notion of Spanish exceptionalism played very well into Franco's hands. It explained why Spaniards, unlike other Europeans, could not live in democracy: because democracy was an unSpanish, and thus dangerous, foreign system. According to the dictatorship, other nations, particularly France and Britain, were permanent enemies of Spain, as they could not forgive its past glories and staunch Catholicism. They promoted freedom as a means to destroy Spain. In addition, another foreign political tool, Communism, supposedly defeated in Spain during the war, was an ever-present menace threatening to come back. According to official propaganda, the Red Beast could not accept that, for the first time, it had been forced to let go of a nation once firmly in its sights—perhaps forgetting what had happened in Finland in 1918, and in Hungary and Germany in 1919. Many foreign friends of the regime agreed with this.

Behind the Francoist ideology of Spanish exceptionalism ran a dark undercurrent of personal bigotry and resentment on the part of Franco himself. Indeed, the depth of the dictator's hatred and xenophobic prejudices was sometimes astonishing. There is no more revealing evidence of this than a surprisingly long series of forty-two articles he wrote between 1946 and 1951 that was published in the newspaper *Arriba*. Franco signed the articles using an improbable pseudonym, Jakin Boor. The story gets even more convoluted, however. At one point, the press reported on a visit that this J. Boor had paid to the Caudillo. A subject of particular importance to Franco was Freemasonry, which the dictator claimed was an anti-Spanish and anti-Catholic organization that cooperated with Communism. The matter obsessed him: in these articles, most of Franco's enemies, both Spanish and foreign—including most leaders of the United States, Britain, and France—were denounced as high-ranking Freemasons. Here are some of Boor's (Franco's) thoughts:

> Freemasonry is a British product, the same way that Communism is a Russian product [...] For England it was the way to activate the dismembering of an empire [the Spanish] that shadowed hers; for France, the best system to eliminate its southern border and a rival. To neither of the two nations was a strong Spain convenient, and they played together to achieve this.[43]
>
> It could not pass unnoticed to Moscow, who ruled the Occident, the Masonic affiliation of Roosevelt and his advisers; who decided, with or without responsibility, in Europe and America, and besieged the fortress, and obviously took it. Russia controlled Roosevelt's and other American rulers' Masonic circles and for a long time had a decisive influence.[44]

This was the same man that, who as we shall see in the next chapter, was about to become one of Cold War America's "good dictators".

A captured future

Why would millions of Spaniards support Franco during the crucial years of 1939 to 1947, a period of immense social hardship, political repression and threats from abroad? The answer lies in a combination of fear and deep social division. But not just fear of the leader or the regime—a sentiment which, although significant, was probably felt only by a large minority; rather, it was a society *afraid of itself*, a feeling that was almost universally shared by the Spanish population. This fear, this deep insecurity over "what is wrong with us", permeated all social strata, thereby deepening the fractures that separated those who had profited, materially and spiritually, from the Caudillo's victory and those who felt defeated. The regime was able to manipulate this fear, thus moving the majority of the apolitical population towards Franco's side. In sum, the Caudillo's power benefited from both the different fears of the much-divided Spaniards and the widespread hope that life might improve. Throughout the dictatorship, the official propaganda machine made sure Spaniards never forgot what was at stake. Behind the image of normalcy Spain remained a suffocating country, of which Franco was the master of both the present and the future.

An indication of how deeply post-war Spanish society was divided and afraid of violence can be seen in the letters that ordinary Spaniards sent to Franco in the 1940s. In these missives, those who felt that they were on the winning side asked the Caudillo for justice, often interpreted as a sort of compensation for the sacrifices and pain suffered under the Republic and during the war. Those who were the defeated wrote to the dictator mainly asking him for pity, as they understood and confirmed to him that he had total control over their fate. The horror of the war loomed over all of these letters, as did the open wounds the conflict had left in society. The regime did little to heal these wounds: on the contrary, it made sure that they never closed. Moreover, Francoism demanded complete submission from its defeated enemies and in exchange for their recognition that they were completely wrong, offered, at best, a very limited pardon. Such a mean and vengeful attitude appears, for example, in a 1940 book of poetry written by political prisoners. On one hand, the prisoners had to laud their tormentor, the Caudillo, and, on the other, request his supposedly magnanimous pardon.

In the prologue of this book, the editor, José María Sánchez de Muniain, a member of the council running the work-for-reduced-sentence scheme (he was also a prominent militant of Catholic Action), explained that:

> Spain is in a magnificent position to be again an instrument of providence [...] We are the envy of peoples and we are guided by the cleanest sword of modern times. This is not boasting but the truest of truths.[45]

The cleanest sword belonged to Franco, to whom the vanquished had to pay homage. From Soria prison Juan Bautista Llorca ended his poem entitled "Spain" with the following verse:

> Honour to the Caudillo who brought fortune!
> Honour to his ancestry, clear crib!
> To whom History opens glass doors!
> Because of you Spain is Grand, Free and One!
> Franco, Franco, Franco! Hail General![46]

From an unnamed prison, Félix Paredes, in "Gratitude towards the Caudillo", explained the anxieties of prisoners as they hoped for his Excellency's pardon:

> And pardon arrives, it arrives! And the inmate welcomes it,
> like the one who welcomes dawn as dawn revives him
> and facing that sign of peace and consolation
> the eloquent minute carrying the task
> that introduced in the prisoner's anxiety the surprise
> and always sure of the truth that he signs,
> ratifies with pride that the Caudillo pardons.[47]

This attitude towards prisoners was based on the conviction that the "reds" had committed atrocious crimes against good Spaniards, the nation, and its Catholic heritage. The Church (with many individual exceptions, mostly at parish level) was one of the most ardent defenders of this view, and that is why Franco's (in)justice was repeatedly endorsed by clerics. Having lost nearly 8,000 of its clergy to the republicans, the post-war Church, while advocating a spiritual rather than legal pardon, made very clear that such a pardon also meant submission to both Franco and God. In 1939, Father José A. Pérez del Pulgar, a Jesuit who also was a senior administrator of the penal justice system, explained that by working, prisoners not only "contribute to repair the damage done by their cooperation with the Marxist rebellion", but also "reconcile themselves and their families with religion, society and the Fatherland, without need to request amnesties that would degrade and devaluate Authority".[48] For the Church, remembering and harshly punishing, not pardon and reconciliation, was the best policy.

Even the execution of "red" criminals was, according to some priests, a most humane policy. Father Martín Torrent, the chaplain of Barcelona prison, explained in 1942 how he had seen "prisoners condemned because of rebellion to die [in front of the firing squad] with their extended arm and yelling Long Life to Franco! and Up with Spain!" This proved, so he claimed, that "the average prisoner today only trusts the Caudillo's magnanimity". This same cleric also defended the idea that those executed at dawn were lucky souls because, knowing when their death was coming, they could prepare themselves for the afterlife by means of confession.[49] As for forgetting, Father José Echeandía explained in 1945 that "those who use arguments of unconscious conformists, tricks of hidden and dangerous enemies, to which our generous and forgetting ears could pay easy attention" were, in fact, opening the door to a new round of mass crimes.[50]

The Church was not alone in perpetuating this dynamic of victimization, humiliation and uncompromising punishment. As the letters to Franco show, ordinary people such as farmers, middle- and even lower-class individuals, saw themselves as the past and possibly the future victims of the "reds", and the Caudillo himself, rather than his regime, as the best guarantee that this tragedy would not be repeated. Important sectors of society shared this opinion. For example, according to the police, when the dictator visited Barcelona in May 1942, local businessmen made it clear that their:

> sympathy was only for the Caudillo, that they want to know nothing of the Falange. As for the un-political middle class, in spite of lamenting their privations and having repeatedly criticized current polices, particularly in the rationing system,

when they saw the Caudillo they remembered again the tragic
moments of "red domination" and praised the Caudillo's sincerity
when he declared how aware he was of all the on-going social
suffering.[51]

Similar observations were made in reports the following year from
Melilla, and in 1944 from Zaragoza, and were corroborated not
only by the regime's own opinion analyses but also by the often
well-informed British consuls and diplomats. As if they needed
further proof, people had seen Italy descend into chaos after the
fall of Mussolini in July 1943 and reached their own conclusions.
Anyone who had supported or profited from the regime saw the
writing on the wall: liberated Europe was not just a happy dance
floor but also a place of reprisal, particularly brutal in the East,
though still extremely violent in the West. Spain's violent past
could become the present again any moment. Only Franco could
guarantee this would not happen.

The dictator not only manipulated fear, he also profited from
people's hopes. To achieve this, the Caudillo justified most difficulties
as being legacies of the past, while, at the same time, he presented
himself as a modest ruler always tirelessly working for his nation's
welfare. For example, in 1946, on the tenth anniversary of the
July uprising and more than seven years after the end of the war,
he gave an interview to "a Spanish journalist". Even this moment
of self-promotion was presented as a sacrifice since "in spite of
being a man of deeds more than of words", he had to force himself to
talk because "public men cannot avoid dialogue and presenting to
others affairs of public interest or transcendence".[52] After thanking
God for "the protection that he has been offering to Spain", Franco
proceeded to explain the country's economic situation. He made
clear that "my love and ambitions for Spain are so many and so
great, that I will never be satisfied even if a lot is achieved".
Among the many sources of blame for the country's ongoing economic "difficulties" (in reality, it was nothing short of a disaster)
Franco heaped scorn upon: the "reds", whose overcirculation of
banknotes (even if republican money had already been declared
invalid during the war) had caused the present inflationary crisis;
the destruction caused by the "reds" in the war (he did not blame the
war, but only the other side); the persistent drought, which "had

caused a severe lack of food that had prevented the country from having a complete harvest in six years" (false); most damaging was the "happy and trusting attitude" of governments in the previous fifty years, which allowed the country's resources to be wasted; the lack of gold reserves, taken to Russia by the "reds", etc. Later in this interview, in a passage that is nothing short of an Orwellian masterpiece, he described the extent of his never sufficiently recognized efforts and achievements:

> People only know what they have gone through and the deficiencies and sacrifices, but they ignore in reality all the sleepless vigils, the provisions, the efforts and almost miraculous means by which [these deficiencies] were overcome [...] Keep in mind that my Government and myself, in spite of what can be said abroad, are men of work and not of propaganda [...] It is paradoxical that when other nations had spent billions in killing and destroying each other [...] we spent in Spain's re-birth and in social justice [...] The [food] intervention, bad and imperfect that it may be, is the only life saver of the poor [...] There are those who claim, mendaciously, that high prices are a product of our increases of [workers'] salaries [...] You can tell your readers that a better harvest is in sight [that the Government will track] the problem of high prices [...] and that all sacrifices will result in a better purchasing power of our currency.[53]

Franco ended the interview by reminding readers of "his constant memory for those who died for our re-birth, making sure that nothing will render sterile their sacrifice" and he asked Spaniards "to be on guard in defence of the martyrs' legacy to us".[54] Even in the moments of self-praise and supposed hope he could not restrain himself from reminding Spaniards that peace, or rather civil war, was at stake. Spaniards had to be on guard against other Spaniards and foreign forces.

The trauma of the war, the deep social and cultural fractures, the unequal distribution of the fruits of victory, and the fears and hopes about the future help to explain how Franco was able to preserve, and even increase, his mystique amongst both his supporters and apolitical Spaniards, a mystique that remained intact even in the most adverse circumstances. He became the master of the nation's future, and the depository of its hope. For many Spaniards reality was seen through the idea of what Franco might think or desire, and these thoughts were sometimes more meaningful than their own daily experience. They were ready to be part of a play, of a mass representation filled with reflecting mirrors, in order to please the Caudillo. For example, in the spring of 1943, the great man visited the province of Almería, an area where poverty took its steepest toll in the form of ongoing starvation and illnesses such as typhus and conjunctivitis. Four years after the area's "liberation" (the province was one of the last to be taken by rebel forces in 1939) the new regime had few good things to show for itself in Almería. In fact, material conditions were getting worse. But since the saviour sent by God was coming, the local authorities rushed to create good news, or rather, to create a new, if ephemeral, reality for Franco; it was encapsulated in an all-Spanish rather pathetic version of the so-called Potemkin village.[55]

It was known long before the Civil War that beneath the dry and often barren fields of the area known as Campo de Dalías, in the west of the province, that there were vast quantities of untapped subterranean water. If used, they could radically transform the area into a food-producing zone. Having done nothing to date, the authorities, and more specifically the provincial governor, found the scarce resources necessary to show Franco that "the works have already started, with the possibility that he may visit them". On April 10, 1943, the authorities requested an engineer from Valencia to dig a well in the Campo de Dalías, not by chance right by the side of the Málaga–Almería road, with work commencing on the 28th. The governor, in these days of chronic petrol and transportation shortages, lent the engineer a truck to bring the equipment from Valencia (almost 500 kilometres away). By May 9, the day the Caudillo arrived in the province, the well was already 25 metres deep. It was 6.30 pm when the climactic moment arrived: the Caudillo's motorcade approached the well, the engineer later reported, and "even if he did not stop, we are sure that he had a perfect view of the installations, because he answered our salutes as we stood next to the drilling tower".[56] Later that day, at the School of the Arts, Franco spent 10 minutes inspecting the plans for the irrigation project and asking the thrilled engineer about the possibilities of finding enough water in the region. The only other plans he enquired about were for the social housing projects the governor had told him about, which he inspected for 5 minutes before leaving.

The next day the local newspaper carried pictures of enthusiastic crowds, with many people wearing little more than rags, welcoming the Caudillo to the city of Almería. By then the dictator was already on his way back to Granada. Passing the well once again, Franco waved back at the drilling crew, who seemed to notice—or so they liked to believe—how the car slowed, and Franco had "noticeable pleasure in his face". Shortly afterwards, in nearby Granada, Franco summarized his thoughts on what he saw in Almería: " ... thirsty land of disgusting caves, there I saw the plenitude of our good achievements: the immense new neighbourhoods in frenetic construction; engineers who drill the land in search of the liquid veins that fertilize the fields".[57] A mirage created for the dictator now became, in his lips, an official truth and a message of hope. Almería's Campo de Dalías agrarian region would not be developed until the early 1960s. As for housing, a small, insufficient number of tiny, poorly constructed homes were made available in that city in the 1950s.

The appropriation of memory

The Caudillo not only was master of the present and the future he was also the main interpreter of the past. Furthermore, the narrative of his life was supposed to encapsulate Spain's story, its suffering and its redemption. He was the main force and the thematic axis behind the regime's efforts to forge a suitable historical memory and to impose it on Spaniards. The discursive line of this project was to manipulate and decontextualize the material and human damage caused by the Civil War—responsibility for which was pinned solely on the republicans—and to compare it with the damage that the unstable Republic had both caused and threatened to cause to the nation: the killing of a mythical one million good Spaniards, and the imminent mass killing of millions more, by an atheistic, Soviet-style government born out of the February 1936 elections. Refusing to accept this terrible fate for Spain, dictated in Moscow, Franco, the exceptional hero chosen by God, became the leader of the Saviour National Movement of July 18, 1936. In keeping with this narrative, the numbers of pro-Franco dead were inflated, as part of a mythology that claimed their martyrdom as the price of Spain's redemption. Their young blood irrigated the fields that after 1939 offered Spaniards the fruits of peace and prosperity. At the same time, the dictatorship not only denied its enemies the status of victims, but also erased them from public memory, and from the historical record as well. And thus, all the people who died in the war fell either fighting for Franco or murdered by the "reds" while blessing God's and Spain's (the Caudillo's) names. They were the *Caídos por Dios y por España* (Fallen for God and for Spain).

The clearest, and most grandiose, example of the Caudillo's appropriation and manipulation of Spain's tragedy was (and still is, see Chapter 6) the Valley of the Fallen. Excavated out of granite rock not far from King Philip II's great sixteenth-century monastery El Escorial, in the mountains north of Madrid, it is a monument of gargantuan dimensions. It has a church 300 metres long, topped by a cross 150 metres tall. There is an abbey and a hostel, plus grand gardens and esplanades. Started in 1940 and inaugurated in 1959, in a location personally chosen by the dictator, it was constructed by hundreds of political prisoners as well as free workers, and consumed much-needed cement and steel in the economically depressed post-war period. Conceived as a monument for those killed on the nationalist side, the remains of some 40,000 to 70,000 victims of the war were placed in a catacomb next to the church. However, the bodies were so poorly identified that nobody really knows who, exactly, or even how many, are buried there. At the last moment, the regime decided to include the remains of a few hundred republican soldiers as well, but without their families' consent. These soldiers were considered to be innocent, if misguided, Spaniards who had been led to their death by corrupt, coward and manipulative republican leaders.

The monument would become a gathering place for the regime and its supporters, and the symbol of Franco's exceptional role as the saviour of a martyred Spain. Even before work had started, the Valley offered further proof of Franco's role as a man of destiny acting under God's commands. Fray Justo Pérez de Urbel, a well-known regime propagandist and first prior of the abbey located at back of the complex, explained how the Caudillo chose the site. Shortly after the end of the war, Franco saw the place in the distance and started climbing Madrid's Guadarrama Mountains followed by a breathless General Moscardó:

> You are not going to force us to climb there, said the hero of the Alcázar de Toledo. Not today, no: but we shall climb another day; and dare to expect that many Spaniards will go there.[58]

And thus the Valley became another of the Caudillo's fulfilled prophecies. But what did he intend with this construction? Fray Justo described the monument's meaning as follows:

> A beautiful idea. It was inspired not by an aim of personal exaltation or by narrow partisan spirit but by a deep religious sense of life and integral concept for the fatherland. The war ended happily with the victory of true Spain against the destructive forces that came from outside ... [59]

The principal victim belonging to true Spain to be buried in the Valley was the founder of the Falange, the once young and dashing José Antonio Primo de Rivera, who was executed by the republicans in Alicante on November 20, 1936. His execution was only officially recognized by the rebel authorities two years later, when the date of his death was made a holiday—the Day of Pain. In 1939, José Antonio's body was recovered from his grave in Alicante and buried at El Escorial following an impressive, several hundred kilometres-long march of torch-bearing Falangists as the funeral procession slowly moved from the Mediterranean city towards central Castile.[60] Along the way, some imprisoned republicans were taken from local jails and "spontaneously" murdered by Falangists who were avenging their beloved leader. Franco was present at José Antonio's reburial in 1939, and again when his body was moved to the recently finished Valley of the Fallen in 1959. In the meantime, the supposed aura of destiny that surrounded the handsome José Antonio all his short life—like Christ, he was only thirty-three at the time of his death—was conferred on the less than physically dashing dictator; who had became the administrator of the young Fascist leader's heroic death and political legacy (in reality, they deeply disliked each other).

The official message that explained the meaning of the Valley remained unchanged throughout the dictatorship. In 1959, the Ministry of Propaganda (*Ministerio de Información y Turismo*) described the relationship between Spain's tragedy and Franco's project in a pamphlet that was also published in French and English. Twenty years after the end of the Civil War, the regime said that the conflict had been the product of a "planned Marxist revolution" by the [*sic*] "Komintern". It added that the Valley was meant as homage to "all the victims of Marxist terror and all who died in combat". The pain for the victims was "felt with most intensity [by Franco] because he was the Caudillo of the national forces". This is why the Caudillo "in solidarity with the sentiments of those families who gave heroes to the fronts and martyrs in the rear-guard" conceived the idea of the Valley. In victory, he was magnanimous: political prisoners were given "the opportunity to collaborate with the works". However, there were machinations everywhere, including in Rome, against the project, which was presented "as a unilateral monument to the victor". Nothing could be farther from the truth, since "nobody can say without being called publicly a slanderer and a liar" that the Valley was going to be Franco's mausoleum. "This idea is criminal because there is not the slightest indication that the Valley is expected, not even in the distant future, as a possible place of eternal rest for today's Chief of State".[61] Franco would be buried there in 1975.

The annual funeral mass and ceremony for José Antonio and the other fallen held every November 20 was not just a symbol of the Caudillo's control over José Antonio's legacy or over the collective pain of Spaniards; it was also a reminder of the horrors of the war, the precarious nature of peace and, finally, of Franco's pivotal role in keeping the country free from strife.[62] The regime established the pattern surrounding every Day of Pain ceremony very early on. Newspaper articles published on November 20 praised José Antonio; the next day they talked about the Caudillo presiding over the ceremony. Similar local ceremonies took place in the mini-valleys that were established by the thousands everywhere across Spain in the form of crosses and plaques to those "Fallen for God and for Spain", bearing the names of the Francoist victims of the war.

Many of those plaques were installed inside churches. José Antonio's name was often engraved on the outside walls of the temples. With this, Church and State sent a powerful message to Spaniards: God has sent his son, Christ, to the people only to be murdered at the age of thirty-three, but also to create a Church led by the Pope. Spain sent her beloved son, José Antonio, to be murdered also at the age of thirty-three by bad Spaniards and foreigners, but also to create a new nation led by his chosen saviour and leader: the Caudillo.

One problem with this religious and political version of the past was, of course, the inconvenient memories of the republicans killed in the war or assassinated by Franco's supporters. But these memories had a disadvantage over official celebrations: there was no physical place where these republicans could be honoured, or even remembered. The dictator's supposed piety and much-publicized forgiveness never reached his victims. No military cemeteries existed for those killed in combat and, of course, for those assassinated by the Caudillo's supporters; they remained in the unmarked mass graves where they had been dumped. People were barred from leaving flowers or messages on them, even if they knew where they lay. Private memories among family and friends survived, of course, but their transmission to the next generation was problematic. Telling the truth to children was risky: not only because they could talk and put everybody at risk but also because for these children knowledge of the truth, in a sense, made them part of the problem that tormented their elders. Many preferred to preserve the younger generations' innocence from the terror of the past even if this allowed the dictatorship's version of Spaniards' pain to remain largely unchallenged, while memories of the regime's victims faded in time.

The Day of Pain was part of a wider project of Francoist Historical Memory. There were other official holidays to the dictator's, and his regime's, glory. There was Caudillo Day (October 1), and the anniversary of the beginning of the war—or, as the regime called it, the day of the beginning of national rebirth (July 18). This was the day when official buildings or housing projects were inaugurated by authorities; people got the day off from work and a double monthly pay (more on this in the next chapter). The regime's media amply propagated all of these festivities, as well as Franco's more or less normal official activities.

Both Franco's public image and the building of an imposed Historical Memory were greatly helped by a new powerful tool of propaganda and manipulation introduced by the dictatorship in January 1943: the newsreels. They were called NO-DO (for *Noticias Documentales*) and their exhibition was mandatory in all cinemas before any feature film. Since Spaniards were among the world's most frequent moviegoers, and because television did not reach the majority of households until the late 1960s, Franco's likeness greeted many millions of Spaniards via NO-DO newsreels. The tone of the Caudillo's appearances in NO-DO was set in the first 1943 issue. A five-minute report introduced the newsreel to Spaniards while at the same time making an analysis of the country's state of affairs: an orderly nation, each person in their right place, all of this presided over by Franco. The dictator was then introduced as the cameras entered his palace-residence, *El Pardo*, whose doors opened almost magically, moved by no visible hand, for the first time to millions of eyes. The Caudillo was shown working in his office, seated at a desk with a crucifix on it. The image reflected what propaganda had been saying for years about him: a calm, tireless man devoted to Spaniards' welfare (the regime's propaganda often referred to *la lucecita de El Pardo*: like Mussolini's office at Palazzo Venezia Franco's studio lamp was said always to be on during the night). The narrator explained how "In the days of supreme danger for the Fatherland, he knew how to save it". Images of Civil War battles followed, and then of the Victory Day parade, with people clapping as the triumphant troops marched by. The off-camera voice explained again: "The doors of Spain are opened to a new era of national honour and greatness"; "Each one in his position has a duty to offer his personal effort", as Franco obviously was doing from his privileged, well-deserved place.[63] Later that year, long NO-DO documentaries such as *Spaniards Remember … 1936–1939* (47 minutes) and *March 28, 1939* (36 minutes) portrayed the chaos that led to the "red crimes", as well as the "liberation" of Madrid.

The Caudillo and the memory of the Spanish Civil War became permanent themes in the NO-DO newsreels. There were also frequent documentaries on peace and reconstruction. At the centre of many of the national news broadcast, either present or casting his shadow over how to interpret them, stood Franco. In total:

> Between 1943 and 1975, Franco appeared [in NO-DO] 154
> times inaugurating dams, social housing, agrarian projects or
> factories. Documented also in 375 pieces of news were his official
> visits to different places, receptions, awarding of medals or
> prizes and non-military events. As head of the government or
> Chief of State he appeared another 215 times ... [64]

Franco's image was carefully managed. When reporting on Spain's
relationship with other states, he was called Head of State (*Jefe del
Estado*) or Generalissimo; but when referring to the Spanish Civil
War or its consequences he was called the Caudillo, though when
referring to the conquest of a town during the past conflict he was also,
albeit less often, called Liberator (*Libertador*) or Saviour (*Salvador*).[65]

The role of the masses in these pieces of visual propaganda was
that of providing "popular" enthusiasm. In NO-DO films ordinary
Spaniards were rarely presented as individuals. When the Caudillo
appeared, people were shown looking at him, admiring his successful
deeds, gratefully clapping or waving flags, signs or just hand-
kerchiefs. One of NO-DO's first releases set this pattern. In May
1943 Franco visited Zamora, a poor, depopulated and conservative
Castilian province. There he inaugurated a hydroelectric project,
one of the dozens that he would attend in the following decades
(in this case, given the date, it was probably one started by the
Republic). These kinds of projects belonged to the myth of Spain's
reconstruction and in particular to the supposed redemption
of Spain's countryside not by radical land distribution, as the
republicans had done, but by expanding irrigation and internal
colonization (see Chapter 4). In the images, a triumphant Franco
entered a rural town. After the inauguration of the reservoir,
he passed near a group of workers who raised their hands in the
Fascist salute. They said nothing, they had no individual faces;
they were either part of the set or reduced to the role of hailing
the presiding priest of every ceremony: the Caudillo.[66]

While conveying this double message of peace and Franco's serene
rule, NO-DO, like the rest of the regime's propaganda machine,
was a useful tool for re-writing the past, and particularly the truth
of Franco–Axis relations. Inconvenient historical events, such as
the presence of the Blue Division on the Eastern Front, and even
the role of Axis troops in the Civil War, did not appear. Images of

Italian and German troops in the Victory Parade where Franco got his *Laureada* were excised, while the false version of the meeting with Hitler would be repeated over and over. The main objective of the propaganda machine during this period was the promotion of the myth of Franco the wise "man of peace": the opportunistic yet hugely successful image the dictator had clearly promoted since the last months of World War II. However, the message of peace and progress was always shackled to the regime's foundational claim to legitimacy: its victory against the anti-Spanish forces during the Civil War. The dictatorship constantly remembered this victory as the necessary precondition for peace. For Spaniards, the meaning of the Caudillo could not and would not be separated from the long shadow of past violence that loomed always over the future. When he or his propagandists used the word peace they were, in fact, referring to civil war. While not always understood abroad, this was perfectly and terribly clear to all Spaniards, as it was clear to them who owned their past and controlled their lives.

Notes

1 20-5-1939, "Franco, Padre de la patria y héroe supremo de la guerra, recibe la Gran Cruz Laureada de San Fernando", *ABC*.
2 January 1941, "Pesimista informe de la DGS", *Documentos Inéditos para una Historia del Generalísimo Franco (DIHGF)*, vol. II, Madrid, Azor, 1992, pp. 19–22.
3 November 1941, *Boletín Informativo de la S.G. de Falange: Información, comentarios, bulos, ambiente*, Archivo de la Fundación Francisco Franco (AFFF) 27032.
4 20-8-1942, *D.G. de Seguridad. Serv. de Información: División del ambiente político en Asturias* ... , AFFF 27177.
5 November 1941, *Boletín Informativo* ... *doc. cit.*
6 31-8-1942, *Secretaría General del Movimiento. Informe de Fermín Sanz Orrio sobre Abastos*, Archivo General de la Administración, Sección de Presdiencia (AGA-P) 9.
7 Francisco Franco Bahamonde [Jaime de Andrade], *Raza*, Barcelona, Planeta, 1997.
8 Alberto Reig Tapia, "La autoimagen de Franco: la estética de la raza y el imperio", in Vicente Sánchez-Biosca (coord.), *Materiales para una iconografía de Francisco Franco. Archivos de la Filmoteca*, 42–42 (2002–2003), I, pp. 97–121.
9 20-9-1940, *Informe de Higinio París Eguilaz sobre los fallos en la política económica* ... , Archivo de la Fundación Francisco Franco (AFFF) 27070.
10 Jesús Palacios, *Las cartas de Franco. La correspondencia desconocida que marcó el destino de España*, Madrid, La Esfera de los Libros, 2005, pp. 136–139.

11 Ibid., p. 139.

12 David Wingate Pike, *Franco and the Axis Stigma*, Houndmills, Palmgrave, 2008, pp. 70–72.

13 December 1940, *Alto Estado Mayor. Plan de Campaña nº 1, previniendo una invasión {sic} desde Portugal*, AFFF 2803.

14 Francisco Franco Bahamonde, *Discurso del Caudillo ante el III Consejo Nacional*, Madrid, Art. Graf. Larra, 1942. pp. 6, 7, 8, 12.

15 Francisco Franco Bahamonde, *The Caudillo's speech at the opening of the Spanish "Cortes"*, Madrid, Ediciones de la Vicesecretaría de Ecuación Popular, 1943.

16 19-11-1944, *Informe de la Secretaría de Carrero Blanco; "Consideraciones sobre una futura constitución política del mundo"*, AFFF 105.

17 24-2-1945, *Nota adjunta a la memoria complementaria sobre propaganda exterior de España*, AFFF 6634.

18 Quoted in Pike, *Franco*, p. 126.

19 Ibid., pp. 16–19.

20 Ibid., p. 130.

21 Agustín del Río Cisneros, *España, rumbo a la post-guerra. La paz Española de Franco*, Madrid, Afrodisio Aguado, 1947.

22 Ibid., p. 11.

23 Ibid., p. 12.

24 Ibid., p. 13.

25 Ibid., pp. 355–356.

26 8-10-1945, *Embassy of the United States of America, Subject: An appreciation of the Spanish Political Situation*, National Archives College Park (NACP), State Department, Lot Files 6635, 59/250/852/8.

27 6-11-1945, *Embassy of the United States of America, Transmitting memorandum on "Allied-Axis Wartime Balance Sheet with Spain"*, NACP, State Department, Lot Files 6336, 59/250/852/8.

28 3-12-1945, *Embassy of the United States of America, Ambassador Armour's Farewell Conversations with General Franco and Foreign Minister Martin Artajo; Reception of Military Attaché by General Franco*, NACP, State Department, Lot Files 6336, 59/250/852/8.

29 Ibid.

30 Jacobo Israel Garzón, "El Archivo Judaico del Franquismo", *Raíces*, 33 (1997): 57–60.

31 Richard Wigg, *Churchill and Spain. The Survival of the Franco Regime, 1940–1945*, Brighton, Sussex UP, 2008, p. 181.

32 23-3-1945, *Military Intelligence Division W.G.G.S.*, NACP, State Department, Lot Files 6634, 59/250/852/8.

33 15-2-1946, *Incoming telegram 936*, NACP, State Department, Lot Files 6337, 59/250/852/8.

34 15-2-1946, *Embassy of the United States of America, Subject: Transmitting Embassy's Political Report for Year 1945*, NACP, State Department, Lot Files 6337, 59/250/852/8.

35 1-5-1947, *The Foreign Service of the Unites States of America, American Embassy*, Madrid, NACP, State Department, Lot Files 6340, 59/250/852/8.

36 8-5-1947, *Embassy of the United States of America, Subject: Transmitting Embassy's Political Report for 1946*, NACP, State Department, Lot Files 6340, 59/250/852/8.

37 Pike, *Franco*, pp. 136–139.

38 George H. Gallup, *The Gallup Poll. Public Opinion 1935–1971. Volume One, 1935–1948*, New York, Random House, 1972, pp. 520, 579–580, 612–613, 661.

39 Ibid., p. 151.

40 10-7-1947, *American Consulate, Malaga, Subject: Spanish Referendum*, NACP, State Department, Lot Files 6340, 59/250/852/8.

41 See, Mark Byrnes, "Unfinished Business: the United States and Franco's Spain, 1944–47", *Diplomacy & Statecraft*, 1 (March 2000): 129–162.

42 30-12-1947, "The Chargé in Spain (Culberston) to the Secretary of State", Department of State, *Foreign Relations of the United States (FRUS)*, Washington, US Government Printing Office, 1946–1975, 1947, Europe, vol. III, pp. 1099–1101

43 Francisco Franco Bahamonde [Jakin Boor], *Masonería. El libro secreto*, Barcelona, Ojeda, 2003, p. 9. First edition 1952.

44 Ibid., p. 212.

45 *Musa Redimida. Poesías de los presos en la Nueva España*, Madrid, Editorial Redención, 1940, p. 10.

46 Ibid., p. 94.

47 Ibid., p. 99

48 José A. Pérez del Pulgar, *La solución que España da al problema de sus presos políticos*, Librería Santarén, Valladolid, 1939, pp. 50–51.

49 Martín Torrent, *¿Qué me dice usted de los presos?*, Talleres Penitenciarios, Alcalá de Henares, 1942, pp. 51, 53, 67–68.

50 José Echeandía, *La persecución roja en el País Vasco*, Fidel Rodríguez, Barcelona, 1945, p. 10.

51 5-2-1942, "Informacion interior, Barcelona", Fundación Nacional Francisco Franco, *Documentos Inéditos para una Historia del Generalísimo Franco (DIHGF)*, Madrid, Azor, 1992–1994, 5 vols, vol. III, pp. 249–252.

52 Francisco Franco Bahamonde, *Declaraciones de Franco a un periodista español*, Madrid, Publicaciones Españolas, 1946, s.p.

53 Ibid.

54 Ibid.

55 The name comes from Catherine the Great's Russia and refers to the Prime Minister and lover Prince Potemkin's building nice but fake dwellings for the occasion of the rulers passing by.

56 17-5-1943, *Instituto Nacional de Colonización, Jefatura Nacional de Colonización, Jefatura Delegación Regional de Levante e islas-Valencia*, Archivo IRYDA, 24321. I am most thankful to Sofia Rodríguez López and Oscar Rodríguez Barreira for making this document available to me.

57 Ibid.

58 Fray Justo Pérez de Urbel, *El Monumento de Santa Cruz del Valle de los Caídos*, Madrid, Instituto de Estudios Madrileños, 1959, p. 7.

59 Ibid., p. 5.
60 22-11-1939, "Por las carreteras de España, cubiertas de mirto y de flores, los restos de José Antonio, alumbrados por centenares de antorchas, reciben el impresionante homenaje de las multitudes", *ABC*.
61 Ministerio de Información y Turismo, *Nota informativa sobre el Valle de los Caídos*, Madrid, Ministerio de Información y Turismo, 1959, pp. 5–6, 9, 11.
62 20-11-1940, "De la vida y de la muerte de José Antonio", *ABC*; 21-11-1940, "El Caudillo ofrendó ayer, sobre la tumba del fundador de la Falange, la Palma de Oro", *ABC*; 20-11-1941, "Vida breve pero infinita", *ABC*; 21-11-1941, "Con el dolor, siempre renovado, de España, el Caudillo, Jefe Nacional de la Falange, rinde ante la tumba del Fundador el homenaje conmovido del país", ABC; 21-11-1941, "El Caudillo, Jefe Nacional de FET de las JONS, rindió ayer ante la tumba del Fundador, el homenaje del dolor de España", *ABC*.
63 Rafael R. Tranche and Vicente Sánchez-Biosca, *NO-DO. El Tiempo y la Memoria*, Madrid, Cátedra, 2000, pp. 196–198.
64 Saturnino Rodríguez Martínez, *NO-DO: catecismo social de una época*, Madrid, Universidad Complutense, 1999, p. 216.
65 Ibid., pp. 215.
66 Ibid., pp. 114–115.

4   Moderate ruler, 1947–1961

The lonely anti-Communist

During the 1940s, and indeed even later, the Caudillo had very few respectable international allies. Throughout the decade deeply rooted anti-Franco sentiments predominated in the United States, Britain, France and other Western nations. Many people in these countries supposed that a minority of Spaniards supported Franco and his regime, and that the dictatorship survived only because of its extensive use of terror. This was, in many ways, a convenient belief. For many Europeans the regime's existence was an unpleasant reminder of the past, in particular of how widespread support had been in some of their own societies for dictators like Hitler, Mussolini and Pétain. In terms of what we now call Historical Memory, Franco, then only a relatively young man in his mid-fifties, was a walking skeleton that refused to go into the closet of European history. As such, even though he was the ruler of a relatively marginal, impoverished country, the Caudillo's international shadow loomed surprisingly large. This situation had dreadful and immediate consequences for poor Spaniards. As long as European and American public opinion opposed Franco, the country would not be included in the newly emerging international organizations of the period, nor would it benefit from the 1947 Marshall Plan, which helped to feed Europeans and to speed the economic recovery of most of the Western part of the continent.

This painful international isolation explains both the official reception and the popular excitement that met Evita Perón when she came to Spain in the summer of 1947. The visit was a sensation, and not only because of the huge propaganda and organizational machine that enveloped Argentina's First Lady; it was so significant to Spaniards because Evita's presence reminded them of a lost prosperity, while at the same time bringing promises of help in the form of both financial aid and wheat for the starving population. From the moment Evita's plane, escorted by dozens of dilapidated Spanish fighter planes, landed in Madrid on June 9, the Caudillo and his equally prudish wife, Carmen, did not waste many opportunities to be seen next to this overtly sexual former actress. Followed by a long entourage of limousines, she was greeted by tens of thousands of ordinary Spaniards. The next day, schools, workshops and offices were officially closed for four hours, while the tightly controlled official unions incited workers to go to a demonstration in support of Franco and Juan Domingo Perón. NO-DO produced several official newsreels on the trip showing Evita's meetings with Franco, her visits to the country's historical monuments, cathedrals, Civil War battlefields, and, of course, the cheering crowds that followed her wherever she went. The generic name of these special issues was "Messenger of Peace" (*Mensajera de la Paz*). A few years later, this enthusiasm was replaced by diplomatic rows and orchestrated press campaigns in which Franco and Perón used journalists as proxies to attack each other. But this would not occur until the early 1950s, by which time the international situation of the Spanish dictatorship was much improved.

The international notoriety of the Franco regime largely evaporated in the three years that followed Evita's visit. In this short time, the dictatorship—that international pariah of 1946–1947—quietly became more acceptable in the eyes of Western governments, and even to some sectors of public opinion. The main reason for this reversal was the onset of the Cold War, a time when the Western public focused its attention on much bigger problems (for example, the Korean War, or the nuclear arms race), and the policies of the nations that were then the main international players: the Soviet Union, the United States, Germany, Britain and France.[1] However, as we shall see, other factors, which are too often overlooked by scholars, influenced this normalization of the regime's image.

The United States played the key role in normalizing Spain's international presence through a dual process of rendering Franco less notorious and his country less visible. This was achieved for the most part by the American discourse over the two countries' supposedly common interest in fighting Communism. Already in October of 1947, the State Department had decided that "national interest required a modification of US policy toward Spain in the direction of normalizing US–Spanish relations".[2] When this policy was first formulated American policy-makers had to move cautiously as the memory of Franco's duplicitous behaviour during the past war was still fresh amongst Western governments and the general public. The Cold War partially erased this memory. By January 1949 the American government was exploring the possible reaction of European governments and non-Communist parties and unions to a formal "repeal of the operative parts of the 1946 Resolution [adopted by the United Nations] and, if so, how serious such a reaction would be". In the case of France, for example, American officials concluded that "the Spanish question arouses much less active interest in the general French public than it did a few years previously". Reports from the Benelux countries and Britain were very similar. By contrast, in Scandinavia popular opposition to normalizing relations with the Franco regime remained fairly strong.[3] But the real battle for the American government was not abroad but at home, with its own voters and with the remnants of its own anti-Fascist ideology.

In the late 1940s, both the American government and the media were moving public opinion in the desired direction. Again, the rising tide of anti-Communism in the United States provided the backdrop, but, as we shall soon see, there were also specific pro-Franco campaigns that helped to lift the Caudillo's image and to make his regime more palatable to the general public. This objective was achieved rather quickly. Already in a 1950 opinion poll, 57 per cent of Americans said that the United States should send military and economic aid to Spain in return for the country's promise to help in case of a confrontation with the Soviet Union, while a stubborn 23 per cent of those interviewed still said no. The following year, the proportion of those who said yes had risen to 65 per cent; those against it also grew, albeit less so, to 26 per cent.[4] A significant but determined minority of Americans always opposed Franco, but the general population went along with the political elite's decision to rehabilitate the Caudillo's image, transforming him from a fierce Fascist thug into a moderate Christian statesman.

Franco had not been a passive pawn in his own international rehabilitation. On the contrary, since the dark days of 1947 the dictator had been sending clear signals, directed at both the American government and public, of what he could offer in the supposedly shared struggle against Moscow (that is, while at the same time publishing his notorious articles under the name of J. Boor, accusing the American State Department of being in the hands of Freemasons and Communists). In a February 1947 interview with the American newspaper *Evening Star*, the moderate and modest ruler surfaced with his usual peculiar arguments to prove that the victors of World War II had treated his regime unfairly. "I am a man who never had any ambitions, neither of command, nor of power," he started, modestly. "Since my youth, life tested me hard, taking charge of positions of command and responsibility well superior to my age and rank." This was followed by the predictable demand for "respect" for Spain's uniqueness: "We cannot judge and compare one country with another"; then by self-congratulation: "We have tried to repair both the physical and spiritual damage [caused by the Civil War]. I dare to say that Spain is the country that finds itself today in the better situation, in all aspects, among all the European people"; finally, there were explanations for some of the country's economic difficulties:

> In the past ten years, our population has increased by nearly three million more Spaniards. This is why demand is higher than supply, both scarcity and our difficulties to import products are the causes of the black market [...] But the State rules in favour of the middle and modest classes.[5]

But there were even more sensational revelations, such as the one in which the moderate ruler told American readers how he had protected Spain from the Nazis:

> At Nuremberg, the same documents that have been used to justify the most terrible of charges against Germany show in the clearest and most conclusive way the efforts by the Axis powers to force Spain to enter the war, without result.

And the final twist: yes, there had been Spanish volunteers fighting the Soviets alongside the Nazis; but British and Americans, too, had fought the Soviets alongside the Finns during the "Winter War"

(1939–1940); and "during this other universal war there were many Spaniards fighting among British and American soldiers against the Axis nations".[6] In saying this Franco was taking credit for tens of thousands of exiled republican soldiers and anti-Fascists—men who had enlisted mainly in the French Army, far less in the Soviet forces, and very rarely in the British or American militaries—who had fought against the Axis to prove Spain's good will and contribution towards a post-war new order! His regime, the dictator implied, was just another normal post-war European political system. The interview was quickly translated into Spanish and printed by the official propaganda-publishing house.

In April 1947, it was the turn of the British *Sunday Times* to publish a friendly interview with the Caudillo. The formal topic of conversation was the passing by the dictator's rubber-stamp parliament (the *Cortes*) of the Succession Law, which, as we have seen, made Franco regent for life:

> The reception of the law by the country could not be better [...] The Spanish press has freely expressed its opinions [about the law], and we must admit that the majority of the studies and commentaries that have been made in this regard have maintained a high level of quality [...] Freedom of the press [...] in Spain has few limitations. The vigilance exercised over the press is aimed solely to prevent it from going off-track [...] I believe that all the problems of our nation are just problems of our people's education [...] I ask Britons of good will that before making judgments about our nation, to visit us and learn [the reality] by themselves.[7]

As the reports that reached his office prove, the truth was rather grimmer than the Caudillo's words would suggest. In 1947, eight years after the end of the war, there were still very acute social problems in Spain. The scarcity of food for the poor continued to be particularly appalling. These dire conditions were reflected in a contemporary report from the Governor of Valencia—by no means the worse-off province in the country—claiming:

> the situation of discontent will soon lead to a situation of passivity of both the working population and the middle class

because of the lack of adequate food as they only get through official rationing 50 per cent of the calories they need ...

The report also claimed that the black market prices were out of their reach. People lived "hungry and in despair". To the lack of food, the Valencia Governor's confidential report added the lack of affordable housing, clothing and most articles that normally are associated with "a decent life".[8]

Of course, the Caudillo never admitted any of this, either to Spaniards or to foreigners. For the former, his discourses were mainly about the shadows of war wrapped in references to peace; for the latter, his invaluable contribution to the fight against Communism. This was his only international card and he played it repeatedly. In a 1948 interview with *The New York Times*, when asked what Spain might offer to the then forming Atlantic alliance, the General responded with the usual self-glorification:

This alliance is, without Spain, like an omelette without eggs [...] Where but in Spain could the USA find bases and safe storage in case of war in Europe? We are the only Europeans that fight Communism at no cost.[9]

No cost to himself, at least, he might have added.

Some of the interviews Franco gave to the American media, or the declarations made by American conservatives—often Catholic politicians—in favour of his regime were not as spontaneous and disinterested as all involved pretended. To start with there was a generously funded lobby campaign in the United States, which helped to transform the dictator's image among both elites and the public. Coordinating these efforts was José Félix de Lequerica, the former ambassador to Vichy, an erstwhile friend of Pierre Laval (whom he abandoned after World War II, when Laval sought refuge in Spain) and, since March 1948, "inspector" of embassies residing in Washington—a title that only partially obscured the fact that in 1945 the United States had refused to accredit him as an ambassador. Lequerica, a man with a reputation for cynicism and manipulation, used a fund of nearly 200,000 dollars a year to hire public relations firms well connected to power circles, feting senators, journalists and powerbrokers.

From the American side, opportunistic racism greatly helped the process by convincing officials of the rationality of making friends with a dictator who until very recently had been despised as a Fascist. Paul Culbertson, the chargé d'Affaires in Madrid, was central to this approach; but he was not alone. Racist and cultural prejudice allowed Culbertson to explain, for example in a June 1949 document, why Spaniards could not enjoy the benefits of a democratic system:

> I am not a supporter of the idea that we should base policy on the concept of molding the rest of the world in our own democratic image [...] people the world over are not the same and won't mold the same. Certainly not the Spaniards [...] Franco is not to blame for all the things that are wrong here in Spain and, while he himself is a devout Catholic, there is no indication that he or the members of his regime support that old inquisition spirit found in the Spanish Catholic Church and among the people. [...] Franco may be a dictator but he would never get by with any crusade on behalf of Protestants. So, on religion I think we should give the devil his due.[10]

Now, on top of being an asset in the fight against Communism, Franco was also the moderator of a nation of inquisitorial retrogrades. The intended recipient for such a message was President Truman, whose last major objection to the normalization of relations with the dictatorship hinged on the persecution and harassment of Protestants in Spain. However, the most important reason for the change of American policy towards Spain was not racial or cultural prejudice but realism. The former was a convenient alibi used to justify a strategic need: that Americans wanted military bases in Spain. The racial/cultural discourse gave a patina of intellectual respectability (racism, in spite of Auschwitz, was still a respectable opinion) that fitted both American needs and the political reality in Spain. The Americans knew that the Caudillo was there to stay, and they preferred accommodation to risking the dangers of a forceful political transition. This strategic need became a reason for finding more political and human virtues in the Caudillo than in his people. According to Culbertson's annual report on the country for 1949, "Franco admittedly has a feeling for what he thinks his people want [...] he considers himself a sort of father to the people and seems to believe that he is making them happier than anybody could do". As for the religious intolerance existing in Spain, Culbertson stated that it was due to "factors not altogether under the control of General Franco".[11] The same dictator who had established a ruthless police state supposedly did not control his henchmen and officials: but at least he kept the uneducated mobs calm, and that was good enough.

The good dictator

Once the Americans decided that Franco was there to stay, it was easy to predict the immediate future of the dictatorship. As the Caudillo's loyal right-hand man, Carrero Blanco, wrote to him in 1950, the dictatorship not only felt internally secure but was also convinced that the Americans "needed" Franco, and that the passage of time would only strengthen the regime's position in any future negotiations. The economy was bad, and ordinary people's suffering went unabated, but Carrero, and presumably Franco, believed that "the Spanish people are ready to embrace with enthusiasm economic sacrifices before accepting any political subordination [to foreigners], the incoming battle will be completely won, and this will be the culmination of Your Excellency's extraordinary work during the last difficult years". So convinced was Carrero of the Americans' need for Franco that he believed Spain was going to win crucial economic help, and he even mused about a possible restitution of Gibraltar as a result of the negotiations.[12] To prepare his camp for decisive talks with the United States, in July 1951 the Caudillo shuffled his cabinet. The next year the new ministers started to introduce a new set of mild economic reforms that corrected some of the most untenable policies of the autarkic system.

However, for the United States (as well as for Franco) this trans-Atlantic relationship was always a matter of need not of love. While courting the Caudillo, the Americans could also be very dismissive of him. The same Culbertson who had written that the dictator was a moderator of his people's base instincts could describe him as a "Gallegan [who] listens to what he wants to hear, [and then, when convenient] shuts his mind and ear altogether". Moreover, "Franco is the kind of Spaniard who likes to get into the movie without paying the ticket. He has certainly given no evidence of willingness to pay any price for admission to the West". With this Culbertson was referring to the American suggestions of political liberalization in Spain on which they had all but given up hope. Nevertheless, Culbertson showed that harbouring prejudice does not preclude possessing a sharp mind when he explained that the freeloader had wide support in Spain, which "can be as negative as it is positive in some quarters but, either negative or positive, there is fear of the risk of the uncertainties of change. To the world Franco personifies the Regime. Not completely so in Spain".[13]

Some American officials, however, came to genuinely appreciate Franco. In 1951, the recently appointed ambassador Stanton Griffis, who was not always fooled by the Caudillo's easy and seemingly never-ending talk, confidentially reported to Washington a certain degree of admiration for the man: "Franco is hard working", "there is evidence of recent improvement of [...] religious freedom". He also believed that Franco was sincere when during an interview the Caudillo had said that in case of a Soviet attack he was ready to send troops to defend the West beyond the Pyrenees.[14] Was he aware of the fact that the Caudillo had made the same pledge several times to the Nazis, during World War II, of two million Spanish bayonets to save Berlin from the Soviets?

In the early 1950s, time was clearly on Franco's side. Since the end of World War II, so potentially catastrophic for him, the Caudillo had been waiting for the Free World to come his way without paying the price of the "ticket" (relinquishing power) or even making cosmetic reforms. Ordinary Spaniards had paid the price in the form of social and economic misery. But this inconvenient fact did not interfere with the Caudillo's increasing prestige in the United States, which was too far away for his people to see Spaniards' daily misery (and where, still today, the mass starvation that Spain suffered in the early 1940s is mostly unknown even among professional historians). Instead of the sad truth, the American public got a very different version of Spain's contemporary reality: Franco's version.

Ordinary Americans got their first taste of the face and words of the good dictator-in-the-making thanks to an interview that Franco gave to the CBS correspondent in Madrid, Mr Schoenbrum, in 1951. In the interview, the Caudillo expressed his empathy for the

Americans' ignorance of the Spanish situation: "I understand that it is difficult for some sectors of the American people, because of the circumstances of their lives and democratic sense, to understand the political events that take place under other meridians." The Caudillo was not only a very understanding person; he was also the quintessential proud, Quixotic Spaniard: "Spain feels secure in itself, that nobody could ever break its resistance. To submit its twenty-eight million people to the yoke, many millions will fall along the way."[15] In this interview, there were no questions about hardship or prisons.

The always-cunning Caudillo was playing his cards carefully: showing the face that he thought would better manipulate the other side. The Americans would be wrong to believe that they had him for free. When asked by *The New York Times* a year later, in January 1952, if Spain would fight alongside NATO forces in the case of a Soviet attack, the Caudillo said that "in spite of the moral considerations [...] he could not consider the question" because Spain had no formal alliance with any other country "except with Portugal". When asked if he would consider signing a bilateral agreement with the United States, the astute dictator became a team-player, almost a leader of a constitutional system, when he said that he was convinced that both "my Government and the *Cortes* would consider the issue with their best will". However, he had a problem with NATO and the rest of the West: unlike Spain, they "lacked the spirit needed for great enterprises".[16] In reality, as the State Department knew all too well, Franco's regime had long been hoping, and would continue to hope, for an invitation to join NATO. In 1951, for example, the Caudillo had told an American envoy that even if Spain did not join the organization, if his army was re-equipped "Spain would be bound by all the NATO commitments including those relating to the initiation of hostilities against any NATO member by the USSR".[17] However, both the Americans and the Spanish authorities knew that a number of countries would oppose Spain's entry. He would prefer to wait rather than risk a humiliating rejection.[18]

The Caudillo's patience was successful. When, in 1953, Spain signed a series of defence and cooperation agreements with the United States, Franco did not have to pay the "ticket" to democracy. Instead, in exchange for military and economic aid, he ceded several military bases to the Americans. By then, friendly coverage of the Spanish dictatorship was already the norm in the American media. Typical in this regard was the *Longines Chronoscope*, a CBS television program. In an episode broadcast in 1951, Republican Senator Owen Brewster had described anti-Franco sentiments as follows: "I think it is emotional and ah, ideological. The French and the British governments now in power have ah, been very critical of the Franco regime and there are many elements in this country who agree". Then he pointed to the prestige of the anti-Fascist and anti-Communist Winston Churchill to back his own position:

> Churchill, who was all through the war, knows thoroughly the Spanish picture, and I've discussed it with him this summer and I know that he fully agrees with those in this country who consider Spain as the cornerstone of European defence.[19]

Not only republicans supported the new policies. In a program broadcast by CBS in early 1953, Adolf A. Berle Jr, former United States Assistant Secretary of State under President Roosevelt, said:

> I know of course that there are many people who believe that the United States government should never negotiate treaties with governments of which it doesn't approve, that rather limits your ability to act in international affairs [...] Now, in the Spanish case, the Spanish people undoubtedly want to be protected against, to have defence against Russian aggression either direct by an army or by reason of a packaged revolution exported to them. We have a common interest in having them protected [...] To that extent therefore and up to that point, the Spanish people and the American people have a common interest.[20]

While Mr Berle claimed to know what the Spanish people "wanted", other diplomats, playing as anthropologists, knew why nice and subtle things such as democracy was not suited for Spaniards. In a 1956 briefing on Spain for their ambassador to the UN, which started with an explanation of Spain's "incomparable strategic position", State Department officials explained how:

Lying in the periphery of Europe and occupied for several hundred years by African peoples […] Spain was only slightly influenced by three of the experiences which are fundamental to the philosophical, political and social outlook of the United States and of most of Western Europe: Protestant Reformation, the ideas of the 18th century rationalism and the French Revolution, and the 19th Century Industrial Revolution.[21]

Americans and Spaniards might have had the same interests but they were different people with a very different history and socio-political needs. In 1956, 10 years after the closing of the French–Spanish border and two decades since the beginning of the Civil War, the American people watched newsreels that praised the alliance with Franco's Spain:

Ambassador John Lodge and Spanish military leaders are on hand as American-made tanks and other military equipment arrived at Cartagena. Representing America's part of the long-term treaty under which Spain extends the use of base facilities to the United States' Sixth Fleet, this modern war materiel significantly strengthens Spain's Armed Forces. America fulfils its part of the bargain, tanks for bases to bar the spread of Red Aggression.[22]

Listening to such words, it seemed as if the Cold War had started in 1936. It would get worse. The next year, in April 1957, the Francoist Victory Parade was described by CBS news as follows:

Spain celebrates the 18th anniversary of the termination of the Spanish revolution and victory over communism. The nation's military might, much of it of American manufacture acquired in return for bases, is on display for the occasion. Señora Franco and her daughter are among the distinguished guests as is the Generalissimo himself. One of the colourful contingents is made up of the Moorish guards. As a crack unit of paratroopers passes in review, the Caudillo looks on with pride; 18 years of peace and rebuilding.[23]

In international affairs, nothing is offered for free. The warm relationship between the Francoist regime and the big American

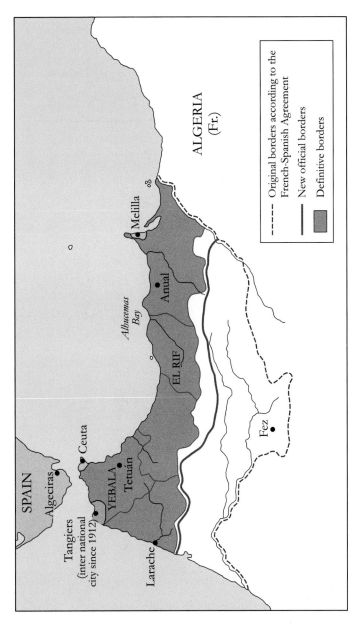

Plate 1 Map of Spanish Morocco from 1902–1927

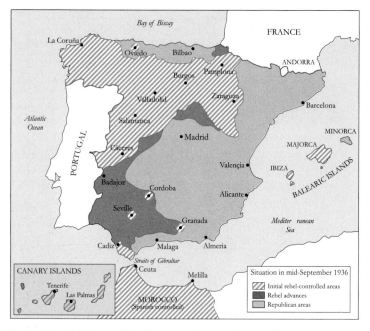

Plate 2 Map of the Spanish Civil War, July–September 1936

Plate 3 The last rival for power. Franco and Mola in 1936

Plate 4 Franco in his study in 1940 (Hitler's portrait is on the table)

Plate 5 Measuring the Soviet threat. Franco in the 1950s

Plate 6 The gentle dictator. Franco sitting with his family in 1960

Plate 7 Juan Carlos, Prince of Spain, and Francisco Franco in the early 1970s

Plate 8 The Valley of the Fallen. Franco's tomb is inside the complex's basilica

media companies in the 1950s was not based solely on their shared anti-Communism. Those companies saw in Spain a nearly virgin market ready for development. The regime tried to lure those corporations with concessions that sometimes bordered on bribery. For example, in January 1956, the Vice-President of United Press presented Franco a memorandum requesting permission to increase their presence in Spain. In a highly laudatory tone, the document declared "the enormous change in world opinion regarding Spain, its increased prestige abroad, all of this being the result of the significant work of His Excellency in the national renaissance". In the same text, United Press did not forget to thank the Caudillo for the concession of a very favourable exchange rate, which was flexible at the time. United Press was repatriating its profits from Spain at the very advantageous exchange rate of 10.9 pesetas per dollar, a third of the average exchange rate. The company asked Franco to allow it to continue enjoying the same conditions in the future.[24]

Spain's, and the Caudillo's, return to international normalcy also had a more popular and authentic dimension. Towards the end of the 1940s individual travellers started to appear in the country. At first they were not ordinary people but writers, militants, academics, even bohemians who came to see and understand the extraordinary, even exotic country of the Civil War, the International Brigades, and the mysterious Franco regime. In many senses, these travellers were looking for answers to their own political and cultural questions, as well as inspiration for their work. Gerald Brenan, the noted British novelist, was one of them. He returned to Spain in 1953 in an attempt to make sense, from a humanistic and progressive view, of all the violence that war brought to the country (an anti-Francoist, he had already published *The Spanish Labyrinth* in 1943.) Others, such as his compatriot, the anthropologist Julian Pitt-Rivers, who went to the country in 1950, rehashed arguments already expressed at the beginning of the Civil War that portrayed the democratic Second Republic as an aberration of Spanish history. Pitt-Rivers explained Franco's regime as the continuation of a more authentic tradition of authoritarianism that was necessary to keep Spain, "a country unlike any other", functioning.[25]

In the 1950s interpretations of reality may have differed, but what was plain for the whole world to see was that the Spanish people had not revolted in spite of the country's terrible economic situation. Even some anti-Fascists were already thinking that there was more to Franco's hold on power than his regime's repression. By this time, a new liberal American identity had emerged that accepted the need for political compromises with dictatorial anti-Communist regimes. Mildred Adams was one of these liberals. She was a celebrated journalist, a literary critic and a feminist who wrote for *The New York Times* and *The Economist*. Like the two previously cited authors, Adams had a prior interest in Spain. She was an acquaintance of the celebrated poet and playwright Federico García Lorca (who was executed by the rebels in 1936) and had translated the works of Spain's most famous philosopher, the liberal José Ortega y Gasset. In 1959 Adams wrote a piece on Spain for *Foreign Affairs*. The gist of Adams' argument was that there was no doubt about the origins of Franco's power and that political repression existed, but the crucial question for her was whether "the dictator-run political state" was a form of government "sympathetic to the Latin temperament". Having posed such a question, her conclusion was predictable:

> Spain at heart, in history and religion [is] schooled to a hier-archical society with little movement back and forth between levels. It has enormous arrears of tradition, which make an undifferentiated democracy seem to its people alien as well as difficult. The present system [...] is a recognition of this ancient factor in the national character.[26]

Other American liberals, of a very different background, begged to differ. The celebrated African-American novelist Richard Wright had published in 1957 *Pagan Spain*, where he dissected daily life under Franco's regime. A former Communist who had grown in the American South under the notorious Jim Crow system, he did not look for cultural or ethnic arguments to explain the dictatorship. According to Wright, there was not much difference between Spain and his own country's segregationist states: what he saw was a cruel and repressive society that, with the willing help of the Catholic Church, simply humiliated its marginalized citizens. This book was never translated into Spanish.

By the time Adams, Wright and others were explaining to their readers Franco's Spain, a growing number of tourists (mostly

Europeans) were seeing the country for themselves. In 1951, 1.26 million visitors went to Spain; in 1960 there were 6.1 million, and rising. This re-connection between Spain and the rest of Europe helped the regime to advance its claim, supposedly confirmed by millions of happy tourists, that it was ruling a moderate Catholic, developing, and exotic, but normal country. Many Europeans seemed to agree, at least in part. For example, in a Gallup poll conducted in Britain in early 1946, 60 per cent of those consulted favoured severing diplomatic relations with Spain, with 16 per cent disapproving. By 1961 answers were very different and more nuanced: while 14 per cent still wanted "little to do" with Spain, 29 per cent said that the country should be treated as any other, while 29 per cent supported closer relations, and 28 per cent had no opinion.[27]

Spain was allowed to join the United Nations in 1955. It was a tremendous political victory for the regime. However, the real climax of Franco's personal international semi-rehabilitation as a Cold War ally—for it never went much beyond that— came four years later, when in December 1959 President Dwight Eisenhower visited Madrid. Newspapers reported that an improbable 1.5 million people greeted him. (The population of the Spanish capital was only a little over two million at the time.) These media also depicted both men as fighters for peace, thus portraying the democratically elected president and the dictator as moral and political equals.[28] Although he was initially timid, the massive public attention the American president received warmed him to Franco, as was reflected in the pictures that showed their embrace at Madrid's airport moments before Eisenhower's departure. In this way history had, in a rather ironic sense, gone full-circle, with the popular *Ike*, the man who commanded the Western armies that defeated Hitler in 1945, now smiling at and embracing the man who shook hands with Hitler at Hendaye in 1940.

The talker

A person living in an open, democratic society would likely have difficulty understanding the symbolic power and the impact on the people of the discourses uttered by a dictator, specially the incessant repetition and insistence on the truthfulness and wisdom of his words. Unlike in free countries, in dictatorships there are very few external references to either validate or question such claims. Nor can a citizen of a peaceful society fully appreciate the impact of references to violence, past or future, in a country still traumatized by a recent civil war and living under the threat of repression, as was the case in Franco's Spain. The words and the images invoked by the Caudillo's discourses—even if they were spoken with his high-pitched nasal voice and were full of banal commonalities— possessed a force that in a different context and in a different country would have been absent, or would even have sounded ridiculous. What made the Caudillo's words important was not what they said or how they were translated into action, but how they invoked the memories, fears and expectations of the people. Franco's words were, in a sense, also the story of the meaning of the dictatorship; they reflected both the collective traumas and the deep fractures of Spanish society. That is why it is so important to pay close attention to the "what, where and why" of Franco's discourse, in order to fully comprehend the function and impact of his words.

Franco frequently used what George Orwell, in his novel *1984*, called doublespeak. To start with, he employed a different discourse depending on whether he was speaking to Americans and other foreign publics, or to his own people. To the former—as we have seen already—he made constant appeals for moderation, respect for political and cultural diversity, and the common cause of anti-Communism. To the latter, he presented himself as leader of a national revolution that, paid for with a generous sacrifice of blood, had restored Spain's forfeited imperial heritage. However, his words to Spaniards—and this is the essence of his doublespeak—often contradicted his polices. The Caudillo was basically a manipulative ultra-reactionary who, while he pretended to speak for the whole of Spain, systematically excluded millions of Spaniards from his recollections of the past as well as the material rewards of his regime.

For the socio-economic side of his discourses to the Spanish people, the dictator employed a pseudo-Fascist and Catholic corporative language that in practice did not interfere with the policy of protecting the more mundane interests of the coalition of forces that had supported the rebel side during the Civil War. In addition, and more crucially for most people, regardless of what the Caudillo repeated over and over again in the 1940s and 1950s, the regime's policies, often made life worse, not better, for millions of ordinary Spaniards. These policies not only failed to bring more equality or the reversal of injustices but, on the contrary, one of their main objectives was to roll back many social rights and achievements that groups such as workers and women had enjoyed under the Republic. The historical side of Franco's discourses, particularly when addressing the Civil War, was based on mixing harsh, uncompromising Catholic imagery and concepts with raw militaristic values. His religious images invoked the fall of the nation, a crusade of redemption, the good and young blood spilled and, finally, the submission/expiation of the defeated to the true faith and light: Franco himself. When using militarist concepts, he affirmed the exclusive right that the Caudillo and his men had over the fruits of victory, because they, the Army of Spain, had heroically and against all odds won a hard-fought war against the spurious forces of anti-Spain.

Doublespeak meant that in Franco's Spain words and deeds often marched down different paths. During his thirty-nine years in power, truth was never an impediment to the Caudillo. Facts were manipulated or denied, the past doctored, data altered and explanations changed, all in order to serve a crucial, unchangeable tenet of the regime's propaganda, which millions of people shared too: that Franco was always right. The dictator and his sycophants would call this axiom Spain's (i.e. Franco's) "truth". In this paradigm, the Caudillo supposedly embodied the whole nation; and every achievement was a product of his genius while every failure or limitation was a result of the actions of Spain's (Franco's) enemies, internal or, preferably, external. Moreover, the main voice in praise of the Caudillo was Franco's. Even in the most adverse circumstances, the dictator had no hesitations in trumpeting his role as both prophet and miracle-maker. For example, in December 1948, during his end of the year speech, while Spain was practically isolated from the rest of the Western world and its economy was in shambles, the Caudillo declared: "In the exterior [...] events continue to prove during this year our increased prestige and authority and the increased strength of our reason".[29] By "our" he meant "my". Next, he presented the catastrophic failure of his policy of autarky as the successful continuation of a number of economic plans launched during the Civil War:

The plans that in several aspects have been done or are being implemented, were developed in Burgos [his capital during most of the Civil War]. Not one of the problems that Spain faces today escaped our attention then or we did not seek out a solution to it at the time.[30]

The political history of Spain was a constant in Franco's discourses, and here again he had no problem falsifying the record. For example, in 1949, at the inauguration of the new *Cortes*, the Caudillo declared: "For the first time in our History, a third legislative period starts."[31] This was not true: the Second Republic had three legislative periods between 1931 and 1936 (the third one was interrupted by the military rebellion), and there were several more during the Restoration (1876–1923). While those of the Second Republic were flawed in many respects, and the political system of the Restoration was deeply corrupt, these legislatures were still freer, and more representative of popular opinion than anything Francoism would ever achieve, or want to achieve. A monopoly over the media allowed Franco to boast and to talk at length again and again about the history of Spain since the Middle Ages (another of his favourite themes), to ridicule the country's liberal past, and to express self praise for the institutions of his own creation. To the rubber stamp parliament that he was addressing in 1949 he said:

The quality and quantity of the legal dispositions, the favourable commentary that some of the main ones have caused in foreign technical publications, and the fact that some of them [the laws passed] have been adopted abroad afterwards, are clear proof of the efficiency of the system ... [32]

The world, according to Franco, was imitating the Caudillo; though not only did the world not recognize his creations but it refused to acknowledge the uniqueness of his regime and his impressive achievements. Envy and bad faith explained why Spain had been rebuilt in forced isolation, with no foreign help.[33]

The next year, in 1950, the Caudillo went to Bilbao. In the past, the Basque nationalist movement and the working class organizations, mostly Socialist, had been strong there.[34] Only three years before, in 1947, there had been a harshly repressed general strike.

However, Franco spoke in Bilbao about very different matters. On this occasion, he displayed another of his obsessions—xenophobia mixed with contempt for democratic values:

> [Democracy] was a happy formula for foreign countries and a disgrace for us [...] Spain, which once dictated her laws to the universe, which was several centuries ahead in the practice of democracy, already in the XIV and XV centuries the kings called representatives of cities when they needed money, while the rest [of the world], some lived under medieval tyranny and others walked in the forest wearing just a cloth over their loins. [The editors of the pamphlet that recounts the visit then added: "Great applause and cheers."][35]

This acidic, cheap mocking of both Europeans and Americans was soon followed by a discussion of the Cold War and the dictator's sacrifices for the country, which he felt were not appreciated by common, indolent Spaniards. This was another of his recurrent themes: people just ignored how taxing the situation's demands were on his heroic persona. This side of his discourse—Franco as an insufficiently recognized/thanked hero/victim—was expressed, using at times the royal "we", during the same trip to Bilbao, but now in front of a select audience at the Yacht Club (*Club Marítimo del Abra*):

> I do not know, because I am a lover of deeds and I like to escape from words, if we have been too succinct and we need further explanations, but several times I have noticed Spaniards do not realize the days and times we live in [...] We are experiencing what is called the Cold War [...] and it is similar to military battles: soldiers sleep soundly while their commander keeps vigil and is watching, evaluating all the risks and threats that may occur. This is today's reality [...] we do not want to create more concern among you, but perhaps you should know ... [36]

He later added:

> Spain had not mattered [in international affairs] for a century and a half. Spain had been the fiefdom of other nations, and all the programs made abroad proposed a peasant Spain, poor,

forced to sell its riches at basement prices, so afterwards we would
have to buy their manufactured goods [...] This is no tale I am
telling you. When we have gone to foreign countries to get
assistance and patents for our factories, to make our own trucks
or build our own tractors, they have frankly said that their
plans included the non-industrialization of Spain .... [The editors
added: "The cheers and enthusiastic applauses are endless."][37]

In fact, the opposite was true. After the Civil War, the regime rejected
British and American offers of economic assistance, including the
building of new factories. At the time, Franco was expecting a
German-dominated world. But that truth was inconvenient; what
was important was that Franco needed enemies to justify his
regime's shortcomings. To the foreign attempt to boycott Spain's
economic renaissance, and particularly its industrialization, the
Caudillo recalled again his own tireless and visionary work carried
out already during the war, and his most recent plans. He was
talking now about the Socio-Economic Ordination Plans [*Planes de
Ordenación Económico-Social*], which "directed by the State, executed
by technicians and perfectly studied, allow us to develop a government project to redeem our people".[38] Made in the late 1940s,
as a local alternative to the Marshall Plan, and thankfully never
implemented, the Plans would have been a failed attempt to
reinvigorate the catastrophic autarkic experiment.

Another of Franco's favourite themes was his own supposed prophetic power. This idea was always present when discussing both
international and national events; and there was no hint of modesty
in his self-praise. In a speech given in Madrid in December 1950
he said:

The year that ends has confirmed, once again, that the Spanish
Regime has fulfilled in terms of universal history a vanguard
mission, in which a prophetic spirit gave breath to our endeav-
ours and aspirations [...] What for many may enter the
category of surprise, for us is part of an old lesson that we
cannot forget.[39]

And then he listed his successes, logical products of his farsighted
wisdom: "rectification by the United Nations but without any

substantial change of our doctrine or positions"; "a wise internal policy"; "a fruitful year of national recuperation because of our socio-economic achievements", even if Spain was not being helped "by foreign nations" [he was referring here to the Marshall Plan], "It is so easy to rebuild and recover when all kinds of external help rains! [...] If we were not able to provide a better welfare it is because of a lack of understanding by foreign countries". More achievements followed: "Our social legislation [...] we see with satisfaction is followed by some foreign countries"; "When the history of these years will be written, it will include the housing projects and new neighbourhoods built for all kinds of social groups; they will be a stone monument ... "; the Army "has perfected its means and equipment"; and the Navy's concentration of ships in the Strait of Gibraltar that year was the "biggest since Trafalgar".[40]

Spain, the post-war laggard of the West, was in the Caudillo's words some sort of economic and military tiger. According to him, his promises had been fulfilled. But even when he talked about economics, he was never talking solely about economics. Any situation, any achievement or any problem, always reverted to the central theme: his providential role in saving Spain and, the next logical step, what might happen to Spain if any attempt was made to remove him, the Caudillo, from power. In reality he was always, implicitly or explicitly, talking about the Civil War and the threat of a future conflict. It was both a reminiscence and a threat, and it applied to both followers and enemies. In this regard he was never more blunt than when talking to his comrades-in-arms and to former combatants of his army. In October 1952, for example, he presided over the Meeting of Veterans that took place in Segovia. Later he addressed those gathered for the occasion at the *Alto de los Leones* mountain pass, where one of the fiercest battles of the Civil War had taken place in July 1936, as General Mola's rebel forces tried to reach Madrid from the north. The place had become a symbol of the Nationalists' courage. The Caudillo started by addressing "all the veterans" of the Crusade. However, in his doublespeak, when he said "veterans" he meant only the members of *his* Army. This was made plain later in the speech, when Franco referred to the nearby Valley of the Fallen, still under construction: "I would have liked to see the end of the works in this grandiose monument that we are erecting in honour of our heroes and the martyrs of our Crusade".[41] However, the gist of Franco's message at the *Alto de los Leones* gathering was the war:

> Victory belongs to all of us and it is administrated for all of us. You know well how, facing your trenches and positions, the nerve of the enemy army was constituted by the international Communist brigades [...] If martyrs and heroes [...] in Heaven form a legion to guard over our victory, it is here on Earth to you, combatants of our Crusade, to ensure that [our Fatherland] is not lost, as so many times throughout History, and recently we saw it lost in the European fields [...] Since victory made possible the re-birth of Spain and a firm will to be became obvious, it started the eternal conspiracy of the anti-Spain.[42]

With these words the Caudillo was doing two things: reminding his followers of their privileged position, and appropriating the collective suffering of Spaniards for the regime, that is for himself. If the dead heroes belonged to Franco it was because he deserved that, and more, as payment for his selfless work and suffering for the good of Spain. He was not shy about this. In 1959, giving a speech to Castilian peasants, Franco told the assembled mass that they should be grateful to him for recently completed local agrarian projects, which consisted of concentrating scattered properties by means of a land exchange (*concentración parcelaria*) because this was a project that "you, the beneficiaries, have not thought of". This project was only possible because he, the Caudillo—again using the self-pitying argument about the ingratitude towards him, the hero—had been working to improve the life of Spanish peasants. However, now, after more than twenty years of effort and success, and the fact that he was there to listen to the people, "the world still calls us dictators [...] Where is there true democracy? [...] never in the History of Spain has a more fruitful democracy been conceived".[43]

The core of the dictator's political and historical discourse remained essentially unchanged until the regime's last days: self-pitying and self-glorifying; never accepting responsibility for any problems while congratulating himself for all the supposed successes. At Christmas 1961, after two years of deep economic reforms (the 1959 *Plan de*

Estabilización) that had caused a sharp contraction of business and a sudden rise in unemployment, Franco addressed Spaniards about the future. The overall success of the reforms was still uncertain. In the printed version of the speech, the anonymously written introduction once again reminded Spaniards that Franco's words are "sober, removed from empty rhetoric and pompous lyrical pretensions".[44] Then the Caudillo reminded the people, hinting at the Civil War once again, what was at stake and why Spain needed him:

> we are living in an ample period of political stability, social and economic progress, and of order in the middle of the convulsions that brought about the world war and the violence of a post-war condition that nobody dared to call peace, which continue as a historical event [...] The ship has to respond to the skill of the captain and the unity and discipline of the crew; all of this is necessary during the crossing, and even this is not enough without God's will to protect us from what is unpredictable.[45]

God was always behind him. And yet Franco's speeches could easily include, next to threats and references to the divine, the most risible banalities. In the same 1961 Christmas address the Caudillo offered peculiar, selective, and shallow proof of his successes. He said how happy he was with his regime's achievements, as the statistics about the decline of crime showed. The reason for this was his social justice. Here is the example:

> In one of my trips I stopped in a small Andalusian village to visit a small social project of houses and family orchards for journeymen, and during the event the judge and local authorities manifested their satisfaction because of the changes the village had experienced, because from 350 crimes against property there had declined to just five after that small social project had been completed.[46]

Throughout his rule Franco would never flinch from self-praise, from resorting to the flimsiest of arguments to "prove" both the success and transcendence of his regime, and from using the threat of civil war. In spite of all the suffering that his regime had inflicted upon the population this is how, in 1961, he described the balance of his twenty-two years of absolute rule:

> The main conquest of these years has been the unity of a country previously divided by separatism and class struggle [...] The greatness of the Crusade, which only dim people cannot see, is to have achieved the active participation of all good Spaniards [...] in the most glorious epic of our History [...] I believe it never existed in the History of Spain a State more legitimate, more popular and more representative one than the one we started to forge almost a quarter of a century ago [...] Without our Victory the evolution of the last world war would have been different [...] the allies and the Christian world, in general, have a debt towards Spain. We are not debtors, but creditors.[47]

In essence, what Franco said was that not just Spain but the world had a huge debt of gratitude towards the Caudillo.

New hagiographies

The unassailable hero/martyr Caudillo had a very long list of courtiers whose profitable task was to glorify him and to fabricate the past. His most faithful followers competed with each other in explaining the man's greatness and foresight to Spaniards and the rest of the world. For the Caudillo's glory, the sky was the limit. For example, a 1954 anthology of speeches made by Franco in the late 1930s and 1940s, started with this brief biographical note on the dictator:

> The Caudillo of Spain's life has been, since the beginning and without interruption, a total and permanent dedication to the highest designs of the Fatherland, and in addition, it has exposed the highest military virtues in several circumstances and actions, which can be called only heroic and exceptional.[48]

Such an exceptional hero deserved new appropriate and updated biographies.

The best-known hagiography of the Caudillo in the 1950s was entitled "Sentinel of the West" (*Centinela de Occidente*). The book was written in 1956 by Luis de Galinsoga, a journalist (first with

ABC, then with *La Vanguardia*) as well as a politician (twice "elected" to Franco's self-styled parliament). He had the cooperation of Franco's cousin and long-serving military aid, Francisco Franco Salgado-Araujo, familiarly known as *Pacón*.[49] (It must be said that at the time, privately, *Pacón* was writing a very different portrait of his cousin, which only appeared in 1976 after both men were dead, and which will be described later in this chapter.) The Caudillo provided key information for the book, and as such Galinsoga's hagiography is very important. Because it was published towards the end of the period of autarky and the persistent dislocations of Spain's post-war economy, it was the last comprehensive "biography" of the dictator before he could claim, with some veracity, that he was also the maker of Spain's economic progress. This affected the author's arguments, which were limited by the obvious lack of material achievements after Franco's two decades in power. Accordingly, there was no room in the text for unfavourable topics such as the appalling lack of food and adequate shelter, poor educational levels, etc., which affected the country. This dispensation with earthy things may explain why the book used so many pseudo-religious arguments and metaphors. This was a Cold War version of Spain's history, always at the service of the country's Saviour.

The title of "Sentinel" comes from one of those self-praising and self-pitying sentences so dear to the modest Caudillo, in this case the speech he gave at the Army Museum in March 1947: "I am the sentinel that is never replaced, the one that gets the unpleasant telegrams and dictates the solutions; the one who invigilates while others sleep."[50] The book's two main ideas do not lack ambition: one, present through the whole narrative, is that long before 1936 Spain had been waiting for the Caudillo as its saviour, and, two, as it is explained in the final pages, that Franco, because of his actions during and after the Civil War, saved the West from falling into the hands of the Soviet Union.

According to Galinsoga (as well as Franco's cousin, and the Caudillo himself), Franco had been a daring hero since the time of his youth. But Galinsoga went even further than the wartime hagiographies written by Arrarás and Ruiz Albéniz. Indeed, in Galinsoga's eyes Franco demonstrated his courage and messianic mission even before going to Africa. For example, one day he showed precocious determination and wisdom when he ordered a little boat to travel during a storm between La Coruña and his home town of El Ferrol, located at the end of a long fjord—all of this against the wishes of the local veteran sailors and *Pacón*, who were amazed by the young man's determination. However, in keeping with the already well-established Francoist canon, Africa was the main proof of Franco's virtues and the beginning of the road to a destiny that could not be blocked by lesser forces, people and obscure enemies. For example, the reader is informed that when Captain Franco was wounded in 1916 he should have obtained the *Laureada*, but the government was unfair to him (instead, he received a different medal and was promoted to major at the age of twenty-three). In any case, the fact that he survived his wound could only be explained by two intertwined reasons: that "God" worked "imperturbably" to save his life and that the Creator had in store for him a *Laureada* that would come as a result of an even bigger feat: Victory in the Civil War.[51] Soon afterwards the hero was posted to Asturias. There, in addition to pursuing his relationship with Carmen Polo, Franco devoted his time to the study of history, economics, politics and society. The result was that "in a few months" he learned the secret of how to become a "Statesman".[52]

Following the 1921 Annual débâcle, the nation "desire[d] [major] Franco!" to save the desperate situation of Melilla. In 1922 the Saviour wrote a fundamental piece about the use of tanks in warfare and "as the specialized reader and any expert in the matter can see, time has given him reason".[53] This put Franco ahead of other classic thinkers on the use of tanks such as Mikhail Tukhachevski, Heinz Guderian, Basil Liddell Hart or Charles de Gaulle. Franco's military prowess did not stop at the technical level, however. As a commander, "his art was beyond mere technique", because he was a "genius" in the league of people such as "Alexander the Great, Hannibal Barca, Julius Caesar or Napoleon Bonaparte". When there was a problem, other officers knew that the matter was to be left in Franco's hands.[54] However, in spite of his being a genius, or precisely because of this fact, Spain's different "governments were always cheap and sordid towards him".[55] In spite of this ingratitude, Franco kept multiplying his favours to the nation. He conceived and executed the 1925 Alhucemas landing.[56] But fighting was only part of the young Caudillo's greatness. In 1927, in a casual conversation with the Minister of Finance, José Calvo Sotelo—at which the dictator Miguel Primo de Rivera was present—Franco, now a brigadier general, unmasked himself as an expert in economics, and surprised his company by giving "luminous advice to the glorious statesman and financier" Calvo Sotelo.[57]

When the Republic arrived in 1931, this tragic event also proved to be a providential one because it finally allowed the prophet to act. His miracles would now be more revealing, to the point of converting even the unbelievers who were lucky to be near him. How else could one explain the fact that, when he was posted to Tenerife in March 1936, a mob waiting to jeer him at the port was suddenly transformed by his mere presence into a cheering crowd?[58] In the following months, he miraculously survived several "attempts" on his life (no one was ever caught for these actions, however).[59] At the same time, in a subtle, almost seamless way, he organized the July rising. General Mola's name was nowhere in this story.[60] And again in a seamless way, when he flew into Tetuán after the rebellion had started he arrived there miraculously transformed into the "Head of the Movement" (*Jefe del Movimiento*).[61]

During the war, the prophet repeatedly showed his wisdom and magnanimity. In April 1937 he predicted the fighting would last two years. And, of course, it ended in April 1939.[62] The Saviour deeply loved his people: later that year, he did not take Madrid because he did not want to destroy the city.[63] Moreover, concerned with the high number of Spaniards who needed to be corrected, he became an expert in law, particularly in criminal law, devoting long hours to studying every single case of the thousands that his legal adjutant, Major Lorenzo Martínez Fuset, brought before him. When he was not happy with the case proceedings, he sent the documents back to be re-examined.[64]

Up until 1939 the Caudillo's mission had been saving Spain. But shortly after victory, Providence put in his hands the future of Europe, and perhaps of the world. First, at the meeting with Hitler in Hendaye in October 1940, Franco resisted the German dictator's pressure to enter the war. The Caudillo feared nobody, neither the Axis nor the Allies. Moreover, had Hitler dared to attack Spain, Franco would have launched a guerrilla campaign, as had occurred during the Independence (or Peninsular) War of 1808–1814. Second, the Caudillo also abstained from joining

Hitler after the invasion of the Soviet Union—as it turned out, a providential move: had he acted differently, the Communists would have occupied all of Western Europe! Third, if Spain had intervened in November 1942, when the Allies invaded the North of Africa, world history would also have changed its course. But the Spanish troops posted in Morocco did not attack the Allies (luckily for the Anglo-American armies?). At the time, Franco had higher concerns. He wanted to convince the West of the huge mistake that the division of forces meant, Germans and Italians on one side, and the rest on the other. Unfortunately, he was not heard. But his wisdom and foresight helped him navigate all these risks. He knew what was coming and was always vigilant. Throughout all the key moments of World War II, only his prudence saved Europe.[65] This is why, in 1956—in case the reader still ignored this crucial and obvious fact—Franco's office at the Pardo Palace was "the axis of the West and the mediator with the Orient".[66]

Galinsoga's hagiography, albeit full of ridiculous claims, was far from being an extreme example of the personality cult surrounding the Caudillo. In this sense, books for children reached again the higher levels of sycophancy. For example, a 1957 book described the birth of Franco, his mother and his life in terms Catholics use to refer only to the life of Christ. There even was an Annunciation in the text. In this book, the Virgin appeared to Doña Pilar, Franco's mother, and told her:

> You will have a boy that will be spoken about. I will give him a sword and a white horse [the image is obviously taken from Saint James the Slayer of Moors, Spain's patron saint] and I will give him the heart of a Caesar and the wisdom of a Sage, and I will make him smile with such astonishing grace that his smile will give a new faith to the souls of all Spaniards.[67]

A few years later, the Virgin addressed the chosen one, still a child, in a dream:

> With this imperial sword and this white horse, if you are not afraid, you will save Spain and you will fulfil the objective of having in the country not a single home without a fire or bread in the kitchen.[68]

While official, stiff and always ridiculous reverence towards the Caudillo was routine in the 1950s, the cult of the dictator also had a human, direct component, and often a comforting one, at least from the point of view of ordinary Spaniards. Once the excitements of the 1940s were over, the man who had brought victory for a large minority and "peace" for all, had also became a habitual and a gently aging figure in their lives. The ritualization of the Caudillo's official activities (his presence at public commemorations, visits to towns and ongoing public works sites, or his summer holidays) transmitted a sense of normalcy to a country that in its heart was still traumatized by its dreadful past. Both intertwined aspects, routine and trauma, were present in the main commemorative days of the regime's calendar, and two in particular: Victory Day on April 1, and the double festivity of the Exaltation of the National Movement and National Work Day on July 18.

The high point of Victory Day was a military parade (which, starting in 1958, would take place on a Sunday in May to avoid April's unpredictable weather). It symbolized Franco's crucial achievement: the destruction of Spain's enemies and the salvation of the Fatherland. The tightly controlled official media used the occasion both to report the event—although little of novelty was shown until American weapons arrived in the mid-1950s, before which the same deteriorating and progressively obsolete German and Italian-made armaments from the 1930s kept passing year after year—but also to include pieces of "memory" in the form of articles and particularly newsreels to explain to Spaniards the meaning of the commemoration, and to remind them that the dictatorship was ready to face its enemies.

However, the most important day of the Francoist political calendar was July 18. On this date the regime celebrated two things. One was work and reconstruction (Work Day); the other the beginning of Spain's liberation, i.e., the Civil War (National Movement Day). The leisure and dread, the celebration of peace and the bitter memories of the past, filled the journey. That day saw Franco's picture appear on the front page of all newspapers, which also carried articles full of praise for the Caudillo and his peace. To celebrate both, the regime showed the last harvests of fruits reaped by the National-Syndicalist Revolution. This included the official inauguration that day of public buildings. The problem was that too often there was nothing new to inaugurate. This was a consequence of the regime's meagre budgets and lack of economic resources until the 1960s. Often, the solution was to re-inaugurate some building already in use, or to pretend that a first stone laid in a construction site was actually going to become a building sometime soon. To encourage people to celebrate progress and national redemption, that month's pay-cheque was doubled. With some money in their pockets and the day off (it was also a bank holiday) many Spaniards went to the beaches or to a picnic. No other day better captured the Caudillo's contradictory standing among Spaniards or reminded them of the fragile nature of their peace.

Far less important was a ceremony established in 1958: the Unions' Demonstration. The chosen day was May 1, International Workers' Day, but re-branded by the regime with the religiously safe and socially innocuous name of Day of Saint Joseph the Artisan (the dictatorship always used the positive, less menacing term of "producer" instead of the revolutionary-sounding "worker"). The Demonstration was a folkloric and sportive event held at the Real Madrid soccer stadium in which the official unions brought workers to show Franco their sporting and folkloric abilities, discipline, and loyalty. The performers were there to pay homage to the Caudillo who, seated on a highly placed tribune in the stadium, was the focal point of the celebration. The show ended with fireworks and large banners that exclaimed the producers' gratitude towards Franco.

The role of the Caudillo as the overseer of popular events also became a fixture in some sports, especially football. As the game became more popular, particularly in the late 1950s and early 1960s, when Real Madrid became Europe's most successful team, Franco's presence at important matches, and at the final of the Generalissimo's Cup, which normally took place in Madrid, was an occasion of both popular joy and excitement. (Founded in 1902, the Cup is Spain's oldest football competition.) The moment of the Caudillo's appearance on the authorities' balcony, his passing of the cup to the winning team, and his departure from the stadium were all greeted with enthusiastic clapping and cheers by the spectators, and dutifully reported by the media.

Franco's regular holidays also became a central theme in the regime's propaganda. It became a tradition that conveyed the message that

Spain was a normal country at peace (and perhaps a prosperous one where people could take a holiday). The supposedly tireless, well-meaning ruler enjoyed very long summer rests in cooler Northern Spain. Normally, he went first to his native La Coruña province where he stayed at a restored seigniorial mansion (Pazo de Meirás) given to him during the war through an officially enforced campaign of popular contributions. This was the semi-private part of his vacationing. All summer he had at his disposition the yacht *Azor*, from which he could indulge his passion for the sea and for fishing. The Caudillo also enjoyed hunting—as we shall soon see, far more than the general public was led to believe. In the carefully edited news and images of his activities, people could also see how he relaxed playing golf, painting, or, less often, interacting—rather than playing—with his grandchildren (his daughter had married in 1950 an aristocratic surgeon, Cristóbal Martínez-Bordiú; they had seven children). More public and active was the end of the summer holiday, which often went into late September, in San Sebastián (Basque Country), where his presence revolutionized the town. Basque nationalists now often prefer to remember how the "usual suspects" were arrested or questioned by the police before every visit, but they frequently forget the very enthusiastic reactions of the general population to the Caudillo's public appearances, or how much the dictator enjoyed and patronized traditional Basque folklore, culture and sports.

The Caudillo's continuous presence in the media, in which he was portrayed doing normal things year after year implied routine; but it also meant that, at least for millions of Spaniards, his image was softening, becoming more and more that of a respected elder (he started to be called *Tío Paco* or Uncle Frank). This benevolent side of Franco's persona increasingly became part of the officially orchestrated image of the Caudillo. This image corresponded, totally or partially, with reality. For example, by the late 1950s, it was obvious that Franco was getting old as he approached the age of seventy; it was also evident that he had a normal, growing (and presumably happy) family; also, and thanks to NO-DO newsreels, Spaniards could see that he was still tirelessly working at his desk. The old man cares for us, millions thought. But behind the carefully constructed image of the Caudillo stood a very different and all too real man. We now know what Franco and his entourage were really like and what the dictator said in private thanks to a cascade of books (see Chapter 6) that appeared shortly after his death. However, no testimony is more revealing than that of his cousin *Pacón*'s, which dealt with the period from 1954 to 1971, when he was one of the Caudillo's closest collaborators. The Franco that *Pacón* portrayed was, as in his speeches, a self-assured and self-centred pedant who had definitive, if variable, opinions about everything and everybody. He was obsessed with conspiracies, particularly by the Masons, and deeply xenophobic. He was also a seemingly sincere believer in the veracity of the official story of the past, becoming exasperated on numerous occasions when, for example, someone questioned the regime's canonical historical version of his role in the organization of the July 18, 1936 revolt, the true nature of his conversation with Hitler in October 1940, or his friendship with the Axis powers. In private, as in public, he was increasingly distant and cold, even with his boyhood friends, particularly when his wife was present.

Very different from the Caudillo's official public image were other less pleasant aspects of this supposedly gentle and hardworking man. Among other things, *Pacón* recorded his cousin's remarks, full of contempt, resentment and even envy towards many of his fallen comrades and former protectors, such as Generals Berenguer, Sanjurjo, Mola and King Alfonso XIII. Moreover, the life of his family and entourage was not nearly as austere as the propaganda would insist. Doña Carmen's stiffness, aristocratic pretensions and lack of empathy were compounded by her taste for expensive jewels and antiques, for which she was reluctant to pay. Their son-in-law Cristóbal soon gained a reputation among well-informed insiders as a ladies' man, as well as for his penchant for profitable shady businesses, in which members of his family and other collaborators of the Caudillo's were involved. Flatterers, timeservers and sycophants constantly surrounded the dictator. Perhaps more important for the running of the administration, the supposedly tireless worker actually devoted little time to work. Hunting and other recreational activities took an enormous proportion of his time and energy. In 1955 *Pacón* estimated that the Generalissimo did not work more than ten days per month, while easily hunting for an average of twelve, often accompanied by several of his ministers who obviously were also absent from their desks. In 1959 the Caudillo told his cousin that in his last hunting spree he had "broken a record" by killing "nearly five thousand partridges".[69]

Twenty years of peace

Spain's reality did not justify the Caudillo's self-satisfaction, the flattering words of his courtiers, or the image of both the man and the country presented by his propaganda. In political, legal, economic and social matters the achievements of the first two decades of the dictatorship were extremely meagre. The key to this abysmal performance was the regime's political structure. To start with, the whole institutional system could not be separated from Franco. The Caudillo was both Head of State and his own Prime Minister. He was also the Generalissimo of the Army and chief of the weak single-party, FET-JONS. There was no constitution. Only in 1958 did the regime pass a fundamental or organic law (*Ley de Principios del Movimiento Nacional*) on the juridical and ideological principles of the state, which was followed in 1967 by another law (*Ley Orgánica del Estado*) defining the powers of the Chief of State. Until then, Franco ruled using a set of *ad hoc* laws and institutions such as the parliament (*Cortes*, opened in 1943) that limited itself to endorsing his government's decisions. Spain had a charter of rights (*Fuero de los Españoles*) adopted in 1945, but its provisions could be suspended by the executive (Franco) at any time.

In addition to the lack of any clear institutional or political counterbalance to Franco's power, there was also permanent uncertainty about the future. The country was, according to the law voted on in the 1947 referendum, a monarchy with a regent for life (Franco), and an organic democracy (thus making both terms, monarchy and democracy, meaningless). Moreover, according to the 1947 law, the Caudillo had the right to decide who would replace him, and when. Finally, Franco's charisma in the armed forces and among wide segments of the population was very high, making it possible for him to justify his rule by appealing to sentiments such as loyalty and fear of the enemy instead of having to show practical results. All the previous factors combined gave the Caudillo a power that was perhaps the most extensive of any modern dictator. This was a disgrace: the dictator's ignorance, prejudices and interests shaped the regime's flawed institutions and policies.

In economic matters, the dictatorship's performance up to 1959 was catastrophic.[70] The 1940s had been a disaster for Spain, to the point that some economists consider this decade the country's true Great Depression. Under autarky industrial production stagnated and did not recover its pre-war levels until 1950–1952. The modernization of agriculture not only stopped but was put in reverse as farmers were forced to use techniques and ways of production that had been abandoned decades before; and as a result, for a long period after the war, subsistence farms did better than export-oriented ones. Trade was deeply distorted, with high prices, scarcity and a rampant black market. Until the late 1950s, basic products such as wheat and olive oil were sold in larger amounts through the black market than the official one. Currency control also strangled business and fuelled corruption. In sum, Spain missed the first fifteen years of Europe's post-war recovery, and the country became an economic laggard. Whereas in 1930, per capita income in Spain was 13 per cent below that of Italy, in 1950 it was 40 per cent.

Economic underperformance caused deep social fractures and untold suffering. Starvation started to wane after 1945, but hardship remained very high throughout the 1950s. For example, an officially endorsed report from 1953 on the condition of landless labourers in Sevilla province revealed that the real average daily salary was close to 40 pesetas, when a family needed at least 200 to buy their food. Not surprisingly, there was widespread malnutrition, chronic illness, and early senility among these peasants, as well as severe physical and intellectual underdevelopment among their children.[71]

However, the long post-war period was not necessarily bad for business; in fact, it was a time of capital accumulation. People who had property and/or employed workers did very well. There were three main factors behind the existing socio-economic disparities. One was that the Spanish economy was closed to competition, and thus high prices could be passed on to consumers. The second, more dramatic, factor was that employees saw their real wages reduced to between half and one-third of their pre-1936 levels, depending on the sector. The purchasing power of pre-war salaries did not recover until the early 1960s. The third factor was that direct taxes remained extremely low, with no income tax and minimal property levies. This meant that the Francoist state could not, even if it wanted to, supplement the income of workers and landless peasants by means of transfers of services and wealth.

This social tragedy was no accident, but rather the logical outcome of ultra-reactionary policies. The Second Republic had passed numerous laws to improve worker's lives. The regime repealed most of them. The Republic also tried to improve the lot of hired hands and poor peasants (at a time when their salaries were much higher) and attempted a failed agrarian reform to give them land. After the Popular Front's electoral victory in February 1936, and without waiting for new laws, peasant unions occupied hundreds of thousands of hectares. This dynamic was aborted by the July 1936 rising. Occupied lands were returned to their owners and peasants' unions dissolved by the rebels, a process that often included the murder of both leaders and militants. However, the Francoist regime soon came up with its own plan: rural colonization, which became one of the pillars of the dictatorship's discourse on "social justice" and of the Caudillo's benevolent image. The plan was to bring as many arid lands as possible into irrigation, and then sell some of this land on credit to good, honest peasant families. The objective of colonization was to build a new rural Spain free from social conflicts and with a peasantry loyal to the regime.

The achievements of over three decades of rural colonization would be very small. Throughout the dictatorship, an average of only a few dozen families a year received new land and a total of nearly one hundred new villages were built. However, the symbolic power of colonization was very important (some of the new towns were given the Caudillo's name). In his visits to the provinces, the dictator usually inaugurated some of the ongoing projects—irrespective of whether they were already completed or still had to wait years to start—which provided some golden opportunities for the regime's propaganda. One of the dictator's favourite images of himself in photographs and newsreels, was when he presided, satisfied, over the opening of the spillways of dams, or when he turned the keys that allowed water to run through canals or from perforations. The refreshing rush of water that then emanated seemed to come directly from Franco's hands: it was not just progress but the re-birth of dry, poor Spain under his serene but tireless command. It also meant that when Franco was present, his promises were fulfilled. Another crucial propaganda moment was when Franco would be filmed giving title deeds and keys to the houses to humble, though grateful, peasants. He also did the same for public housing projects in the cities. In both cases the message was simple: the good Caudillo cared for the common folk.

A good example of what both the dictator and the dictatorship said they wanted for the countryside was the *Plan Badajoz*. Initially planned for 1952–1965, it was a colonization project much touted by the propaganda machine. A pamphlet published in 1956 contains numerous pictures that illustrate life at Guadiana del Caudillo, a colonization village showing the new reality of a culturally and socially conflict-free community created by the Plan: a well-attended mass at the parish church; about 40 children quietly reading at the three-seated desks of their new school; the mandatory photos of Franco and José Antonio and a crucifix hanging on the class-room wall; an intimate moment of family peace in the newly-built home, with the rather smartly dressed mother cooking near the chimney, and the father, wearing his Sunday best, at the table, feeding one of their two children seated on his lap; children in regional costumes dancing to folk music at the central square; the Three Wise Men Epiphany parade passing in front of the church; a parade of peasants dressed in traditional costumes ... [72] This might have been the type of countryside the regime mused it was making, but the majority of local landless peasants knew better. In spite of the Plan, in the 1950s and 1960s, tens of thousands of poor people from Badajoz migrated elsewhere in an attempt to escape their poverty. They knew all too well the difference between the words and images of the regime and their own abject reality.

By the mid-1950s the failure of the regime's economic policies to deliver prosperity to most Spaniards had created an atmosphere of deep dissatisfaction towards the regime among the population. Franco knew this all too well, as he was very much aware that the economy was near collapse. For example, in 1956 the dictator received a police report on prices, salaries and living conditions in the country. The analysis was based on official prices, which were well below real ones because of the widespread black market. The report mentioned the escalating inflation, and how salaries, which had just been raised, nevertheless kept lagging behind price increases. As a result, the commentaries by low and middle class Spaniards were "truly unpleasant [...] blaming the regime for this situation". People compared their situation with those of "other European nations that had been able to [...] steadily increase family incomes and even to allow workers to save and to have mass access to holidays abroad without ruining the national economy".[73] Finally, after a wave of strikes in the country's industrial areas in 1956 and 1957, Franco very reluctantly accepted the termination of his policy of autarky. That year, the reformers in his government, mostly technocrats linked to the Catholic Opus Dei organization, started to prepare the 1959 Stabilization Plan.

However, before life started to become better (after about 1961) it became worse as the Stabilization Plan cut government expenditure and thus further reduced people's purchasing power. This sharp contraction of living standards did not prevent the regime from trumpeting its own success, which then was reduced to two main achievements: 20 years of survival for the dictatorship and Franco's peculiar "Peace". This is the context in which the 1959 Twenty Years of Peace propaganda campaign was launched. It was of necessity a low budget celebration, in which out-of-proportion claims and inflated rhetoric barely hid the grim truth.

The campaign took the form mostly of talks, mass political rallies and, in particular, the publication of provincial and nationals surveys listing all the material achievements of the previous two decades. The propaganda machine piled statistic upon statistic relating to public investment in order to prove the huge change that the country had undergone since the end of the war. The numbers might have been impressive if they represented a few years' growth but not two decades.[74] Moreover, the data was provided by the local branches of the party and by civil governments. It was not verified by independent sources.[75] It did not matter: oblivious to the fact that the economy was in disarray, local Falangists from Albacete complained that in spite of "the deep transformation of the life of the nation" as a result of the "gigantic effort realized under the Caudillo's providential mandate [...] many Spaniards [still] do not realize the extent of this transformation". Progress was everywhere to be seen, something "that all Spaniards owe only and exclusively to our Caudillo, always deeply concerned with the re-birth of all the peoples of Spain".[76]

In the book about Logroño, Franco was thanked because "under your command and the protection of the National Movement the wasted land had become a garden and, in their daily works, villages and cities have seen their hope reborn as the sources of prosperity multiply".[77] This quasi-religious tone was well justified at least in one respect, religion—a situation that repeated itself in several other provinces. According to the local authorities' own figures, in the previous two decades, the money spent on religious buildings had been greater than that allocated to schools (10,234,975 pesetas compared to 10,149,603 pesetas). It was much worse in Salamanca, where the money spent on religious buildings had been 210,464,934 pesetas, while a mere 15,339,890 had been assigned to schools; in other words, for every peseta invested in new schools in Salamanca province fourteen went to churches and parish houses.[78]

According to propaganda, Spain's progress was evident everywhere: from the North to the South. In the Basque land of Guipúzcoa, where "people are always intrepid, always honest, and always resilient", nobody doubted that all this "unequalled and unrivalled development and progress" had its roots in the "Peace" of a period which "History" will call "Franco's Era".[79] In the very Castilian Segovia "today, many humble dwellings have easy and abundant comforts not reserved just for the few privileged ones".[80] In Southern Murcia, "in spite of the destruction caused by the War of Liberation" (a curious reference since the province had been well behind the republican lines during the whole conflict) the local authorities had "difficulties in collecting data about so many material achievements" from the last 20 years of "Peace and Work".[81] And from the North African city of Melilla—the *Adelantada*, or first one to join the Movement in 1936—Spaniards could see "how without forgetting the vigil of our arms, it has been re-built, stone by stone, the Fatherland's economy", and "appear and appear new villages, happy, healthy, and cared for. The cities are surrounded by extended belts of new houses, a product of a well meditated plan".[82]

The Twenty Years of Peace propaganda campaign came right before Spain's big economic boom in the 1960s. While the propaganda machine stressed success, in private, the regime showed its insecurity about this claim when, for example, it instructed the press to emphasize a number of ideas to counteract "the insidious campaigns that our enemies promote". According to the instructions, the victory in the war was to be presented as almost a miracle because a powerful army was created from scratch, with no means or help (no German or Italian troops, planes and tanks). The reconstruction of Spain had supposedly started during the war, when Franco assembled specialists in Burgos to plan the economic re-birth of the nation. But damage caused by the war was massive, to the point that "the red leaders when retiring from Spain said the country was unviable, empty of life, that it could never rise again and they trusted", in spite of the destruction that they had caused, that they would be put back in power by foreign powers.[83]

In 1959, as in 1939, there were misery and lies aplenty, but there was no foreign pressure or any internal force capable of unseating the Caudillo. Political opposition had been devastated and socially isolated. As Franco knew all too well, a majority of Spaniards continued to trust or to accept him, and they feared another civil war more than anything. Even if they were unhappy about their standard of living, very few wanted to or dared to protest. They mostly described themselves as apolitical. However, the dictator also knew that a strong nucleus of dissent existed among the working population and liberal middle class, and among a growing minority of university students. As the scarce and distorted studies on public opinion from this time show, even if workers wanted little to do with politics, they certainly had deep grievances with the system, and were very much aware of their exploitation.[84] And they were not always quiet: there had been important strikes in the Basque Country in 1947, in Barcelona in 1951, and in several industrial areas in 1956 and 1957. Moreover, quite often, as the police reported, popular opinion in many other parts of Spain sympathized with the protesters—at least the few who managed to learn what was happening in the country.

Workers, even if called "producers", never had been among the regime's strongest supporters. More worrisome was that students, the country's future elites, were becoming increasingly restless. A study on Madrid's students sent to Franco in 1955 revealed a surprisingly (given their often-privileged social origins) strong nucleus of dissenters from the regime. The data was striking: 38 per cent of students declared themselves politically progressive and 40 per cent conservative; 85 per cent considered themselves culturally liberal; 85 per cent accused the political elites of incompetence; and 74 per cent of corruption; and, finally, 55 per cent of students were against the "socio-economic, political and cultural situation".[85] The following year there were major confrontations in Madrid's streets between students and Fascist thugs and policemen.

Indifferent to reality, Franco had no problem with reporting a very different, but always self-serving, balance of the two decades of his rule. As he said in the *Cortes* in 1958:

> The overall balance [is] in absolute numbers such that it cannot be compared with anybody's before us […] This is why, when due to the impossibility of preventing circumstances […] as a result of the growing crisis, which thank God we are fortunate enough to confront, there are some difficulties […] there is no reasonable motive for pessimism. [As for] the working population, we always had and we maintain our faith in them. It is possible that on occasion they can be surprised and momentarily disoriented […] but they know how to react with the dignity and good sense that normally characterizes those who have to earn their bread every day with their work and sweat on their foreheads.[86]

The economy was in disarray: inflation was skyrocketing; salaries lagged behind prices; schools were too few and too poorly equipped; there was a chronic housing shortage; the systematic answer to any protest was repression; the country was still gripped by the fear caused by the war and the dictatorship; and freedom was a word that made sense only beyond the Pyrenees. But luckily for Spaniards, the Caudillo still trusted them.

Notes

1 Jill Edwards, *Anglo-American Relations and the Franco Question, 1945–1955*, New York, Clarendon Press, 1999; William Buchanan and Hadley Cantril, *How Nations See Each Other. A Study in Public Opinion*, Westport, Greenwood Press, 1953, p. 120. 1973 edition.

2 1-3-1949, "Suggested United States Position on Spain at April Session of United Nations General Assembly", *FRUS*, Western Europe, vol. IV, 1949, pp. 731–734.

3 19-1-1949, "Relations of the United States with Spain: The Spanish question at the United Nations; United States economic policy towards Spain; United States interest in the activities of various Spanish exile groups; attempt to coordinate policy toward Spain with France and the United Kingdom", *FRUS*, Western Europe, vol. IV, 1949, pp. 721–724.

4 George H. Gallup, *The Gallup Poll. Public Opinion 1935–1971. Volume One, 1935–1948*, New York, Random House, 1972, pp. 938, 986.

5 Francisco Franco Bahamonde, *Declaraciones de su Excelencia el jefe del estado Español al periódico Norteamericano "The Evening Star"*, Madrid, Publicaciones Españolas, 1947, s.p., passim.

6 Ibid.

7 Francisco Franco Bahamonde, *Declaraciones de S. E. El Jefe del Estado al "Sunday Times"*, Madrid, Publicaciones Españolas, 1947, s.p., passim.

8 1947, *Informe del Gobernador de Valencia sobre difícil situación en este provincia por la elevación de precios ...* , AFFF 789.

9 Quoted in Matilde Eiroa San Francisco, *Política Internacional y Comunicación en España (1939–1975). Las cumbres de Franco con Jefes de Estado*, Madrid, Ministerio de Asuntos Exteriores y de Cooperación, 2009, pp. 53–54.

10 22-6-1949, "The Chargé in Spain (Culbertson) to the Secretary of State", *FRUS*, Western Europe, vol. IV, 1949, pp. 750–753.

11 26-1-1950, *Foreign Service of the United States of America, Subject: Annual Political Report for Spain: An Estimate of the Situation in 1949*, NACP, State Department, Lot Files 3704, 59/250/40/9/4.

12 4-4-1951, *Nota, seguramente de Carrero, sobre situación política y necesidad de cambiar el Gobierno*, AFFF 807.

13 10-6-1950, "The Chargé in Spain (Culbertson) to the Secretary of State", *FRUS*, Western Europe, vol. III, 1950, pp. 1563–1566.

14 24-4-1951, "The Ambassador in Spain (Griffis) to the Secretary of State", *FRUS*, Western Europe, vol. IV, 1951, pp. 814–816.

15 Francisco Franco Bahamonde, *Discursos y mensajes del Jefe del Estado, 1951–1954*, Madrid, Publicaciones Españolas, 1955, pp. 21–24.

16 Ibid., pp. 131–136.

17 24-5-1951, *Foreign Aid Presentation to Congress, Spain*, NACP, State Department, Lot files 1400, 59/250/49/28/4, box 8.

18 Circa 1956, *Confidential, Position of NATO members on Spain's Joining NATO*, NACP, State Department, Lot files 3094, 59/250/49/28/4, box 8.

19 *Sen. Owen Brewster (R-ME) from Chronoscope* (Columbia Broadcasting System, 1951) 14:40.

20 *Adolph A. Berle from Chronoscope* (Columbia Broadcasting System, 1953) 14:36.

21 December 1956, *Notes on Spain (From briefing for use by the Ambassador with the US Delegation in the 10th UN General Assembly in December {sic} 1955)*, NACP, State Department, Lot Files 5295, 59/250/852/8, box 1.

22 *Universal Newsreels*, Release 18, February 27, 1956 from Universal Newsreel, Hollywood, CA, Universal Pictures Company Inc., 1956, 6:43.

23 *Universal Newsreels*, Release 30, April 8, 1957 from Universal Newsreel, Hollywood, CA, Universal Pictures Company Inc., 1957, 8:44.

24 January 1955, *Memorandum confidencial presentado al Jefe del Estado: Oferta de United Press, por medio ...* , AFFF 16139.

25 Tom Buchanan, *The Impact of the Spanish Civil War on Britain. War, Loss and Memory*, Brighton, Sussex Academic Press, 2007, pp. 158–168.

26 Mildred Adams, "Twenty Years of Franco", *Foreign Affairs*, vol. 37, no. 2 (Jan. 1959): 257–268.

27 Buchanan, *Impact*, p. 160.

28 22-12-1959, "El viajante de la paz", *ABC*; 22-12-1959; "La entrevista Eisenhower-Franco una de las más importantes celebradas por el Presidente", *ABC*.

29 Francisco Franco Bahamonde, *Mensaje de S.E. El Jefe del Estado a los españoles*, Madrid, Publicaciones Españolas, 1949, p. 6.

30 Ibid., p. 12.

31 Francisco Franco Bahamonde, *El Caudillo dice ... Discurso del Jefe del Estado en la inauguración de las Cortes Españolas. Año 1949*, Madrid, Hidalgo, 1949, p. 3.

32 Ibid., p. 4.

33 Ibid., pp. 37–38.

34 1950, *Gobierno Civil de Vizcaya, Secretaría General: Consultas en relación con el programa de estancia ... .*, AFFF 22074.

35 Francisco Franco Bahamonde, *El Caudillo habla en Vizcaya*, Bilbao, Escuela Gráfica de la Santa Casa de Misericordia, 1950, p. 6.

36 Ibid., p. 15.

37 Ibid., p. 5.

38 Ibid., p. 17.

39 Francisco Franco Bahamonde, *Discursos y mensajes del Jefe del Estado, 1951–1954*, Madrid, Publicaciones Españolas, 1955, p. 7.

40 Ibid., pp. 8–10, 14–15.

41 Francisco Franco Bahamonde, *Alto de los Leones de Castilla. Concentración regional de excombatientes de las Dos Castillas*, Valladolid, Gerper, 1952, pp. 15–16.

42 Ibid., pp. 16–18.

43 Ministerio de Agricultura, Servicio Nacional del Trigo, Delegación Nacional, *Viaje por Castilla de S.E. el Jefe del Estado, Señor Don Francisco Franco Bahamonde ... *, Madrid, Ministerio de Agricultura, 1959, s.p.

44 Francisco Franco Bahamonde, *Ante 1962. Mensaje de Franco al pueblo español*, Madrid, Ediciones del Movimiento, 1962, p. 5.

45 Ibid., 10.

46 Ibid., p. 13.

47 Francisco Franco Bahamonde, *Discurso de apertura de la VII etapa legislativa de las Cortes Españolas*, Madrid, Imprenta BOE, 1961, pp. 7–9, 16.

48 Francisco Franco Bahamonde, *Pensamientos políticos de Francisco Franco*, Madrid, Delegación Nacional de Sindicatos, 1954, p. 1.

49 Luis de Galinsoga, with Teniente General Franco Salgado, *Centinela de Occidente (Semblanza Biográfica de Francisco Franco)*, Barcelona, AHR, 1956.

50 Ibid., [p. 9].

51 Ibid., pp. 30–31.

52 Ibid., p. 34.

53 Ibid., pp. 52, 68–69.

54 Ibid., p. 76.

55 Ibid., p. 81.

56 Ibid., pp. 110–112.

57 Ibid., pp. 125–127.
58 Ibid., pp. 192–193.
59 Ibid., pp. 196–197.
60 Ibid., p. 209.
61 Ibid., p. 233.
62 Ibid., pp. 273–274.
63 Ibid., pp. 275–276.
64 Ibid., pp. 283–284, 302–303.
65 Ibid., pp. 367–386.
66 Ibid., p. 445.
67 J. Manuel Useros, *El hombre en el paredón*, Valencia, Editorial Bello, 1957, p. 54.
68 Ibid., p. 58.
69 Francisco Franco Salgado-Araujo, *Mis conversaciones privadas con Franco*, Barcelona, Planeta, 1976, pp. 131–132, 143–144.
70 Antonio Cazorla Sánchez, *Fear and Progress: Ordinary Lives in Franco's Spain, 1939–1975*, Oxford, Wiley-Blackwell, 2010, pp. 57–94.
71 Acción Católica, *Los problemas sociales del campo andaluz*, Madrid, Acción Católica, 1953, pp. 204–242.
72 Intituto Nacional de Industria, Secretaría del Plan Badajoz, *El Plan Badajoz*, Madrid, E. Casado, 1958.
73 October 1956, *Dirección General de Seguridad. Boletín de Información: Comentarios al aumento de precios y al desnivel … ,* AFFF 24804.
74 A summary of the investments can be found in 19-11-1960, *Ejemplar de la revista Documenta del Ministerio de Información y Turismo*, AFFF 2892.
75 Circa 1959, *Breve referencia para el jefe del estado sobre libro "Veinte años de Paz en el Movimiento nacional bajo el mando de Franco"*, AFFF 24390.
76 Jefatura Provincial del Movimiento de Albacete, *Veinte años de Paz en el Movimiento Nacional bajo el Mando de Franco*, Albacete, Jefatura Provincial del Movimiento, 1959, s.p.
77 Jefatura Provincial del Movimiento de Logroño, *20 años de Paz en el Movimiento Nacional bajo el Mando de Franco*, Logroño, Jefatura Provincial del Movimiento, 1959, s.p.
78 Jefatura Provincial del Movimiento de Salamanca, *Veinte años de Paz en el Movimiento Nacional bajo el Mando de Franco*, Salamanca, Jefatura Provincial del Movimiento, 1959, s.p.
79 Jefatura Provincial del Movimiento de Guipúzcoa, *Veinte años de Paz en el Movimiento Nacional bajo el Mando de Franco*, Guipúzcoa, Jefatura Provincial del Movimiento, 1959, s.p.
80 Jefatura Provincial del Movimiento de Segovia, *Veinte años de Paz en el Movimiento Nacional bajo el Mando de Franco*, Segovia, Jefatura Provincial del Movimiento, 1959, s.p.
81 Jefatura Provincial del Movimiento de Murcia, *Veinte años de Paz en el Movimiento Nacional bajo el Mando de Franco*, Murcia, Jefatura Provincial del Movimiento, 1959, s.p.
82 Jefatura del Movimiento de Melilla, *Veinte años de Paz en el Movimiento Nacional bajo el Mando de Franco*, Melilla, Jefatura del Movimiento, 1959, s.p.

83   1959, *Notas sobre distintos puntos que la prensa debe tratar en una labor de contrapropaganda a las campañas insidiosas y de olvidos que fomentan nuestros enemigos*, AFFF 24861.

84   "Un sondeo en el alma del trabajador", *Ecclessia*, 542 (1951): 11–12.

85   1955, *Informe sobre "Las actitudes sociales de los universitarios de Madrid in 1955"*, AFFF 22962.

86   Francisco Franco Bahamonde, *Discurso pronunciado por S. E. el Jefe del Estado ante las Cortes Españolas al inaugurar la VI Legislatura y Promulgación de los Principios del Movimiento Nacional*, Madrid, Publicaciones Españolas, 1958, pp. 10, 25.

5 Bestower of prosperity, 1961–1975

Twenty-five years of peace

What came to be known as the "Golden Era" of Francoism did not start well. On Christmas Eve, 1961, while pursuing his passion for hunting, the Caudillo suffered a serious accident that almost cost him his left hand, not to mention his life. Admittedly, there had been positive developments that year. The economy had suddenly boomed. It was the first sign of the "Spanish Miracle": between the early 1960s and 1974, the nation's GDP grew at an impressive rate, close to 7 per cent each year—the world leader after Japan. Yet, perhaps because things started to look better, the many years of exploitation and suffering among workers and other poor segments of the population resulted in an explosion of protests in the spring of 1962. It started in the traditionally combative region of Asturias, where miners in several coal pits went on strike in April demanding that salaries and other benefits match consumer prices. The harsh repression by both the companies and the authorities only fuelled further protest, resulting in the largest strike under the dictatorship up to that time; workers in places such as the Basque Country, Catalonia and even Madrid joined in. In response, the government declared martial law in several provinces, thus suspending the formal rights Spaniards possessed according to the 1945 *Fuero de los Españoles*. Arrests multiplied, and the police did not hesitate to use torture. Franco was the main proponent of repression. The dictatorship blamed "Europe", "masons", "Communists" and the exiled "red" government as being behind the strikes, which were supposed to be part of a "strategy against the Spanish regime".[1]

By September most strikers were back at work, but there were isolated conflicts during the following months.

As the government tried to control labour unrest, a new front opened in June 1962 when over one hundred democratic opposition leaders met in Munich. Some of those present at the meeting were former supporters of the July 1936 uprising who now embraced dialogue and cooperation with their former republican enemies. The Communists did not attend this gathering. Enraged by the encounter, the Caudillo deported dozens of well-known opposition members to far-flung parts of Spain. The hysterical over-reaction of the official media backfired and Franco's international reputation sank to a new low. It was a public relations disaster and as a result, in July 1962, the Caudillo replaced his clumsy Minister of Information and Tourism (propaganda and tourism) with the clever and ambitious Manuel Fraga Iribarne (later, after the re-establishment of democracy, Fraga would be the founder of Spain's Popular Party, now in government). However, Fraga's first moves in the job were not very auspicious.

A third event reminded both Spaniards and the world about the half-hidden reality behind Franco's peace. In November 1962, a Communist leader by the name of Julián Grimau, who had been sent back to Spain by the party from France, was captured, tortured, and then formally charged with having being a sadistic assassin, "a chekist", during the Civil War. Conducted by a military court instead of a civil court, Grimau's trial was full of irregularities. The military prosecutor was later shown not to have a law degree. In addition, Manuel Fraga, who was the person in charge of explaining the course of the trial to the world, expressed himself often in inappropriate terms, for instance when he called Grimau a criminal before he was sentenced. In spite of international calls for clemency (hundreds of thousands of telegrams and petitions were sent to Franco by a variety of world personalities, including Pope John XXIII and Queen Elizabeth II), Grimau was executed in April 1963, twenty-four years after the Civil War was supposed to have ended.

To counter the international campaign to spare Grimau, and the fact that his regime had been internationally reviled for its cruelty and authoritarian ways, the Caudillo resorted to refreshing Spaniards' fears. In his 1963 end of the year speech, he recalled the horrors his supporters had suffered during the Civil War in the following terms: "Just look back towards the years that preceded our Crusade, to the martyrs of our cause, to their persecutions and sufferings in the Red zone … "[2] He would admit no concessions:

> The world is so crazy and hard headed that it does not manage to defend itself from this political war [against Communism]. Life is a permanent battle, in which we cannot sleep, and peace, a conquest that we must nurture and protect.

At bottom, everything could be explained by the secular hatred against Spain by foreign nations and bad Spaniards:

> How sad it is to see that throughout the History of the Black Legend against our country it was always fed by resentful Spaniards who had failed in linking themselves to the national community.

As for Grimau's unmentioned execution: "Never in Spain nor in any other nation, has Justice enjoyed a greater independence."[3]

Many, both inside and outside of Spain, agreed. In October 1963 the European far right, presenting itself as an honest association of World War II veterans (European Confederation of Ex-Combatants), met in both Madrid and at the Valley of the Fallen. Delegates from France, Germany, Italy, Belgium, and Luxemburg were present. Collaborating with the association were veterans from Portugal and from the United States. Spain had joined this association in 1961. The idea behind the meeting was to show "the real Christian spirit, anti-Communist and of union between the peoples of free Europe".[4] It pretended to gather veterans regardless of their experiences and roles in World War II, as good gentlemanly comrades who fought a noble conflict in a sporting manner. For example, the Free French (and active pro-Zionist) General Koenig was seated not far from the last German military Governor of Paris, General Von Choltitz, a man who had dutifully carried out Hitler's order to mass murder Jews on the Eastern Front. In his speech, the organization's vice-president, the Frenchman M. Rigoine de Fougerolles, traced a parallel between France's recent fights (and defeats) in Vietnam and Algeria with the Spanish rebels'1936 rising, because "General Franco and those who fought on his side fought for the freedom of the Free World and they [Spaniards] are perhaps the first combatants of the Free World".[5] A grateful Franco replied:

> When we speak of freedom and human dignity, of respect for the individual and conscience of the superior common good, of objective rules of justice and requirement of a moral behaviour of the State, we know we are reverting to that common denominator of our European fidelity.[6]

In the Spain of the 1960s, fear, a past that would not go away, progress and lies were never far apart. A few weeks after Grimau's execution, on July 18, 1963, Manuel Fraga accompanied the dictator during the inauguration of the splendid new installations that housed Spain's official, and then only, television network. Franco's image and words were now entering into ordinary Spaniards' living rooms. But there were more innovations in the making. The ebullient Fraga also had a new idea in mind to celebrate the regime's achievements and to pay homage to his master: a campaign to celebrate "Twenty-Five Years of Peace". Franco's Peace, until then a concept used and understood in a rather narrow and, in many ways pessimistic, sense as an avoidance of strife, would be redefined in a more appealing and positive direction: the transformation and prosperity of Spain under the Caudillo.

This new interpretation marked the culmination of a narrative that started in the first months of the Civil War, and referred to the meaning and importance for Spain of Franco's life. This new Franco, now a grandfather both literally and figuratively, would fit the period of progress and optimism that prevailed in Spanish society during the 1960s, enjoying the rewards of a good life after years of hard work and sufferings for the Fatherland. While this new interpretation could not make Spaniards completely forget the misery of the 1940s and 1950s, it would, nonetheless, present this period as one collective heroic effort, which under the direction of the Caudillo was now beginning to bear fruit. However, as some sceptics pointed out at the time, the shift in the official ideology carried risks because it was bound to bring new values and cultural realities that would test the ability of the regime, and its ally the

Church, to adapt. Another additional risk was that by linking political legitimacy to economic wellbeing, any serious economic downturn would undermine the dictatorship's claim to rightfully represent Spain.

Behind this glorification of progress there was plenty of improvisation. The 1964 "Twenty-Five Years of Peace" campaign was organized in a rush in late 1963. The reason was that the campaign had been cancelled before, after the adoption of the 1959 Stabilization Plan that caused the imposition of severe budgetary cuts. The original project, as described in two decrees passed in 1958 and 1959, was very ambitious and included "the construction of buildings of various types and the investment of 2,000 million pesetas".[7] The cancellation of this first plan clearly showed that the government did not expect the sudden economic boom of the early 1960s. It was only when the recovery was clearly and surprisingly robust that the celebration of progress was deemed appropriate. This celebration of both peace and prosperity supposedly proved that the Caudillo had always been right. As Fraga put it in the September 1963 report that launched the new scaled-down project, "we should adopt some urgent steps" with the objective of making clear that "the National Movement, during the years of peace, has created and greatly developed the foundations to accustom Spaniards to a peaceful coexistence that had not existed for over a century".[8] This was one of the key themes of the campaign: Franco's Peace had fed progress and this progress was now making Spaniards less violent.

Conducted by two of Fraga's main collaborators, the first meeting of the committee that organized the 1964 events took place only on November 13, 1963.[9] In the following weeks, a number of events were organized. All of them were expected to take place during the period between April 1 (Victory Day) and July 18 (National Movement Day). Since there was no money and no time for new buildings, a lot of effort was put into low-cost events such as poems, novels, movies, documentaries, radio programs, television programs, concerts, articles in newspapers and magazines, posters, and union and youth gatherings.

As planned, on April 1, 1964 Spanish television and public and private radio stations broadcast the last wartime communiqué that on April 1, 1939 had announced the surrender of the republican troops and the end of the war. That same morning, presided over by the Caudillo, a mass was celebrated at the Valley of the Fallen. This marked the beginning of a number of political, cultural and sporting activities that took place in the following months. One major event was the exhibition called "Spain 1964: 25 Years of Peace", which was meant to "show the main achievements of these XXV years". The exhibition lasted throughout the months of May and June. Located, after some last-minute changes, in the arcade of the patio of Madrid's *Nuevos Ministerios* administrative complex (built under the Republic), it basically contained a collection of photographs representing each of the ministries, though some private companies were also represented. The exhibition later travelled to other important cities. The main message of the exhibition was the trilogy "A people united", "A country at peace" and "A better fatherland". Next to pictures of daily life, the signs of progress, and the smooth running of national institutions, it also included a photo of the 1959 Franco–Eisenhower embrace and of Pope Paul VI receiving the Spanish ambassador to the Holy See. Photos of factories, new schools and hospitals, reservoirs, graphs showing rising cultural indicators, and the increase of tourists to Spain, etc., all proved that Franco's peace had brought both happiness and progress to Spaniards. Another key moment in the campaign was the May 1 "Unions Show" at Real Madrid soccer stadium, an event at which 200,000 participants were said to be present, and which was meant to be "a homage to his Excellency the Head of State by the Spanish people". Then, on May 24, a large military Victory Parade took place in Madrid's streets.[10]

Books played an important role in the campaign. The most important one, called *Spain Reaches Twenty-Five Years of Peace*, was a summary of all the material, spiritual and political achievements of the regime. Setting a new pattern of using the names of political enemies for propaganda reasons, the book included highly selective and de-contextualized verses written by exiled and/or until then banned or barely tolerated poets. The idea was to show how incomplete these individuals' existence was without Spain, and also to contrast their pain with Spain's present happy and free life.[11] However, the book that was crafted to praise Spain's progress under Franco also had to be careful not to let slip the obvious fact that the economic achievements of the first two decades of the dictatorship had been dismal. In the secret instructions for this and similar books the authorities made it clear that "under no circumstance" should the impression be given that:

> some Governments have been more efficient than others, because it must be always present that the President [Prime Minister] of all those Governments has always been the same person [...] at the same time, it is convenient to point out all the difficulties of the past because of the inherited situation [from the war] and the lack of resources.[12]

One of the main activities in the campaign was the "Concert of the XXV Years of Peace". This included the commission of pieces by well-known composers. The concert included "La Atlántida", a piece based on a poem written in Catalan by Jacint Verdaguer in the late nineteenth-century, and adapted but never completed by Spain's most famous composer of the century, Manuel de Falla. The problem with using Falla's music was that, disgusted by both the Civil War and the Franco regime, he had died in exile in Argentina in 1946. Instead, the pamphlet that presented the Peace Concert, explained that he had died away from Spain only by coincidence.[13]

Poetry also had a role. In December, a competition took place in Madrid in which several bards presented their poems of peace. The queen of the awards ceremony was the Caudillo's eldest grand-daughter, María del Carmen. Several other girls from distinguished families were also present as "ladies". The first prize poem, written by the Francoist author Manuel Alcántara, was a homage to the republican poet Antonio Machado, who had died, heartbroken, in exile in France in 1939. The poem explained how the New Spain was, thanks to the existing peace, nothing like the one Machado had left. Again, the regime was appropriating the memory of some of its most illustrious enemies and victims.[14]

Since television was still only available to a minority of Spaniards (this would change by the end of the decade), newsreels were still the main vehicle of transmission of the images of the campaign. Eight special documentaries on Franco's legacy were made, all under the title of "Twenty-Five Years of Peace", each one addressing a particular achievement: *Art, Agriculture, Industry, Spain and the*

World, Shows, [sic] Spain Builds, Spanish Life, Spanish Culture.[15] All of them praised the unity, peace and prosperity brought by Franco. Through these documentaries, the recent social and economic history of the country, an utter disaster during the previous two decades, was being re-invented and manipulated as a heroic period of difficulty before Spain could rise again. This re-invention of the past also included Franco's version of recent history. One documentary, *Spain and the World*, completely whitewashed the regime's behaviour during World War II, fostering the myth of Franco's stubborn refusal to allow Spain to be involved in the war during his meeting with Hitler at Hendaye in October 1940. The documentary also explained how the victorious Allies later repaid the Caudillo's honourable behaviour with international sanctions and affronts to Spain.

These propaganda pieces prepared the road for one of the campaign's high points. This was the documentary *Franco, ese hombre* (Franco, that Man) directed by José Luis Sáenz de Heredia, a cousin of José Antonio Primo de Rivera. Presented in public for the first time in November 1964, it was preceded by a significant publicity campaign. The documentary opens with a scene of a peaceful morning dawn in Madrid, described by the off-screen commentary as "the peaceable miracle of every day: the sun rises". Next the narrator's voice explains that this is the same Madrid that during the Civil War witnessed so many "red" crimes. Today is different. Of course, there are soldiers in the city but only because the day is not an ordinary day: it is Victory Day and Franco's Army—"the soldiers of Spain"—is going to parade through the city's streets, as it has done every year for the past twenty-five years. The main message running throughout the documentary was that Franco, a seemingly normal individual, whose habits were no different from those of any other grandfather, was a hero in war and peace, the natural, unstoppable centre of Spain's history since he first joined the army as a teenager. His courage, sacrifice and wisdom were protected by Providence because he was the chosen one to, first, save Spain in her darkest hour and, second, lead her during her renaissance, which began with the war and was confirmed by peace in 1939. Peace thus arrived with Franco's victorious troops entering Madrid, and thereafter, the nation would follow the pace of order and prosperity marked by that simple yet extraordinary man.

Once again, Franco was not only the recipient of praise during the campaign; he was also his own most enthusiastic propagandist. During his traditional Christmas 1964 address to the nation, he would adapt his image to fit his newfound role as bearer of prosperity to Spain, inserting new themes and new discursive patterns that would continue in the following years. Now, the references to the war would come at the end of his speeches, with the ritualistic tribute to the fallen "heroes" and "martyrs" of the "Crusade".[16] The main message would now be about progress and normalcy. The dictator said that this general progress proved to be the "justification of our intervention in the country's public life. The general consent that you have been showing me substantially reveals that the road taken was the one you desired".[17] Having asserted that he was ruling because of popular desire, the Caudillo then pinned on his chest the merit of leading renovation and change around the world. His reasoning was that after so much incomprehension towards the regime, finally the world had "evolved towards political–economic–social realities very similar to the ones we gave birth to".[18] When he talked about social problems, he mixed warnings with outright misrepresentations. On the one hand, making an oblique reference to some strikes that had taken place, he cautioned workers and employers not to raise salaries in excess. On the other hand, he said that the situation of the hundreds of thousands of Spaniards who had been forced to migrate to richer European countries in search of work was good because of the help of his government. The proof of this was that there were "numerous commentaries by foreign workers who complain of not being so well assisted as our countrymen are". Furthermore, going to work abroad was good for those Spanish workers, since they gained valuable professional training there.[19]

For the Caudillo, 1964 was a year of successes. Even the monarchist pretender, Don Juan de Borbón (son of the last King Alfonso XIII and father of the future king, Juan Carlos I), a onetime proponent of the restoration of democracy with himself as a king, sent a congratulatory message to Franco.[20] The Church also reinforced Franco's image as the man who brought peace to Spain. The Cardinal Primate, Enrique Plá y Deniel, asked the dictator to bestow a pardon on prisoners in March 1964. No specific distinction was made between political prisoners and common criminals. At the same time, Deniel ordered all Spanish churches to celebrate a "Day

of Thanksgiving and pray for peace" on April 5. Franco conceded
the pardon.[21] However, a general amnesty for republicans' real or
supposed crimes had to wait until 1969.

From peace to progress

The new realities of the 1960s demanded new biographies that
re-interpreted the image of the Caudillo. It was time to go beyond
the attitudes of the 1950s, when anti-Communism and the defence
of Christian Civilization, tales of spiritual and political failures,
redemptions and "his peace", sufficed to explain Franco. Now the
Caudillo was to be the exceptional hero who, albeit misunderstood
and treated unfairly at times, not only saved Spain and the West
from Communism, but also modernized the country and brought
happiness to its inhabitants. However, this new "materialistic"
interpretation lagged behind events and became evident only in the
second part of the decade. In 1966, when José María Sánchez-Silva, a
journalist who had helped with the script of the documentary
Franco, that Man published a book of letters to an unspecified,
fictitious Spanish child, the main theme was still Franco's Peace.
He dwelled extensively on the dictator's glorious military past, his
repulsive republican enemies (mostly Azaña), and his great victory;
but economic progress was not specifically addressed.[22] Also in
1966, another minor Spanish author thanked Franco mainly for
"the period of peace we are working under", which "we hope our
children can enjoy too".[23]

The insertion of progress and prosperity into the biographies of
the Caudillo became dominant only in 1967. That year, as we saw
in the introduction, Luis Bolín published *Vital Years*, his account
of Franco's meeting with destiny. At the same time, the new
representation of the image of the Caudillo was publicized by
foreign authors; whose books in turn, served as proof to local
hagiographers that what they had been saying about the providential
man was now recognized by the rest of the world. In this sense,
in 1967 two important books appeared in English, with very
sympathetic accounts of Franco's life and rule. One was George
Hills' *Franco: The Man and His Nation*.[24] Hills was a BBC journalist
who had been visiting Spain since 1950. His book was published
in Spain the following year, albeit not before being purged by

censors. The other book, even more sympathetic to the dictator, was Brian Crozier's *Franco: A Biographical History*.[25] Both biographies represent the high point of a mid-Cold War interpretation of Franco, and both helped to solidify in the minds of Western public opinion some of the myths about Franco elaborated by the regime's propagandists since 1936. The time was now right for a version of the past marked by serenity and a lack of passion: the millions of visitors that flocked to the country every year could see that Spain's economy was booming and that incomes were rising, as were other social indicators such as education, health and housing.

Hills' book opens with the dictator's childhood. It describes both the strained relationship between his parents as well as his frustrated dreams of joining the navy. Then begins a digression into the tormented nature of modern Spanish history. Finally, on page 60, the book follows Franco's version of his studies at the military academy of Toledo, and his meteoric rise in Africa. What is interesting is the author's empathy with many of the claims and grievances of the Africanista officers. One of them was that politicians in Madrid made them "victims of political expediency".[26] He completely ignored the close relationship between some of these politicians and the officers, a relationship from which Franco profited so much. But then, the book was written in the late 1960s, long after it had been established by the Franco regime that liberal politics had betrayed Spain. The re-invention of the past then takes a new twist when describing Franco's presence in Oviedo (Asturias) after 1917, where he participated in putting down strikes. A man who cared mostly about his career and with deeply conservative ideals is supposed to have been moved, according to the interview Franco gave to Hills in 1966, by "the appalling conditions under which employers were making people work [...] So I began to read books on social questions, on political theories and economists, to search out some solution".[27] There is no proof of any of this. As for the workers' situation, it was far better in 1917 than it would become during the first decade, at least, of Franco's rule.

The hero's first great moments were, of course, 1921 and 1925. In 1921, in Melilla, "it was left to the Legion to save the people from themselves".[28] This is a prophecy of what would happen in 1936, when the Army saved Spaniards from themselves. In 1923, Major Franco was given a permit to get married, and he went to visit one of his patrons, the King. The following is how a modest Caudillo remembered in 1966 this episode, as reported by Hills. According to Franco, a depressed King Alfonso wanted to get out of Morocco. Franco replied: "I beg leave to differ." Next, they went to the next room where there was a large map of Africa and Franco pointed at Alhucemas Bay: "We take the war right into the heart of the enemy territory and we capture the capital." After some thinking, Alfonso said: "You must tell Primo de Rivera this." Franco reasoned that it would be better if the King told the dictator in person. Later, Primo de Rivera asked Franco: "What is this plan of yours?" And so, after his wedding, Franco went back to explain to Primo the amphibious assault that, two years later, in 1925, would finally lead to the defeat of Abd-el-Krim.[29] This, according to Hills, is how the young officer's (or rather, the Caudillo's) gallant attitude and brilliant ideas brought victory to Spain and peace to the Moroccan territory.

When the Republic was formed in 1931, the new Minister of War, Manuel Azaña, made serious cuts to the size of the Army. Perhaps this was needed, Hills admits, but he alerted his readers about what this supposed reform truly meant: "Over 100,000 men went into a glutted labour market eventually to be recruited as militias by the Socialists, Anarchists, Carlists and the soon-to-be-born quasi-fascist Falange".[30] (This was a worrisome fact, although, surprisingly, nobody noticed it at the time.) Where Hills got this piece of fantasy is not explained.

Hills then explains how the Civil War was already coming in May 1931, as shown by the burning of some convents, churches and religious schools: "Spanish writers of nearly all political and religious views date the beginning of the Civil War" from this moment.[31] Hills does not produce sources for this surprising analysis. According to Hills, in the middle of all this chaos, which would get much worse over the next five years, Franco refused to take up arms against the government because he believed that the Army's role was to defend the Fatherland against its enemies, not to meddle in politics.[32] But revolution and Communism were coming, no doubt, after the Popular Front victory of February 1936. The writing was on the wall: Spain was going to be either dismembered or forced under the yoke of Communism. All of this forced Franco to became a "reluctant rebel" who early in July told Mola (not the other way around) that "the time had come to strike".[33]

The war, as the Caudillo predicted, would be hard, but he was a good, prudent general. Admittedly, there were executions in the post-war years, "they may well have numbered ten thousand"—in reality they were close to 50,000—but the man behind the killings was Franco's "fanatic" minister and brother-in-law Ramón Serrano Súñer.[34] These were years of tension, however. Franco had to face a hostile world, starting with the pressure exerted by a victorious Hitler to join the Axis in October 1940. According to Hills, Hitler was also the one who had ordered the bombing of Guernica (April 26, 1937) without Franco knowing it. The perfidious Austrian and Mussolini were also responsible for the frequent bombings of Barcelona during the war, again without the Caudillo's permission.[35] Franco, however, knew how to play his cards with Hitler. He made the Führer wait for an hour at the Hendaye train station, and then, at the interview, he out-manoeuvred the German dictator by requesting impossible-to-meet demands, thus saving Spain from the horror of World War II.[36] From then on, in spite of international incomprehension, Spain's reconstruction was assured. By the time of Franco's death in 1975, the book had appeared in four editions in Spanish, and two in English.

Brian Crozier, who was also British, had worked for both *The Economist* and the BBC. He was a deeply anti-Communist Catholic with a military background. In the acknowledgements of his book he thanked Joaquin Arrarás, the pro-Franco propagandist and hagiographer, and Luis Bolín for their help. The Spanish version appeared in 1969. He considers Franco's least "pardonable trait" his "incapacity to forgive his enemies on the side of anti-Spain, though he was always remarkably indulgent towards friends who betrayed him".[37] From him we now learn that Franco loved British things. The unsupported evidence for this was an obscure 1920 story relating the visit to Morocco by a British general: "This precious evidence of Franco's attachment to things British is not without significance."[38]

According to Crozier, Franco became famous for two reasons: his military genius and his courage. Like Hills, Crozier argues that the Caudillo was responsible for conceiving the decisive 1925 Alhucemas Bay landing plan, convincing both Primo de Rivera and the King, and conducting himself courageously during the actual operation.[39] The King loved him, and protected him, but the impact his devotion had on Franco's career is never explained. Unfortunately, the Republic arrived and Azaña commenced his reforms, which Crozier described as "blows" to the Army.[40] It was the beginning of what would become, according to Crozier, the "Mortal Sickness of the Republic".[41] Chaos, crime, subversion—all would lead the loyal, rather apolitical, Franco to rebel. Looking back, it was obvious that he never wanted power for power's sake, since his "dominant emotion has always been patriotism, and power has been his means of indulging it". There is nothing extraordinary in this, because "he deeply resembles Charles de Gaulle", even if the Spaniard's patriotism is "less narcissistic" than the Frenchman. Franco, in fact, "acts by Providential Dispensation".[42]

The Franco of the 1960s was, according to Crozier, a ruler who cared about his people, as evidenced by the fact that he negotiated with the striking miners in 1962 (a claim that was not true). But he also faced "bad publicity"—for example, when in 1963 his regime shot the underground Communist leader Grimau, a man "charged with crimes allegedly committed during the Civil War". Grimau had confessed under "interrogation" (Crozier's words). This execution was an error, but also a choice in favour of "Spanish pride" over the easy way of favourable publicity.[43] Crozier goes on to claim that Franco had done the best he could with a nation of "deeply Manichean people", who have an authoritarian and non-negotiable personality. Moreover, thanks to Franco Spain was freer than Eastern Europe; and in contrast with its chaotic past and traditional poverty Franco had brought order and progress to Spain.[44] He was firmly on the side of the West and indeed he always had been: "it is impossible to exaggerate the contribution his skill and patience made to the Allied victory".[45] The book appeared in four editions in Spanish, one in English, and another in French.

The apparent personal openness shown by Franco towards these foreign biographers was a calculated policy. When a writer tried to dig beneath the official version of history, alarms sounded and measures were taken. In December 1965, for example, Planeta, one of Spain's largest publishers, asked permission to publish *Testimony of Manuel Hedilla*, written by a group of authors led by Maximiano García Venero. The General Director of Information, Carlos Robles Piquer—one of the main organizers of the Twenty-Five Years of Peace campaign—detected passages in the book that failed to present Franco's actions in April of 1937, during the unification of the Falange and the traditionalists, in the usual laudatory tones. During the so-called 1937 Salamanca crisis, Manuel Hedilla, the legal chief of the Falange, was manipulated, bullied and finally imprisoned by Franco as a result of his refusal to accept the creation of a single, reactionary party led by the Generalissimo. This was not the story the regime propaganda machine had been telling for decades. And this is why Robles sent copies of the text to his superior, the Minster of Information, Fraga, who then sent a copy to Franco himself.[46] The Caudillo edited and eliminated the book's "errors", which, once expunged of damaging information, appeared in 1972.

A third notable pro-Franco British biography written by J.W.D. Trythall was published in 1970. Unlike the previous two by Hills and Crozier, this one was not translated into Spanish. For all its shortcomings and repetition of most of the clichés already made popular by others, it is at times a deeply penetrating account, in part because this was perhaps the first attempt to interpret the Caudillo's relationship with ordinary Spaniards. At the time of its publication, the book insulted some critics by pointing to evidence of Franco's widespread popular backing. Trythall used as an example of the Caudillo's popularity the massive and genuine support (albeit strengthened by vote rigging) for the "yes" question in the December 1966 referendum on the passing of the Organic (Fundamental) Law of the State.[47] For Trythall, as for Crozier, Franco was in many senses a normal European ruler, celebrated in excess by the media, but not more than de Gaulle and Churchill were celebrated in their own countries. But what was most interesting about his book was Trythall's analysis of Franco's larger significance. It is this feature that places this biography in the discipline of social and cultural history:

> He [Franco] has become a symbol, and is respected or despised not for what he is but for what he has come to represent, just as the king, regardless of his personality, might be loved by monarchists and hated by republicans.[48]

The book ended by questioning what the Caudillo would end up meaning in Spanish history once he was gone. This was one of the two big questions in the air in the early 1970s as the dictator's aging became more evident (he turned eighty in 1972). The other issue was less cultural and more practical: namely, what would happen to Spain after the Caudillo's death.

In the late 1960s and early 1970s, when confronted with the "biological fact" of Franco's mortality, as the dictator's death was often called inside Spain, pro-Francoist writers increasingly adopted a tone of nostalgia, as if preparing themselves and the country for the sunset of the golden era. In these years, many, if mostly very minor, works reminded readers of the meaning for Spain of the Caudillo/Saviour and they often promised, literally, not to forget the great man's life and deeds.[49] Ricardo de la Cierva, the most prominent historian of the right, published the culmination of this type of work in 1972. De la Cierva came from a well-known conservative family. The republicans had assassinated his father during the notorious Paracuellos del Jarama massacres of November 1936. Under the dictatorship he worked for the Ministry of "Information", where he was both a censor and a sort of in-house intellectual.

De la Cierva was a rather careless and highly partisan writer whose manipulation of facts has been frequently criticized. His 1972 biography started by presenting what he considered to be the "Historical Enigma of Francisco Franco".[50] According to him, a true portrait of the man could not be found in the many biographies of the general that had appeared abroad over the years, since these were often either inaccurate or defamatory (he was referring to books published abroad by Spaniards which the censors made sure almost no one in Spain had access to). This was a situation that Spanish historiography could not "passively contemplate" without reacting: "Franco can be insulted but, up to now, it is impossible to define him". He explored this mystery through a project entitled "Memories of Spain about Franco" with "a deep feeling of respect for the personage".[51] The first issue of the series set the tone for the rest. It started with the year of Franco's birth, describing what happened in 1892 in both Spain and in the world. De la Cierva ignored the troubled marriage of Franco's parents. He then explained what was good and wrong with the Restoration system (there was economic progress but too much division and political infighting). This first issue ended with a number of graphs showing the evolution of Spain's economy and society since the late 1800s until the 1970s. These were intended to demonstrate the progress of the nation, which de la Cierva attributed to the Caudillo.

De la Cierva's work was connected to the last batch of pro-Franco biographies, which appeared as the dictator's life was clearly approaching its end. Two of the most important ones were written in 1974 by the French authors Jean Dumont and Alain Launay, and were quickly translated into Spanish.[52] The intention of both works was to offer homage to Franco's deeds and historical mission. Such an objective was mirrored in the following words by Launay:

> The Spain of 1974 is Franco's Spain [...] This is not an artificial expression because today's Spain, as it appears to our eyes, is the country the man desired and moulded even in its smaller details, spending half of his life, like a medieval artisan, chiselling and polishing his masterwork, with patience, obstinacy and love. And this man's name is Francisco Franco.[53]

A final hagiography of Franco appeared in 1975, when both the author and the subject were dead. Published by the government's official press, it was written by one of the Caudillo's better-known propagandists, the journalist, diplomat and courtier Manuel Aznar (his grandson José María would serve as a conservative Prime Minister of democratic Spain from 1996 to 2004). Aznar, who died ten days before his master, had, among other tasks, corrected the Caudillo's movie script (*Raza*) in 1941. His 1975 book reproduced all of the myths and official lies about the man, his destiny and his legacy, for which, he argued, all Spaniards should be grateful:

> The great compromise with the country and with himself was raising the standard of living of Spaniards through a continuous, never ending strengthening of our economic structures and the strong industrial development of Spain. Towards this ideal he subordinated many things, and to serve it with all his energies he always considered it necessary to keep all power to himself, and to take full responsibility for his initiatives.[54]

This was the final meaning of Franco's nearly four decades of absolute rule: the constant sacrifice of holding absolute power; the selfless hero who had made Spaniards prosperous.

A satisfied ruler

Hagiographers and propagandists repeated the Caudillo's words of self-praise; provincial and local officials' behaviour only imitated their master's. For them, truth was no impediment when it came to the official account of so many successes. Self-criticism was non-existent, and their facts could not be verified by any independent agency and made public to Spaniards. Take the case of the *Plan Jaén*. One of the much-publicized programs of the regime's redemption of the countryside, it was aimed at eliminating the abject poverty of the southern province of Jaén by generating a rapid process of modernization of agriculture and industrialization. The Plan originated in 1951, shortly after a similar one was approved for the equally impoverished province of Badajoz. That year, Franco visited the province, and with his proven capacity to make prophecies said: "I can assure you that the province of Jaén will be first because it was the most abandoned one; like all provinces of Spain, it will see its program realized".[55] In 1952, a government decree launched the Plan. On the walls of many town halls the following words by Franco were plastered: "Jaén causes me sleepless nights" [*Jaén me quita el sueño*].[56]

In 1973, twenty-one years after the *Plan Jaén* was launched, its achievements were very poor. To be sure, the government's policies had resulted in several positive developments such as an increase in irrigation, soil conservation, electrification, limited industrialization, and colonization. But the standard of living of the people remained abysmally low, an inconvenient fact obscured and distorted in the authorities' official discourses. In the mid-1960s, for example, Jaén's Governor, Sr. Pardo Gayoso, pressured the local newspaper to claim that between 1955 and 1960 the province's rank in the nation's per capita income had gone from 47th to 32th. What was not mentioned, however, was the fact that when these words were printed Jaen's position in the national ranking of GDP per person was actually rapidly declining: by 1967 it was already 50th, or last in the country.[57] The sad reality was that the Plan had never been a real plan because it had neither cost estimates nor coherent goals; it was, rather, a cobbling together of different, more or less *ad hoc* projects under a common name. Mild social improvements to the province came not from the Plan, but from the country's overall progress, which was in geographical terms very unequally distributed, as well as from the massive migration from the province to the richer ones, mostly Barcelona and Madrid. Jaén's evolution during the 1950s and 1960s was far from unique. In terms of both socio-economic indicators and migration, it followed a very similar path to provinces such as Almería, Cáceres, Lugo, Orense, and Palencia—provinces that did not "enjoy" any plan, let alone cause the Caudillo's sleepless nights.

For all the talk of development in the 1960s and the "miracle" of the Spanish economy, the regime knew that it had failed to provide poorer Spaniards with decent levels of social services. The reason for this failure was simple: a number of Development Plans (copied from the French model, and first adopted in 1964) had no allocation for social spending. The lack of investment in social matters was not merely the product of a lack of wealth, but rather of how that wealth was distributed. The planners knew that the crux of the problem was Spain's archaic, inefficient and deeply unfair tax system. Yet Francoism still ended its days with no income tax and with no serious penalty for tax fraud. This resulted in low levels of public investment in social services for the majority of people, and in great privileges for the minority.

In spite of all these shortcomings, the Franco of the mid and late 1960s was a satisfied ruler. He worked little and left his advisers, under the leadership of Admiral Carrero Blanco, to do as they pleased, even if the Caudillo maintained constant vigilance over possible threats to his rule. He always had a keen ear for rumour and gossip that could be used against his subordinates; and he was always ready to consider a traitor anyone who advocated any political liberalization. Overall, however, he felt confident both internally and externally. The Caudillo's satisfaction with Spain's progress became personal during his visits to the provinces. On these occasions, Franco could see that his popularity was peaking.

In April 1967, the Falange reported the "enthusiasm" created in Sevilla "among all social classes" by Franco's visit. The three-kilometre stretch between the airport and the cathedral was crowded by hundreds of thousands of people who gave the Caudillo an "apotheosis" of a welcome. Even a "multitude" of foreign tourists recorded the event with their cameras (tourists, not Spaniards, had cameras). Once in the cathedral, people could not contain their excitement, and several times applause filled the sacred space. Sevillanos, according to the local authorities, were also talking about their hope that the Caudillo had seen with his own eyes that "this was the area of the South of Spain most appropriate to place a steel mill, [since] with this all the labour and social problems that affect the south of the nation would be resolved". Sevilla did, indeed, have serious social problems, the report on the visit stated, such as the recent closing of factories and the housing shortage, which caused a great number of "homes in ruins" to be occupied by some 5,000 families. Just before the visit, a ruined house had collapsed, killing a small child.[58] The Civil Governor, the hardliner future minister in charge of the Falange Party, José Utrera Molina, had said that "thousands of new homes have been erected on our soil", "new industries have erected their plants", "the fields have improved" … etc.[59] The province never got the steel mill.

Popular support for the aging and supposedly gentle Caudillo was not just the product of disinterested excitement. When people cheered for Franco, they were also defending their own particular interests. When they expressed their loyalty for the Caudillo they hoped to be repaid in kind. For example, in June 1967, in Peñarroya (Córdoba) about 400 protesting workers of *Papelera del Sur* (a paper mill) and their families, who were locked in a bitter dispute with the company over salaries, demonstrated in the street and marched towards the local union headquarters. The workers carried placards that said "Franco, we helped you with our Yes in the referendum, now you help us", "Peñarroya and Pueblo Nuevo were with you when you triumphed, be with us in our disgrace".[60] The friend of the humble, the justice maker, the great hero, the Caudillo was being asked to fulfil the role that his own propaganda assigned him.

Throughout the late 1960s, admiration for the Caudillo was both intense and widespread as detected, for example, in the confidential reports sent to the Minister of the Interior by the provincial governors. However, the same reports also showed two growing problems. On the one hand, there was concern about what was going to happen once he was gone. On the other hand, the concern was that the person he had designated as his heir in July 1969, Prince Juan Carlos, was little known and little loved. Hard-core Francoists were generally in support of another regency (dictatorship), while monarchists were divided between those who supported Juan Carlos and those who sided with his exiled father, Don Juan. And of course, there were the Carlists, who supported yet another branch of the royal family. This situation would became more complicated in 1972, when Don Juan Carlos' cousin, Alfonso, who also had aspirations to the Crown, married Franco's eldest granddaughter María del Carmen, in a semi-royal wedding. Franco's inner circle, often led by his wife, Doña Carmen, started to pressure the dictator to change his mind regarding his succession. The Caudillo refused.

The highest point of Franco's popularity among Spaniards was probably around 1969. But, as we shall soon see, there were clear signs that there were more than a few malcontents in Spain who challenged the regime with a determination not seen since 1939. The turning point for these individuals and for the regime was 1970. In December nineteen Basque militants (two of whom were clerics) were brought before a military accused of terrorism. The so-called Burgos Trial drew international condemnation, as well as protests inside Spain, particularly after authorities condemned nine of the accused to death. Eventually, the Caudillo commuted the death sentences, arguing that by doing so the regime was showing its strength. These were words that would haunt him less than five years later. Nonetheless, this is how, a few days after the pardon, he explained to Spaniards what had happened:

> Out of the peace and order that we have enjoyed for more than thirty years has arisen the hatred of those forces that were always the enemies of our people's prosperity, our welfare and the progress that Spain is achieving in all orders of national life.[61]

He knew that millions of Spaniards agreed, as a number of well-attended demonstrations supporting him had taken place all over Spain in the previous weeks:

> The clamorous and crowded demonstrations of support that you have offered me on the occasion of my trips and visits to

Barcelona, Valencia, Zaragoza, Cáceres, Galicia, Guipúzcoa, Jerez, Cádiz and Salamanca, and the immense plebiscite of support at the Plaza de Oriente in Madrid and in all of Spain that in the last days you have offered not just to me but also to the Spanish Army and our institutions, has reinforced our authority [and this is why] I used my prerogative of the grace of pardon to the ultimate punishment, in spite of the gravity of the crimes ... [62]

In spite of the mounting challenges, Franco changed nothing, and offered nothing new. The following December (1971), he explained why:

There is no justification for those who, admitting our economic and social development, call, as if it was a new thing, for a political development. This proposition is simply suicidal and the Spanish people have enough experience to flatly reject another blind jump, and it has enough will to continue its path under an organic [dictatorial] system, based on natural institutions ... [63]

And again, in 1972:

The Spanish nation continues to enjoy good health and walks at a good pace down the road of History, deserving growing admiration, not always confessed, by those who with a clear mind contemplate our restless cultural, social and economic development, the solidity of our State born out of the July 18 and the rooting of its institutions, which are a guarantee of the continuity of our policy at the service of the peace and greatness of Spain.[64]

To propose any change was to question him. But in the last years of his life, in spite of both the booming economy (until 1974) and all the popular support for the Caudillo, there was an increasing sense of foreboding, compounded by the approaching certainty that the dictator's reign was ending. Some Francoists thought it was time to start a controlled liberalization before the dictator died or became incapacitated (this last scenario is what happened to Portugal's dictator, Salazar, in 1968). In May 1972, for example, the Minister of the Interior, Tomás Garicano, a man with a past as a hardliner, explained in a report to the Caudillo the need to practise moderation in regard to the new social movements emerging in the country. Radical reaction and violence should be avoided, he wrote. He reasoned that, given the extraordinary prosperity enjoyed by an increasing proportion of Spanish society, the regime faced no real challenges, except from the universities, and that it was necessary to take advantage of this situation to start a process of "change and renovation". This was to include the majority of Spaniards who "did not experience our War of Liberation".[65] His advice was ignored, and things started to spiral out of control. Frustrated, and accused of disloyalty by the Caudillo's inner circle, Garicano resigned the following year.

On December 20, 1973, as Spaniards prepared for Christmas, Basque terrorists assassinated Admiral Carrero Blanco, Franco's right-hand man for over three decades and Prime Minister since the previous June. While offering his condolences to Carrero's widow, Spaniards watched on their televisions the sad spectacle of a weeping old man, their Caudillo. A few days later, a still shaken Franco explained to Spaniards the meaning of recent events in a very short, and rather dark, end-of-the-year address. As always, he pointed to himself as the main reference. To conclude the speech, the faint voice coming out of the Caudillo's fragile body tried to reassure Spaniards that "after thirty seven years at the helm of the state, here I am in front of you, with the same vocation to serve the Fatherland I always had".[66]

Christmas 1974 saw the last of these end-of-the year addresses. This is what Franco had to say about both the sharp deterioration of his health (more on this later in the chapter) as well as the deepening economic crisis:

> At the end of 1974, difficult for all of us, we have proved once again that the institutions have continued to gain in both solidity and trust. [...] The illness that affected me last summer offered a providential occasion to test the mature serenity of the Spanish people and the safe workings of the mechanical provisions of our Fundamental Laws. [...] The Prince of Spain [...] took over as Head of State during my illness. [...] The new economic situation, which had deeply affected the Occidental world, has showed the Achilles' heel of many countries

with high levels of development, and the scarce international solidarity when confronting the need of finding solutions to common problems. [...] This crisis will surely be long and deep [...] but our Government has been dictating the measures to face it. [...] The youth, which did not know the bitter hours of the past and which has lived in the awakening and well-being of the new Fatherland, has the honour and responsibility to continue without any rupture the work that we started.[67]

The regime's decay was becoming evident even in one of its specialties: the provision of masses of cheerful people to greet foreign visitors. This was evident when the American president Gerald Ford visited Madrid in May 1975. Sixteen years after Eisenhower's triumphant visit, Spaniards—not to mention the global image of the United States—had changed. Now America's help was not so desperately needed and anti-Americanism was high, particularly among Spanish youth. More importantly, the Caudillo's popularity was in decline, and the regime's political paralysis nearly complete. To bolster Ford's visit, the authorities used tried and true methods: they brought 590 buses, carrying some 29,000 people, from the more conservative provinces of central Spain. From Madrid province, another 54,000 people were brought to the event. The stipulation was that they would come dressed informally, avoiding the blue shirt of the Falangists, and that any mention of the Caudillo should be greeted with "spontaneous" cries of "Franco, Franco ... ". Despite the regime's efforts, the fact that the numbers had declined in comparison to similar events of the past made the "popular display" of happiness at Ford's arrival look both pathetic and plainly artificial.[68]

The dictatorship challenged

Even during the golden age of the 1960s the regime's official discourse hinted at the existence of internal opposition. Much publicized events such as the 1970 Burgos Trial and the 1973 killing of Admiral Carrero, although not representative of the general mood of the country or even the majority of the regime's opponents, showed that Francoism's enemies were becoming stronger and bolder. Where did this opposition come from? To answer this question one must go back to the Civil War and the subsequent attempts by the dictatorship to destroy civil society. During and after the war, the regime tried to suppress or at least control groups, movements and ideas; those it could not control, it simply banned. However, while institutions could be obliterated, collective memory could not. Beneath the regime's official truth, the rhetoric of unity around the Caudillo of Peace, the ideological and cultural diversity of Spain survived. In this semi-totalitarian context, the Church was the sole institution fully independent of the dictatorship. While during the 1940s and 1950s the Church was overwhelmingly sympathetic to the regime, in the 1960s a very active minority of clerics, both male and female, engaged in the promotion of cultural change and social activism. In the process, the Church became a significant, if somewhat surprising, force behind the return of Spanish civil society.

The first symptoms of this new reality came from the industrial regions of the country's periphery. Already in the early 1950s, many lay Catholics, mainly those involved in the Workers' Brotherhood of Catholic Action (HOAC), had been very active in illegal trade unionism. To the regime's surprise (not to mention that of the old guard of anti-Francoist militants), Catholic activists were increasingly seen—which is to say, arrested—at demonstrations, strikes and other protests. Some of these individuals were even found to be Marxists. Social activism soon linked up with peripheral nationalism. Even in the darkest days of the dictatorship, there was a latent tension between the Church in the Basque Country and Catalonia (regions with a tradition of using and promoting their local languages) and the narrowly Spanish Francoist regime. While there was some cultural and linguistic liberalization during the late 1950s, Spain's multinational character, harshly repressed after 1939, was suppressed even during the happy 1960s. As a 1964 Ministry of the Interior report to the dictator proposed, government policy must "not tolerate or give authorization" to Catalan and Basque nationalist demonstrations, whether of a cultural, political, or any other nature.[69] A contemporary report sent to the Caudillo by his Minister of the Interior, the hardliner General Camilo Alonso Vega, delved into the relationship between resurgent peripheral nationalism and the Church, and more specifically how religious seminars in the Basque Country and Catalonia had become breeding grounds of dissent. As Alonso explained, the Church was becoming increasingly divided between a majority of conservative, pro-Franco elements, and a minority of pro-democratic, or at least anti-Francoist, dissidents.[70]

The reference and turning point for this new Church was the Second Vatican Council (1962–1965). The Council was an embarrassment to the regime. In December 1962, a few months after it started, the conservative Bishop Jacinto Argaya sent Franco a report on the proceedings. It did not look good. According to this report, the Council was dominated by French and central European prelates who, in voicing their progressive views, had attracted the majority of Latin American representatives. Worse still, the man who every one believed was going to be the next Pope, Monsignor Montini (the future Paul VI), sided with them.[71] The post-Council Church would thus live up to the fears of Conservative Spanish bishops and the dictatorship. When a 1966 police report on a meeting of Barcelona's clergy reached Franco's desk, he underlined the following sentences: "they talked about taking off the cassock and dressing as civilians", "the priests should work in factories and shops and live from their salaries", "they will make an opinion poll on celibacy", "conservative priests say […] this dioceses is a disaster".[72]

However, in public Franco continued to pretend that the Church was following his leadership. As he explained modestly in 1964:

> There are people who discover like a novelty the encyclicals by John XXIII and forget that since 1938 Spain has been practicing, and in many aspects surpassing, the Church's social doctrine […] Which regime stimulates more virtues and spiritual actions for peace among men? Who has tried a better marriage between ethics and politics?[73]

Again in 1967, during his traditional televised Christmas address, the dictator expressed a seemingly genuine admiration for the publication of Pope Paul VI's encyclical *Populorum Progressio*, on social and labour rights, the previous March. As Franco said:

> this backs the doctrine that we have been practicing for thirty years […] What a joy for us to see our solutions confirmed from such high places![74]

However, young priests were not interested in the Franco regime's supposedly Catholic-inspired legislation or institutions. Influenced by new movements coming out of Latin America, such as Liberation Theology, they were already beyond compromising with the dictatorship. The regime knew this because its police spent an enormous amount of time and effort spying on Spanish priests, collecting thousands of reports on what these individuals did or said. The reports showed that open dissent was not limited to the historically combative industrial and urban zones of Spain, but was now spreading to remote villages where political apathy and conservative tradition had hitherto prevailed. For example, in 1968, the Civil Guard observed priests in a village in the Southern province of Almería as they explained to young people that "everyone who has property is a thief". The priests also made favourable remarks about Fidel Castro, as well as claiming that "the Vietnam War is just business for the Americans, because of their weapons sales". One of the priests even dared to say that he had voted "No" in Franco's December 1966 referendum, to which he added the almost unheard of opinion that "His Excellency the Head of the State is dated and he is drooling".[75] If these irreverent words could be heard in a semi-isolated village in what was then one of Spain's poorest provinces, then the regime was surely facing a very serious problem.

Franco, moreover, had a difficult relationship with Pope Paul VI. In 1963 the Pope had clearly and publicly expressed his strongest objection to Grimau's execution, which happened shortly after his accession to the Chair of Saint Peter. More decisively, in the following years he proceeded to appoint progressive prelates in Spain to the extent that by 1973 Francoist authorities were estimating that 35 out of the existing 78 sitting bishops could be counted in that category.[76] Of course, not all members of the clergy subscribed to these anti-dictatorial sentiments; in fact, the majority were either avowedly conservative, with the remainder showing great timidity in political matters. Speaking for that mostly silent majority in 1974, the staunchly pro-Franco Bishop of Cuenca, Monsignor Guerra Campos, wrote that Franco "is a son of a Church who has tried to project in his public life his condition as a Christian". Monsignor Guerra denounced those members of the Church that were trying to re-write the past, negating the benefits for the Church that the regime's protection had offered.[77] In any case, by the early 1970s the political marriage between the dictatorship and the Church was, if not definitively over, at least badly damaged.

University students were likewise a thorn in the side of the regime. As elsewhere in the West, a portion of Spanish youth became politically radicalized in the 1960s; in other words, they were anti-Francoist. In 1965, isolated and regarded with contempt, the official student union (SEU), which had controlled and often terrorized campuses since the war, was disbanded. Barcelona University was closed down in the same year and again in 1966, as were some faculties of the universities of Madrid and Sevilla, among others. Although a majority of students were not active in these growing protests, a very active minority effectively turned the universities against the regime. After 1968, the government frequently resorted to anti-riot and political police to violently repress the students' demonstrations. This dynamic of confrontation would continue until the end of the dictatorship. Most Spaniards, however, had little sympathy for the students; in the eyes of many, they were privileged brats looking for trouble.

Partly a result of this youth rebellion, partly a result of the re-birth of peripheral nationalism supported by local clergy, the Basque terrorist organization ETA (Basque Fatherland and Freedom) gained strength during the 1960s. It committed its first murder in 1968. While initially the majority of the Basque population rejected ETA's activities, the regime's often brutal and indiscriminate repression—for example, the imposition of martial law across the entire Basque Country in 1969—led to growing sympathy for the organization's young members, many of whom came to be seen as Basque heroes fighting for social and national redemption. This dynamic of action/repression between ETA and the dictatorship would have very significant consequences in the last years of the regime, conditioning in many ways the transition to democracy that followed. Most of the almost 1000 people murdered by ETA have been assassinated after Franco's death.

Finally, the late 1960s witnessed increasing labour militancy—a phenomenon that cannot be separated from the often-appalling conditions in workers' neighbourhoods. In the 1950s and 1960s millions of Spaniards had migrated to industrialized urban areas that were often unprepared to receive them. Immigrants prospered thanks to their hard work, but this did not translate into the political conformity that was expected by the regime and feared by its opponents. On the contrary, while material progress helped to create a more affluent society, it also created higher expectations. Some of these expectations included better and safer jobs, improved neighbourhoods, schools and hospitals, and often more political freedom. At the same time, workers who migrated to France or Germany (a mass phenomenon after 1962) also experienced both the wellbeing and the freedom of their counterparts there, and started to question why Spain was so different. When they came home, some of these workers spread their newly-acquired ideas. The older guard of political militants, people who had often spent many years in prison and undergone much suffering in the past, were now finding, for the first time since the end of the Civil War, that young workers, as well as students and Catholic militants, were willing to listen to them. During the 1960s these once disparate constituencies worked together in newly-founded neighbourhood associations; many also infiltrated the official unions, where, in essence, they began subverting Francoist institutions from the inside. New and old political cultures and experiences were coming together. In the process, clandestine political groups and unions started to emerge from years of almost complete isolation, and new groups were founded. Opposition to the dictatorship was now plural and, most importantly, it was learning to work together for the cause of the right to political and cultural diversity.

Predictably, the regime tried to present all of this opposition either as Communist or Communist-controlled. In reality, while the Spanish Communist Party (PCE) was the single largest and indeed best-organized political group in Spain, it was always a minority amongst the vast array of forces—whether composed of democratic monarchists or anarchists, Catholics or lay people, etc.—that opposed the dictatorship. This fact was deliberately ignored by Franco's propaganda machine, which employed a discourse of simplistic, Manichean polarization. In this absolute world of black and white, Spain (meaning Franco) stood opposite Communism. With this discourse, Francoism tried to win for the regime two very profitable results. One was to present any form of opposition to the dictatorship as both the equivalent of treason to the nation and pro-Communist subversion. The other was to remind Spaniards that the same democracy that was normal in Europe was a mortal danger at home; that the alternative to Franco's Peace was revolution, civil war and likely a Communist dictatorship. Paradoxically, this proposition thus reinforced the image of the Communists as the only true opposition to Franco. It was a role that, until the early 1960s, the PCE was only too happy to play. In this way, the two forms of political extremism, pseudo-Fascist dictatorship and Communism, actually reinforced each other at the expense of more moderate political values.

The Socialists (PSOE), traditionally the main party of the Spanish left, had long championed the establishment of a two-party dominated parliamentary system, like the ones existing in most other Western countries. They also stood for peaceful political change. As one clandestine member of the party wrote in 1964, the socialists argued that the key to dismantling the dictatorship was to wait for Franco's death. They had renounced any form of violence or open subversion, and placed themselves in a situation of "impotent waiting". The Socialists believed that the majority of Spaniards held latent social-democratic and/or Christian-democratic ideals and, when "the first historical opportunity" arose, these ideals would manifest themselves openly. At the same time, they recognized that the regime had largely abandoned its "bellicose" attitude and evolved in the direction of a somewhat more "modern, civilized and tolerant" rule. They wanted to believe (probably wrongly at the time) that the majority of the people were hostile to the regime. However, in the last years they wrote "the regime has had the talent not to make victims" and most ordinary Spaniards felt safe enough if they did not venture into politics. This, plus most people's desire to improve their material situation during the emerging economic boom, meant that opposition politics were limited to a minority. "People know their strength and limitations", the Socialists stated. As for the Communist threat, they thought that it was overblown, both because the Communists were a minority and because they were evolving, much like the Italian Communist Party of the same period, towards a democratic line independent from Moscow.[78]

The growing support since the late 1960s for the opposition among the urban working class worried the dictatorship. Behind the official messages of optimism lurked the regime's insecurities over its political legitimacy. Francoism depended on an image of Spain in which consensus around the beloved Caudillo was apparent everywhere. This is why it feared any public demonstration of dissent. As the police said in a 1967 report on the upcoming May 1, (Workers' Day) commemoration: "Public demonstrations [by the opposition] have as their main objective to show to the world that there is no peace in our country"; an objective that would be achieved if, as often happened, police had to intervene, arrest demonstrators and take them to be judged by "military authorities". The police were also afraid that these subversives might bring foreign journalists and/or photographers to document the repression of their demonstrations.[79]

Repression worked to an extent, but it was not enough. This is why the Francoist authorities started to dream of re-mobilizing the regime's political supporters and launching their own institutions, from workers' unions to other voluntary associations. The problem was that the dictatorship had so successfully demobilized society that it was now incapable of rallying active support amongst the Spanish population. The Franco regime, which—like other dictatorships from both the right and the left—had once relied on authoritarian command from the top, was now finding it difficult to convince the people to bolster it from below.

Nevertheless, the dictatorship kept trying. With the passing, in January 1967, of the Organic Laws, the Franco regime pretended to have achieved a harmonic functioning of the political system, which supposedly was now more representative and more stable than the rejected democratic one. A cornerstone of this system was the elections to the *Cortes*, which for the first time since its creation in 1943 included the direct election by secret ballot of 100 representatives, 2 for each province. Normally, the *Cortes* had over 500 members, which meant that the number of directly elected representatives was still less than 20 per cent of the total. Furthermore, candidates could be, and often were, vetoed by the authorities. All men or widowed women at the head of a household could vote. In total, the electoral roll contained about 16 million voters. The problem was that most of these potential voters were very timid about expressing their opinions; most knew very little about elections and even less about the candidates. For example, in 1968

Franco received on his desk a study of the upcoming elections to be carried out in Madrid, not exactly Spain's most backward or illiterate province. The study revealed that almost half of those contacted by pollsters either refused to answer or were unable to answer any of the questions put to them. Of those who answered, 90 per cent did not know any of the candidates. The best-known candidate was identified by only 9 per cent; and 82 per cent had absolutely no idea who they were going to vote for.[80]

More menacingly, in the 1960s, anti-Francoist forces progressively occupied the empty political and social spaces abandoned by the dictatorship. By the early 1970s, it had become obvious that organized opposition was growing, and protest, rather than subsiding when answered with repression by the regime, was becoming more socially acceptable; indeed, it was spreading. These developments caused the dictator to resort to his old formula in the last years of his life—that of stoking fear among the population. The word "Peace" was once again spoken in the context of a "Victory" over the regime's opponents, and the spectrum of Communist infiltration, as well as foreign manipulation, was pushed to the forefront of the regime's official discourse. Talking to Falangist leaders on the 38th anniversary of the party's founding in October 1971, the Caudillo declared that "the enemy tries to divide us because it knows that a divided Spain is a vanquished Spain: we cannot forget that the enemy is alive and present".[81]

Three years later, in 1974, the economic boom was over and strikes were increasing. Carrero, whose task had been to control the situation for a physically enfeebled Franco, was dead. The future of the regime looked more than uncertain. It was at this time that the propaganda machine produced yet another book destined to preserve Franco's crucial legacy. The occasion was the 35th anniversary of Victory Day. The work demonstrates a dedication to the weapon of fear, the crucial element in the Official Historical Memory of Francoism up to the last moment.[82] The book's opening statement emphasizes the following message:

> Behind each brilliant epoch [...] there are two unavoidable realities: a rising people and a man who serves it, embodies it, and directs it [...] Franco has been and still is the main manager, the real builder of Spain's peace.[83]

The Civil War—always the war—had been the necessary sacrifice:

> The Spanish peace is an undeniable fact [...] At the historical
> base of every modern nation there is always the image of a civil
> war. Perhaps that image is the price that history demands
> from us to access national fulfilment. This is the case in the
> United States, France, Germany or England. This is, since
> 1936, the case in Spain. Why does this happen? Obviously,
> because the blood and the trauma of the war welds together
> the nation. In the case of Spain, the war was unavoidable for a
> number of reasons; among them, the national decomposition,
> manifested by street violence, regional separatism, politicking
> and class struggle.[84]

The hints to and the comparison with the new reality were obvious.

The war had welded Spaniards' future to the Caudillo, but
Franco was now dying. The last two years of the dictator's life was
thus a time of incertitude and disorientation as Spaniards started
to contemplate their future without him. Public opinion studies
conducted at the time showed that most Spaniards wanted peace
first and foremost. However, this did not necessarily mean that
peace had to be formed in Franco's image, as it had been since the
war, or conducted among the same parameters after the Caudillo's
death. Spaniards, many of whom shared a strong anti-capitalist
bent, had a keen sense of the need to increase equality and
opportunity. They wanted more say over their future, and also to
make their politicians accountable to them. More and more, particularly among the better educated, freedom was regarded as a
right. Franco's Peace was losing ground to the hopes of the people.
However, these hopes were put at risk, or just made impossible to
achieve, precisely by the same intolerant, violent state that Franco
and his followers so vehemently wanted to preserve, even it
sometimes seemed at the cost of more blood spilled.

Franco's final, unintended tribute to freedom occurred when he
reminded Spaniards of the grim future that his regime had in store
for them after his death. One of the Caudillo's last acts was to sign
the death sentences of five militants from terrorist organizations.
In spite of pleas from relatives—some of whom appealed for
clemency as loyal Francoists—and from all over the world,

including Pope Paul VI, the dictator chose death.[85] They were executed on September 27, 1975. As a result, several countries broke off diplomatic relations with Spain. There were demonstrations against the dictatorship in several world capitals; the one in Lisbon ended with the sacking of the Spanish embassy. The fact that the huge crowd, the perennial "one million" according to the devoutly loyal newspapers, gathered at Madrid's Palacio de Oriente on October 1 to cheer for Franco (far less so for the prince standing at his side) could not hide the bitterness and deep sadness over his decision to carry on with the executions was significant among many Spaniards. Regardless of people's opinions, all saw that political killings and international isolation had returned to Spain. Very few wanted now, in the middle of a democratic and affluent Western Europe, a return to the situation of fear and isolation that Spain had experienced from 1936 until the late 1940s. The trauma of the Civil War was now working against the regime. The Caudillo's Peace was expiring along with his life, tainted once again with fresh blood.

Death

Franco's health seriously deteriorated in 1974. In July of that year, he was forced to temporarily surrender his powers to Prince Juan Carlos. The public received news of his illness with concern: for the first time in almost forty years, the Caudillo was not in command. Moreover, this happened at a difficult time, when the country was facing problems that were supposed to have been resolved in the previous good years: episodes of political violence, strikes, increasingly open political protest and dissent, growing unemployment, and spiralling inflation. In addition, neighbouring Portugal had been in turmoil since the previous April, when young army officers toppled the decades' old Estado Novo dictatorship during the "Carnation Revolution".

At the end of the summer, Franco partially recovered, promptly resuming all official roles; but the Caudillo's infirmity helped Spaniards to confront the dictator's mortality. The issue would not go away because throughout 1975 his physical and mental decline became increasingly obvious. During that year, public confusion was furthered by the well-grounded suspicion among Spaniards that Franco was dying and that they were not being informed of the extent of his condition. Only the dictator's shaking hands, caused by Parkinson's disease, as well as his increasingly slurred speech, gave the populace the first hint of the extent of Franco's deteriorating condition.

After the rally of October 1—and perhaps because of this (it had been a very cold day)—the Caudillo's health failed rapidly. There was some ambiguous news about him having the flu. Then, on October 14 he suffered a heart attack. There would be at least two, possibly three, more heart crises that month. Information continued to be scarce and rumours became more abundant, fuelled in part by news published in the foreign press since October 18. To counteract such information, the tightly controlled Spanish media were initially allowed to introduce some indirect news of Franco's condition: this or that dignitary wishing Franco a speedy recovery. Only in late October were the Spanish media allowed to fully report that the Caudillo was very sick. Soon newspapers began printing the first homages to Franco by well-known right-wing historians and public personalities from abroad, such as Brian Crozier, George Hills, the Shah of Iran, and the Chilean dictator Augusto Pinochet, among others.[86]

As if Franco's agony was not enough, Spaniards' anxieties in late October and early November were further exacerbated by a looming diplomatic crisis with Morocco over the Spanish colony of Western Sahara. Tensions ran high: military preparations were made as Morocco was threatening to invade the territory. Franco's life and his legacy of thirty-six years of "peace" almost ended with a war. Prince Don Juan Carlos went to the Western Sahara to raise the colonial army's morale. On November 6 King Hassan II of Morocco, who had already sent some troops into the territory, ordered over 350,000 Moroccan civilians to carry out what he called a "Green March" to cross the international border. The march was stopped when the Spanish Army planted minefields in front of the advancing Moroccans. War had been averted, but in the diplomatic negotiations that followed Spanish diplomats were dismayed when the United States clearly supported Morocco's annexation aims. (As a result, in 1976 Spain would withdraw from the territory, which Morocco illegally occupied in spite of the United Nations' support for the people of Western Sahara's right to self-determination. The problem continues today.)

As the Saharan crisis unfolded, the media informed Spaniards on November 3 that the Caudillo had undergone an urgent operation. He was operated on again four days later. As people suspected, Franco was suffering a long and painful agony, as he was being kept alive—only barely—by means of intrusive, and increasingly desperate, treatments. The daily reports from his doctors (560 of which were made public during the course of Franco's illness) revealed only partial truths. Foreign attention over the events unfolding in Spain was now intense: 130 foreign correspondents kept the world informed.

The imminence of Franco's death began to dawn on Spaniards on the night of November 19, when regular television programming was replaced with a World War II movie, Raoul Walsh's *Objective Burma!* (1945). The dictator was pronounced dead in the early hours of November 20, 1975. That morning, Carrero's replacement as Prime Minister, Carlos Arias Navarro, tearfully delivered the sad news to the nation, beginning with a sentence that immediately became famous: "Spaniards, Franco [a long pause] is dead." The Caudillo was two weeks short of his eighty-third birthday. Newspapermen had their headlines ready: *ABC* read "Alive in history"; *Arriba*, "With the love of his people"; *La Vanguardia*, "Spain's Pain for Franco"; *Informaciones*, "Silence". Spanish television, through an enormous human and technical undertaking, ensured that Franco's funeral, and King Juan Carlos I's coronation, were never-to-be-forgotten events.[87]

Indeed Spain's tightly controlled media provided a quite unified interpretation of the Caudillo's passing. The content of this discourse adhered closely to the latest canonical version of the dictator's life, as expressed in the second half of the 1960s. Franco was a hero, a simple man of unique virtues, who first saved Spain and then gave it peace and prosperity. Outside of the country, assessments of the dictator's legacy were diverse, but they often reproduced uncritically some of the very myths created by the regime. *The New York Times*, for example, distributed on November 20 an article under the title "Dictator ruled with iron hand but improved Spain's standard of living".[88] Another *The New York Times* headline, while critical of many aspects of Franco's personality and rule, likewise insisted that "Out of the Crucible of the Civil War, Franco's Iron Hand Forged a Modern Spain".[89] The *Christian Science Monitor* agreed: "For all his outmoded authoritarianism, General Franco was alert enough in the late 1950s and 1960s to allow a great burst of modernization of Spain."[90] Even the *Guardian* felt compelled to recognize some merit in the man, producing a headline calling him a "patriotic dictator". Perhaps to compensate, it also printed another rather acerbic article titled "Spain: the man who finally died".[91] More soberly, *The Times*, referring to the Caudillo's recently revealed political testament, spoke of "General Franco's deathbed appeal for his enemies to forgive him".[92] At the same time, some of the traditional prejudices regarding Spain, so dear to some sectors of the English-speaking press, resurfaced. The *Toronto Star*, for example, explained to its readers that:

> for more than 36 years, dour, diminutive Gen. Francisco Franco mastered the passions of a divided and volatile nation. He ruled with the soldierly virtues of strength and discipline and paid tribute to one value above all others—order in a land given to chaos.[93]

Yet, for all the foreboding and fear, for all the contempt and scepticism some sectors of the media had for the "unruly" Spanish, there were no mass killings, riots or serious disturbances then or later. Peace was possible without Franco, and for all who wanted to see, it was obvious that Spaniards felt they deserved better.

Perhaps the most intense public homage to the Caudillo in the aftermath of his death was found in an article published in *The New York Times* by John Davis Lodge, the former actor, republican politician, and American ambassador to Madrid from 1955 to 1961. Lodge first claimed that nobody could give lessons to Spain (by which he meant Franco). He then justified the recent executions before repeating the regime's standard lies about the Communist origins of the Civil War and Franco's relationship with Hitler. When giving credit to the Caudillo for the "miracle of Spain", Lodge explained how in many ways the country he departed in 1961 was superior to other countries of the West, including the USA:

> The fact that there is less drug addiction, less crime, less alcoholism, and fewer broken marriages in Spain than in the United States does not mean that the Spaniards have not in

other ways "come into the 20th century", to use an infelicitous cliché.[94]

The next day, the same newspaper published former (disgraced) President Richard Nixon's opinion of Franco:

> General Franco was a loyal friend of the United States. […] after a tragic and bloody civil war, he brought Spain back to economic recovery. He unified a divided nation through a policy of firmness and fairness toward those who had fought against him.[95]

The foreign media reflected what the world officially thought of both the Caudillo and Spain; but his death and legacy were the real and immediate concern of Spaniards. The media (newspapers, radio, and television) showed that millions of them were deeply saddened by Franco's passing. This was not mere propaganda. A previously unpublished poll taken in Madrid, Barcelona and Sevilla on November 21 reflected the public's mood. When asked what they felt upon learning of Franco's death, 49 per cent of the people interviewed (a total of 1249) felt "something similar to the loss of a loved one" and 5 per cent declared they felt "fear" for the future; however, 35 per cent found his passing "normal, given his age", and 5 per cent claimed to feel "nothing"; the rest, about 5 per cent, expressed a variety of opinions. According to this poll, it is reasonable to conclude that while a majority of Spaniards felt sympathy for the deceased dictator, the last three types of answers certainly concealed half-hidden anti-Francoist sentiments, or at the very least indifference among a significant minority.[96] In any case, by putting other feelings ahead of fear, 95 per cent of Spaniards seemed to hope that things would not turn badly after all.

Franco's body was laid in state at the old royal place, Palacio de Oriente, where his supporters had cheered for him so many times in the past, the last time just barely fifty days before. Long queues had already formed on Thursday, November 20, even if the palace was not opened until next morning at eight. Between Friday and Sunday at 8 am, hundreds of thousands of Spaniards paid their final respects to the dictator. Their numbers have been estimated at between 300,000 and 500,000.[97] According to the official propaganda machine, at one point the line-up reached a (rather hard to believe) distance of 20 kilometres.[98] Spanish television, in addition to 16 foreign channels, broadcast live, depositing in the collective memory of Spaniards some images that are difficult to forget: that of the anonymous man in worker's overalls saluting Franco's body Fascist style, refusing to move (he had to be asked several times); or that of an old man from Granada who fainted and died of a heart attack as he was saluting the dictator's body, also in the Fascist style. According to the same source, old and young, male and female, speaking accents from all parts of Spain, even traditionally marginalized groups such as gypsies, came to honour the deceased leader.[99] On November 22, King Juan Carlos I and Queen Sofia also came to view the body; it was their first official act upon coronation.

The next day, Sunday, November 23, Franco's funeral took place in the vast square before the Palacio de Oriente, presided over by the newly-crowned royal couple. Once again, hundreds of thousands of people filled the square, spilling out into the streets of Madrid. Despite whatever sympathy conservatives everywhere had for Franco, a mixture of prudence and concern for their own public images kept most heads of state from attending the Caudillo's funeral. The few who came were from countries with non-parliamentary systems: Prince Rainier of Monaco, King Hussein of Jordan, Bolivia's notorious dictator General Hugo Bánzer, and Chile's even more notorious General Augusto Pinochet, looking sinister in his military tunic. The United States, which for years had been preparing for the occasion, sent Vice President Nelson Rockefeller. Not far from him sat the First Lady of the Philippines, the extravagantly corrupt Imelda Marcos. When the funeral ended, Franco's body was taken to the Valley of the Fallen, where he was laid to rest just a few metres from the Falange's founder, José Antonio (who, by a coincidence of fate, had also died—by execution, in 1936—on November 20, like the Caudillo).

In these days of sadness for many, uncertainty for all, and relief for a significant, if hard to quantify, number of Spaniards, the propaganda machine did not cease to repeat the old myths of the Caudillo. A book hastily published in November, for example, claimed that "his popularity, the clamour of the masses around him, has been a constant reality of Franco's personal trajectory". Furthermore, since his youth, "he was called caudillo. Because it is perhaps this word that best defines Franco's career. This name was given to him, spontaneously by the generals who directed Spain's operations in Africa".[100]

Some time in the last weeks of his life, Franco had written a political testament. It was very brief and contained several spelling mistakes. He pardoned his enemies, he said, who were also Spain's enemies. Nevertheless, he warned Spaniards that the enemies of Spain and of Christian civilization were afoot. He also asked his followers to show the same loyalty to the King that they had shown him. King Juan Carlos was in many ways a mystery to ordinary Spaniards. Most were unaware, for example, that he had been discreetly corresponding with reformers within the regime, members of the opposition, and foreign representatives, most importantly from the United States. In these exchanges he expressed his intentions to initiate some form of political change. However, many opposition leaders and militants did not accept the King, since they considered his rule merely a continuation of Franco's legacy. Republicanism ran high even among many Francoists, most of them Falangists, who did not trust the monarchy. The situation was made more complex because the King had inherited a prime minister, Carlos Arias Navarro, whom he did not trust. Moreover, the Army was filled with senior generals who were staunch anti-democrats.

In late November 1975, no one knew how ordinary Spaniards would react to all of these challenges. There was a worry that old political and social grudges could re-emerge. And certainly nobody could predict how Spaniards would deal with their past and with the memory of Franco. What happened next—the re-establishment of a democratic system, made formal with the free elections of June 1977, the first since 1936—provided the context in which the answers to these questions would emerge. The arrival of democracy was accompanied by a newly-free society learning from a series of political lessons how to deal with the past. This past, of course, included a variety of traumatic memories and experiences, such as hunger, terror, and lies; but it also included more positive ones, such as peace, belated progress, and a sense of security. In any case, the process of learning about this complex history included the understanding that memory without diversity is just another form of tyranny. Within only a few years of the dictator's death, Spaniards' understanding of their country's past, and Franco's role in it, would change dramatically.

Notes

1 1962, *Informe sobre la estrategia contra el Régimen español*, AFFF 3068.
2 Francisco Franco Bahamonde, *Ante 1964. Mensaje de Franco al pueblo español*, Madrid, Ediciones del Movimiento, 1964, p. 9.
3 Ibid., p. 25.
4 Confederación Europea de Antiguos Combatientes, *Asamblea de la Confederación Europea de Antiguos Combatientes*, Madrid, Sección española en la Confederación Europea de Antiguos Combatientes, 1964, p. 13.
5 Ibid., p. 43.
6 Ibid., p. 172.
7 20-9-1963, Ministerio de Información y Turismo. Dirección General de Información, *Informe para el Consejo de los Señores Ministros sobre la conmemoración de los XXV Años de Paz*, AGA-C 38668.
8 Ibid.
9 27-11-1963 [circa], Junta interministerial para la conmemoración del XXV aniversario de la Paz española, *Conclusiones de la Comisión nombrada por la Junta para estudiar el programa de la Exposición*, AGA-C 38668.
10 3-12-1963, *Minuta del acta de la tercera reunión de la Junta interministerial para la conmemoración del XXV aniversario de la Paz española*, AGA-C 38668.
11 Ministerio de Información y Turismo, *España cumple veinticinco años de Paz*, Madrid, Edicolor, 1964.
12 6-11-1964, *Nota sobre las publicaciones conmemorativas de los XXV Años de Paz, por Higinio Paris Eguilaz*, AGA-C 38668.
13 Ministerio de Información y Turismo, *Concierto de la Paz. XXV Aniversario*, Madrid, Ministerio de Información y Turismo, 1964.
14 Ministerio de Información y Turismo, *Justas Poéticas de la Paz*, Madrid, Ministerio de Información y Turismo, 1964.
15 Rafael R. Tranche and Vicente Sánchez-Biosca, *NO-DO. El Tiempo y la Memoria*, Madrid, Cátedra, 2000, pp. 429–432.
16 Francisco Franco Bahamonde, *Ante 1965. Mensaje de Franco al pueblo español*, Madrid, Ediciones del Movimiento, 1965, p. 24.
17 Ibid., p. 11.
18 Ibid., p. 12.
19 Ibid., pp. 16, 17, 20, 21.
20 30-3-1964, *Carta de D. Juan a Franco felicitándole por los 25 años de paz*, AFFF 4242.
21 26-3-1964, *Plá y {sic} Deniels a Franco pidiendo indulto con ocasión de XXV años de paz. Respuesta de Franco*, AFFF 1472.
22 José María Sánchez-Silva, *Cartas a un niño sobre Francisco Franco*, Madrid, Foresa, 1966.
23 Juan del Espino, *La espada de Franco*, Madrid, Imprenta Europa, 1966, p. 8.
24 George Hills, *Franco: The Man and His Nation*, New York, Macmillan, 1967.
25 Brian Crozier, *Franco: A Biographical History*, London, Eyre and Spottiswoode, 1967.
26 Hills, *Franco*, pp. 97–98.

27 Ibid., p. 105.
28 Ibid., p. 124.
29 Ibid., pp. 133–135.
30 Ibid., p. 171.
31 Ibid., p. 173.
32 Ibid., p. 205–206.
33 Ibid., p. 222.
34 Ibid., p. 331.
35 Ibid., p. 338.
36 Ibid., pp. 320–366.
37 Crozier, *Franco*, p. 10.
38 Ibid., pp. 55–56.
39 Ibid., pp. 79–83.
40 Ibid., pp. 122–127.
41 Ibid., p. 149.
42 Ibid., p. 448.
43 Ibid., pp. 470–471.
44 Ibid., p. 502–511.
45 Ibid., p. 510.
46 21-12-1965, *Carlos Robles Piquer a Fraga para que consulte a Franco sobre algunas páginas conflictivas* … , AFFF 322.
47 J.W.D. Trythall, *El Caudillo. A Political Biography of Franco*, New York, MacGraw-Hill, 1970, pp. 263–267.
48 Ibid., p. 269.
49 (18–24)-12-1972, "El mensaje de la vida de Franco", *Tele Radio*, 782, s.p.; Luis Moreno Nieto, *Franco y Toledo*, Toledo, Diputación Provincial, 1972, p. 401; Cecilia Meléndez de Arvas, *¿Franco predestinado?*, Madrid, Gráficas Lux, 1975, pp. 16–21.
50 Ricardo de la Cierva, *Francisco Franco. Un siglo de España. La España de 1892*, Madrid, Editora Nacional, 1972, p. 1.
51 Ibid.
52 Jean Dumont, *Franco y los españoles*, Madrid, Círculo de Amigos de la Historia, 1975, 2 vols.; Alain Launay, with Jean Dumont, *Franco: España y los españoles*, Madrid, Círculo de Amigos de la Historia, 1975.
53 Launay, *Franco*, pp. 16–17.
54 Manuel Aznar, *Franco*, Madrid, Prensa Española, 1975, pp. 172–173.
55 Pedro Ortega Campos, *Dieciséis años del "Plan Jaén". Evaluación Social*, Jaén, Cámara de Comercio, 1973, p. 152.
56 Ibid., p. 210.
57 Ibid., p. 201.
58 20-4-1967, *Informe del Servicio del Movimiento sobre el viaje de Franco a Sevilla*, AFFF 5203.
59 20-4-1967, "La ciudad se dispone a expresar su adhesión entusiasta al salvador de España", *ABC*.
60 7-6-1967, *Información de la D.G. Prensa sobre incidentes laborales en Vizcaya y en Córdoba*, AFFF 5209.

61 Francisco Franco Bahamonde, *Ante 1971. Mensaje de Franco al pueblo español*, Madrid, Ediciones del Movimiento, 1971, p. 13.

62 Ibid., p. 23.

63 Francisco Franco Bahamonde, *Mensaje de Su Excelencia el Jefe del Estado Español en la Navidad de 1971*, Madrid, Ediciones del Movimiento, 1972, p. 8.

64 Francisco Franco Bahamonde, *Horizonte-73. Mensaje de Franco al pueblo español con motivo del nuevo año y comentarios editoriales de Prensa del Movimiento*, Madrid, Ediciones del Movimiento, 1973, p. 11.

65 7-9-1972, *Informe de Tomás Garicano, Ministro de la Gobernación, a Franco*, AFFF 3537.

66 Francisco Franco Bahamonde, *Ante 1974. Mensaje de Franco al pueblo español*, Madrid, Ediciones del Movimiento, 1975, pp. 9, 14.

67 Francisco Franco Bahamonde, *Texto del mensaje de S. E. el Jefe del Estado a los españoles al finalizar el año 1974*, Madrid, Ediciones del Movimiento, 1975, pp. 9–10, 12, 15.

68 Matilde Eiroa San Francisco, *Política Internacional y Comunicación en España (1939–1975). Las cumbres de Franco con Jefes de Estado*, Madrid, Ministerio de Asuntos Exteriores y de Cooperación, 2009, p. 367.

69 1964, *Informe del Ministerio de la Gobernación sobre separatismo catalán*, AFFF 4580.

70 1964, *Informe reservado del Ministro de la Gobernación sobre nacionalismo en Guipúzcoa y Cataluña*, AFFF 1964.

71 10-12-1962, *Informe que pasa Castiella a Franco sobre el Concilio Vaticano II*, AFFF 1146.

72 14-2-1966, *Información de la D.G. de Prensa sobre agitación clerical en Barcelona*, AFFF 4122.

73 Francisco Franco Bahamonde, *IX Consejo Nacional del Movimiento … Discursos del Ministro Secretario General del Movimiento y del Caudillo de España y Jefe Nacional del Movimiento*, Madrid, Ediciones del Movimiento, 1964, p. 27.

74 Francisco Franco Bahamonde, *Ante 1968. Mensaje de Franco al pueblo español*, Madrid, Ediciones del Movimiento, 1968, p. 18.

75 22-4-1968, Dirección General de la Guardia Civil, *Actividades de personal religioso en Almería*, AGA-Cultura (AGA-C) 564.

76 June 1973, *Radiografía urgente del episcopado español*, AGA-C 560.

77 Monseñor Guerra Campos, *Ante el 1 de Octubre. La Iglesia y Francisco Franco*, Madrid, Artes Gráficas EMA, 1971, pp. 3, 29.

78 19-10-1964, D.G. de Seguridad. Servicio de Información, *Informe sobre la situación de los distintos grupos de la oposición, y de su actitud hacia el régimen*, AFFF 19487.

79 28-4-1967, *Informe comentando el ambiente general, dentro del mundo obrero, con motivo de la conmemoración …* , AFFF 22690.

80 1968, Instituto de la Opinión Pública, *Actitudes y comportamientos políticos. Informe sobre la Encuesta realizada en torno a las Elecciones a Procuradores en Cortes por representación Familiar*, AFFF 16124.

81 Francisco Franco Bahamonde, *Acto de conmemoración del XXXVIII aniversario de la fundación de Falange Española … . Discursos*, Madrid, Ediciones del Movimiento, 1971, p. 44.

82 [Prensa del Movimiento. Gabinete de Estudios], *La Paz, patrimonio del pueblo español. Significación del 1 de abril en la obra histórica de Franco*, Madrid, Ediciones del Movimiento, 1974.

83 Ibid., p. 9.

84 Ibid., p. 57.

85 Some of the letters by the relatives can be found in Palacios, Jesús, *Las cartas de Franco. La correspondencia desconocida que marcó el destino de España*, Madrid, La Esfera de los Libros, 2005, pp. 559–565.

86 Dolores Álvarez et al., *Noticia, rumor, bulo: la muerte de Franco*, Madrid, Elías Querejeta ediciones, 1976, pp. 97–120.

87 *Los últimos días de Franco vistos en TVE*, Madrid, TVE, 1975, s.p.

88 Printed, among others, in Toronto's *The Globe and Mail*.

89 20-11-1975, "Out of the Crucible of the Civil War, Franco's Iron Hand Forged a Modern Spain", *The New York Times*.

90 21-11-1975, "What kind of king in Spain?". *The Christian Science Monitor*.

91 21-11-1975, "General Franco, the patriotic dictator", *Guardian*.

92 21-11-1975, "Franco appeal on deathbed for forgiveness by enemies", *The Times*.

93 20-11-1975, "Francisco Franco: The iron juggler of force and guile", *The Toronto Star*.

94 20-11-1975, "Looking at Spain", *The New York Times*.

95 21-11-1975, "Nixon Asserts Franco Won Respect for Spain", *The New York Times*.

96 21-11-1975, *Estudio 1.088, Sondeo sobre el fallecimiento de Su Excelencia el Jefe del Estado*, Archivo del Centro de Investigaciones Sociológicas.

97 Paul Preston, *Franco. A Biography*, London, HarperCollins, 1993, p. 779.

98 *Franco. Dolor de España*, Madrid, Publicaciones Españolas, 1975, p. 62.

99 Ibid., pp. 63–65.

100 Equipo Cinco, *Franco diferente. Diez perfiles históricos. Un álbum para el recuerdo*, Madrid, Sedmay, 1975, p. 159.

6   Memory, 1975–2012

Transitions

On June 15, 1977, just over a year and a half after Franco's death, Spaniards went to the polls. For most people it would be the first time in their lives that they would experience a free vote: the last multi-party elections had taken place in February 1936. When the results of the election were made public, it was obvious that Spaniards had voted for moderation, tolerance and progress. The party that won, with 47 per cent of the vote, the Union of the Democratic Centre (UCD), was a coalition of centrist groups led by Adolfo Suárez, the prime minister chosen by King Juan Carlos in July 1976 to replace the authoritarian, if rather hapless, Carlos Arias. In this role Suárez led the country towards democracy. The second-place party, with over 35 per cent of the vote, was the social-democratic (though formally Marxist) Partido Socialista Obrero Español (PSOE), which was led by the young reformer Felipe González. The right-wing Popular Alliance (AP), led by Manuel Fraga and still quite identified with the Franco regime, garnered barely 7.5 per cent, and the Communists (PCE) even less, only 3.5 per cent. Openly Francoist/Fascist options failed to win enough votes to be represented in parliament. Between the centre-right and the centre-left, if we count other smaller parties, nearly 90 per cent of Spaniards had opted for conciliation. They also had rejected as their future the false duality of Franco's Peace versus the scourge of Communism (even if by then the PCE was an Euro-Communist force).

The elections were thus a cornerstone in Spaniards' liberation from the fears that had engulfed political life since the Civil War.

Furthermore, many of those who voted for moderate parties had clearly come from that half of the population who, in the aftermath of Franco's death, claimed to feel sad or afraid. Astonishingly, in just a few months millions of Spaniards had changed, or at least adapted, their opinions on the dictatorship and the Caudillo. In fact, overtly pro-Francoist parties would never garner more than 3 per cent of the popular vote. Spain remains one of the very few European countries without a far-right political party in its parliament.

Electorally speaking, the centrist UCD all but imploded in October 1982, when the PSOE entered office with an absolute majority, where it stayed until 1996. Fraga's party moved to the centre and eventually rebranded itself as the Popular Party (PP), becoming Spain's main conservative force in parliament. None-theless, opinions on Franco and his regime were not as straight-forwardly negative in 1977—or afterwards—as successive election results might indicate. Many of the people who voted for democratic but conservative parties such as the UCD and the PP, and even some social-democratic voters, were and still are, albeit in different degrees, sympathetic to some aspects of the dictatorship's memory. Ambivalence was and is commonplace. For example, in 2000, twenty-five years after the Caudillo's death, Spain's official Centre for Sociological Research (CIS) published a report on the evolution of people's view of Franco and his regime. This study compared data from the years 1985, 1988, 1995 and 2000. According to the results, in 1985 18 per cent of Spaniards thought that the Francoist period was a positive one for Spain; by 2000 only 10 per cent shared this opinion. In 1985, 46 per cent thought that the Franco period had had both positive and negative aspects; the same percentage of people expressed this opinion in 2000. Finally, the number of people who had a completely negative opinion of the regime increased from 27 per cent in 1985 to 37 per cent in 2000. This means that a wide segment of the population (64 per cent in 1985 and 56 per cent in 2000) were still ready to give the dictatorship some credit for its achievements.[1] This also clearly shows that at least a portion of voters for the left share a certain ambiguity towards the Caudillo.

There are significant factors that help to explain the opinions of people who say they find both positive and negative aspects in the dictatorship. When asked to evaluate the Francoist period,

Spaniards were often also evaluating their own lives, in which obviously there had been both good and bad. Moreover, the material situation of the country during the 1960s left good memories behind, and in many senses, today's Spain is a product of this period (as it is a product of the dreadful, but more remote, 1940s). For example, the 2000 CIS study revealed that Spaniards felt that some things, such as criminality, drug abuse, terrorism, and pollution were better controlled under the dictatorship. Other things had clearly improved by 2000: the economy, the international situation, social equality, and unemployment.

However, according to this study, there was a marked difference between what people thought of the dictatorship (and of their lives under it) and of what they thought of the dictator. In 2000 the figure of the Caudillo was seen in more negative terms than his regime, reversing the tendency that existed during the entirety of the dictatorship and particularly in the late 1960s. Now, 90 per cent of people considered Franco to have been an authoritarian ruler, 76 per cent a Fascist, and 60 per cent a cruel man. Yet here, too, there was ambiguity since there were other aspects of his personality on which people agreed, and which could be considered in a positive light: most notably, 68 per cent said that Franco was a patriot, and 24 per cent an honest man. However, a small minority still felt admiration for Franco: 15 per cent described him as fair, and 14 per cent as an understanding man.[2]

In sum, twenty-five years after his death a majority of Spaniards had a negative, if somewhat contradictory, opinion of the Caudillo. This was no longer the Franco of the official propaganda machine of the late 1930s and 1940s, or the leader cheered by the masses during his tours of the 1960s, or the elder statesmen mourned by the majority of Spaniards upon his death in November 1975. The country was no longer gripped by fear, insecurity and ignorance: Spain had changed. There were two interconnected keys to this transformation in people's perception of the dictator and his legacy: one was freedom; the other was knowledge.

Freedom came rather swiftly. Both King Juan Carlos and Prime Minister Suárez were able to negotiate a number of formal and informal pacts with both the regime's elites and opposition leaders to achieve a controlled transition to democracy. This transition, however, was not merely gifted from the political elite to ordinary

Spaniards; it would have been impossible without the intertwined process of the reconstruction of civil society and the return of political and cultural diversity during the final years of the dictatorship. As part of this process, a growing number of Spaniards learned how to articulate their civil rights and political expectations, either by joining opposition groups or by engaging in social and cultural activism. Ordinary Spaniards were actors in their country's—and their own personal—transformation. They also demonstrated, in the 1977 elections to the constituent assembly, the 1978 constitutional referendum, and the general elections of 1979 and 1982, their clear support for the new democratic system, as well as for consensus politics.

Spaniards also showed their overwhelming agreement with the 1977 Amnesty Law that sought to close the wounds of the war and the dictatorship by legally erasing crimes committed by both sides. Neither economic difficulty, increasing numbers of terrorist attacks (mostly by ETA), or the threat of civil–military conspiracies to destroy the democratic system, were able to break the consensus shared by a majority of citizens that democracy was the best system to solve the country's problems. During the first years after Franco's death, democracy meant hope, peace and integration in the European Community.

However, there were moments when the people's trust in the democratic system faltered. In the late 1970s, it seemed to many Spaniards that the country's economic and political problems were not being solved because of politicking. The enemies of the democratic system believed that they could take advantage of this situation and reverse history. After some aborted conspiracies, they launched a right-wing military coup in February 1981. It failed; and it was the failure of the coup that, somewhat paradoxically, strengthened democracy as people realized what they might have lost had the plot been successful. The King's popular standing also rose, because he was credited with thwarting the coup. From being Franco's appointee, Juan Carlos I now became the defender of democracy. The renewed enthusiasm for democracy resulted in a massive victory for the PSOE in the elections held in October 1982. Under Felipe González's subsequent leadership, Spain became a full and active member of both NATO and the European Union. Spain's praetorian politics, which had affected the country since the early nineteenth century, were put definitively behind it.

While on the surface, the timeline of democratic reform, and the attainment of freedom, in Spain appears rather straightforward, the acquisition of historical knowledge remains more difficult to evaluate. That is because knowledge came from different sources, and appeared in the form of a sudden burst of information: the testimonies of Franco's collaborators, the words of elderly Spaniards who finally started talking about the past, and the publication of historical studies and novels, and movies. What all of these sources of information had in common was that they offered something new and which had been fiercely suppressed during the dictatorship: a true plurality of voices and opinions. They represented a transition from official manipulation and imposed unanimity to diversity and debate.

Immediately after Franco's death, a surprisingly large number of books appeared revealing hitherto unknown details of the deceased dictator's personality and family life. The most significant of these was the already mentioned semi-diary written by the Caudillo's cousin *Pacón*, which offered a very acerbic account of the man behind the mask of the ruler. Franco's sister Pilar, his niece (also called Pilar), his doctors, and even former husbands of his granddaughters, published some sensational, even lurid, accounts of the Caudillo's intimate circle. For example, one early scandal was provoked by the revelation that the dictator's son-in-law, the always-unpopular Cristóbal, was responsible for selling to the press a number of pictures showing Franco's long and painful agony in hospital. There were even books—one hesitates to call them "books"—claiming to have discovered that the dictator had a number children born out of wedlock, or that he was a homosexual.

Former ministers and collaborators also wrote about the Caudillo. Particularly revealing in this regard was Laureano López Rodó's 1977 book, *The Long March Towards the Monarchy*. A former minister and technocrat closely linked to Admiral Carrero, who put him in charge of the regime's development plans during the 1960s, Rodó was a deeply conservative and Catholic man (he was a member of the Opus Dei organization). Of the many valuable pieces of information found in his testimony, perhaps the most relevant were his account of Franco's stubborn resistance to political reform and his claim that the dictator procrastinated for years in the face of many important decisions. These included the reforms that were finally passed in 1959, and which paved the way for the economic boom of the 1960s and for the final myth of the Caudillo as the maker of progress.

Intellectuals also contributed to the dismantling of the myths surrounding Franco. Mere months after the dictator's death, publishers were offering books that seemed more the product of a sudden cultural revolution than of a measured political transition. For example, Spaniards with a taste for high literature could now read the open letter to Franco, originally written in 1971, by the playwright Fernando Arrabal: "I must tell you that you are the man who has harmed me the most. [Yet] I believe you suffer enormously; because only a being who suffers so much can impose so much pain around him".[3] Arrabal's father was an Army officer in North Africa in July 1936; his comrades shot him because he refused to join the rebellion (Franco never responded to Arrabal's mother's pleas to locate the remains of her husband).

Spaniards could also read the first critical, if not strictly biographical, account of Franco's life and rule by the journalist Luciano Rincón, who wrote under the pseudonym Luís Ramírez, a book first published in France in 1964. Or a more recent one, also very acerbic in its criticism of the Caudillo, by the French author Philippe Nourry. In 1976 the first critical study of Franco's popular image appeared, written by the sociologist Amando de Miguel. The following year it was the turn of Franco's script to the movie *Raza* to be dissected as a manifestation of the author's personal frustrations. In many ways, the years of Spain's transition to democracy were also a time for discovering hidden truths, imagined or real, about the Caudillo (for example, the series in which many of the above-cited books were published was called "The Secret History of Francoism").

The desire to discover the past, and to move beyond it, permeated Spanish society. For perhaps the first time in their lives ordinary people, particularly the elderly, spoke freely about their experiences under Franco; and they started to tell family, friends, journalists, and historians what they had witnessed and felt during the long years of dictatorship, and silence.[4] Arts and media figures not only responded to Spaniards' demands; they also frequently led the public in their search to understand the past. The success of newly-founded newspapers, such as *El País* or *Diario 16*, both established in 1976, provides a good example of this environment. The song that launched *El País* was called *Libertad sin ira* (Freedom Without Anger). It was sung by a group of young men and women dressed in a "progressive" way, some sporting a beard, who repeated the theme that it was possible to live in freedom without anger, in spite of what old people said. The song was rather unfair to the older generations but it nevertheless became a massive hit. Magazines that had been in existence since the 1960s, such as *Cuadernos para el Diálogo* (Notebooks for Dialogue), *Triunfo* (Triumph) and *Cambio 16*, carried articles with similarly informative and analytical content.

Many aspects of the Civil War and life under the dictatorship had long attracted the attention of novelists and filmmakers, but the image of Franco was rarely touched. A notable exception was the work of the crime novelist and essayist Manuel Vázquez Montalbán who produced, in 1978 and again 1992, two hard to classify, though nonetheless best selling, books on Franco. The first was an essay on Franco's ideas (or prejudices), the other a novel written in the voice of the dictator. Filmmakers produced at least eight movies, plus some shorts, on Franco as well. One of the best was *Caudillo.* Made clandestinely in 1975, and released only in 1977, the film employed documentary footage to reflect both the man and his times.

It was only in the 1980s when feature films focusing on the Caudillo were finally made. The best of them was probably *Dragon Rapide*, released in 1986. The film explains Franco's actions in the days before July 1936, when as military commander of the Canary Islands he pondered joining the rebellion (the title of the movie comes from the name of the plane that took Franco from the islands to Morocco). The actor who played Franco did an excellent job at portraying the dictator's cold opportunism and his hatred for the Second Republic; certainly no other movie better captures Franco's personality. The rest of the movies, produced in the 1980s and 1990s, are mostly comedies of very uneven quality, which resort to equivocal and absurd situations.

Pro-Francoist publications did not cease after the dictator's passing. During the transition to democracy, an increasingly isolated far right, which had lost control of government but still maintained a significant influence over the state apparatus, tried to fan Spaniards'

fears. The main thrust of their message was the contrast between
the stability and progress enjoyed under Franco's rule with the
growing violence, crime, and economic difficulty that the country
was now facing. It was often claimed Spain was heading for another
civil war. One author, for example, asked rhetorically whether
"during Christmas of 1976, as I write these lines, we cannot find a
disgraceful political landscape parallel to the Spanish political
drama before the war?"[5] Democracy, according to the far right,
was leading the country back to the horrors of the 1930s: corruption,
politicking, revolution, the killing of good citizens, regional
separatism, Communism—precisely those vices that, they claimed,
had been eradicated by the exceptional, "non-political", patriotic
man, the Caudillo.[6] This fear mongering often included anti-
monarchical and anti-clerical denunciations since, as sectors of the
far right maintained, both the new King and the Church had
betrayed Franco's trust. The King was hated for bringing back
democracy; for duping the Caudillo when alive and then ignoring
his testament following his death; and then for supposedly
betraying the Army during the February 1981 coup. The Church's
position was even more incomprehensible to hard-core Francoists,
given how much it suffered during the war and how much it profited
from the regime's policies. As the previously cited author rhetorically
asked: "What had moved the Church to return so much ingratitude
for Franco's forty years of generosity in not denying efforts, laws and
untaxed economic help?"[7] Betrayal and chaos were key themes
among a far right that claimed—sometimes using radical Fascist
and anti-capitalistic rhetoric—that Spain had been led again to a
state of fratricidal division. As another author put it in 1979:

> The country finds itself divided [...] as is habitual in this sad
> destiny, into two irreducible, antagonistic blocks. On the one
> hand, the lackey bourgeoisie of this neo-democratic system
> allied with the very few radical elements that composed
> the anti-Francoist opposition, and on the other, the post-
> Francoists, loyal to his memory and grateful for his good
> governance.[8]

As most Spanish conservatives, including the leading newspaper of
right-wing opinion, the monarchist *ABC*, embraced democracy,

the pro-Franco far right retreated to two fortresses from where it tried to keep the dictator's memory alive. One was the daily *El Alcázar* (which disappeared in 1987), from where the "ultras", as they were called, tried to intoxicate public opinion with anti-monarchical conspiracy theories and dark threats; the other was the Francisco Franco Foundation. The Foundation was, and still is, presided over by Franco's daughter. Following the Caudillo's death, and taking advantage of the government's tolerance, the Foundation illegally gathered the documents from the dictator's office, the so-called Franco Archive. Access to this collection was strictly prohibited for independent researchers until only recently. A far-right historian, the mediaevalist Luís Suárez, became its administrator and sole user. He published five volumes of selected documents from the early 1940s, a number of voluminous books on the dictatorship, as well as a biography of his hero. The rumour among historians was that the most important of Franco's documents were never in that collection having being spirited to safety elsewhere. There were also fears, never proven, that the archive would be purged.

The Foundation has a publishing house called *Azor*, named after the Caudillo's beloved yacht, which has been publishing books, including many by Suárez, with the objective of defending the memory and legacy of the dictator. These books are often formal and dull and they usually sell poorly. They are also often rather cranky, even for current conservative tastes. The unknown author, or authors, of a 1993 volume titled *Franco's Legacy*, claimed that if Franco's policies had been followed after his death Spain would have avoided the "destruction of family and private life", "divorce and, even […] criminal abortion"; it would also have "no drug addiction and no AIDS".[9] Much more successful were books published by commercial houses, which, particularly during the social-democrats' term in office, painted a depiction of post-Franco Spain as a country of opportunistic, careerist, and often-corrupt, politicians with a past to hide. The most relevant among these writers was the novelist-chronicler Fernando Vizcaíno Casas. His satirical books repeatedly contrasted the honesty of both private and public life under the Caudillo with the falsehoods and venality, which he claimed, reigned over democratic Spain.

Historians

Professional historians have played a fundamental role in the spread of knowledge and democratic values in post-Franco Spain. It could be argued that there are very few instances in Europe in which the profession has rendered such an important and immediate service to society. However, it was not an easy task. What Spaniards knew in 1975 about their past remained confined to what the regime's educational system had told them. Furthermore, under the regime, pro-Franco professors controlled the historical profession, and they were not particularly interested in the war, and not at all in analysing the dictatorship. Not surprisingly, what was produced on both periods was deeply biased, anecdotal at best, or both. It was thus very difficult, even for a well-read person, to learn anything with any degree of impartiality or accuracy about the Civil War, and almost impossible to construct a clear picture of the Franco regime's transformation over time.

A look at the Spanish National Library's catalogue during the late 1960s and early 1970s reinforces this image of historical ignorance and manipulation. During those years, Spaniards could consult a surprising array of topics, such as Marxism, Imperialism or social problems, but only as long as this material referred to other countries or to theoretical questions; at the same time, no books analysing post-war Spanish history were allowed, except of course, pamphlets or studies glorifying Franco and his achievements. Between 1965 and 1973, only a few books dealing with the war were published. The only general history available was Ricardo de la Cierva's 1969 *Historia de la Guerra Civil Española*. The author, as explained in the previous chapter, was both a hagiographer of the Caudillo and an employee of the Ministry of "Infomation". The only good books on Spanish history published in those years were printed abroad—either in Paris, where the anti-Francoist Spanish press Ruedo Ibérico had its offices, or in Mexico and Buenos Aires—and these works were, of course, banned in Spain. In 1967, for example, Ruedo Ibérico published the revised edition of Hugh Thomas's *La Guerra Civil Española*, which first appeared in 1962. That same year, a Mexican publisher, Grijalbo, published the first Spanish edition of Gabriel Jackson's excellent history of the Republic and the war.

The work of Thomas, Jackson and others suffered from a lack of access to Spanish archives, of which de la Cierva was the gatekeeper. It was not until 1969 that Spaniards could read a high-quality, impartial account of their history up to 1939 published inside Spain—Sir Raymond Carr's much-celebrated *España, 1808–1939*. The period studied in Carr's book ended just as the dictatorship started, but it nonetheless represented an exception to the dearth of books on the subject to be found in Spain. Though, as we have seen, Spanish society began moving in the direction of more tolerance and diversity in the 1970s, the poverty and manipulation of the available historical literature would basically last until Franco's death. Suddenly, in 1976, things changed. That year, Thomas's book was published in Barcelona. Soon there were also studies by both Spanish and foreign authors—Ángel Viñas, Hilari Raguer, Ramón Salas Larrazábal, Manuel Tuñón de Lara, Stanley Payne, Gabriel Jackson, Paul Preston—which often appeared in cheap editions. Spaniards bought these books in large numbers, even if a majority of them were not great readers.

However, while freedom and books returned to the country, Spanish historians were still largely ill-equipped to provide comprehensive answers to their fellow-citizens' questions about the past. There were two reasons for this. First, their training was still very deficient compared to that of their foreign colleagues. Under the dictatorship, an elite, traditional political history had dominated the academy. As a result, some young historians sought to acquire better techniques and approaches to social and cultural history by going abroad, most notably to Pau, in France, to participate in the workshops organized there between 1970 and 1980 by the exiled, pro-Communist Spanish historian Manuel Tuñón de Lara.

A second problem remained: the lack of archival access. Innumerable documents, most notoriously those of the police, were illegally destroyed during the transition to democracy; those that survived were badly disorganized. Others, particularly those in the hands of both the judiciary and the Army, were restricted for ideological reasons as well as a prevailing bureaucratic inertia: the guardians of these institutions, after all, had been in the habit of saying no to inquiring minds for forty years. The situation gradually improved during the 1980s and 1990s as the government, as well as the regional and local authorities, invested funds in the renovation and creation of archives. In spite of all the difficulty, during the 1980s Spanish historians were already producing high-quality narratives and were training a new, more sophisticated generation of professionals. This allowed them to publish the first accurate and impartial accounts on different aspects of the past, from the Civil War to the Franco regime's final days, which helped to disperse the mist of lies and distortions that the Caudillo's propaganda machine had tried to impose on the minds of Spaniards. Historians, for example, not only focused on one side's reign of terror; on the contrary, they analysed, rigorously and scientifically, both Nationalist and republican repression.

In the last three decades, scores of biographies of Franco have appeared. It is impossible to name them all here. However, it must be said that the one published in 1985 by Juan Pablo Fusi represented a qualitative jump. This was followed in 1992 by a similar work by Javier Tusell, and in 1993 by Paul Preston's monumental work. Soon after, the first studies on the myths surrounding Franco during the war were published. More recently, there have been studies on Franco's personality and psychological profile.

The output of high-quality biographies cannot be separated from the wider context in which historians came to provide a number of sophisticated and subtle accounts of both the war and the dictatorship. The vast majority of them agree that the dictatorship was a very negative period in Spanish history, and that Franco was a cruel ruler; but they are more divided on both the origins and the legacy of the regime. On the first issue, the main questions are related to what caused the demise of the Republic and the onset of the war. Rejecting easy explanations of good versus bad, historians have lately been focusing on the lack of democratic culture in the 1930s among republicans and their enemies alike. On the issue of the legacy of the dictatorship, the debate has revolved around the extent to which today's democratic Spain has dealt with its traumatic past. Another widely explored issue in recent years has been the scale and repercussions of political violence, and the human cost of the Civil War and the Franco years. To be sure, none of these themes—the origins of the war, the political culture of the 1930s, memory, and the effects of violence—are merely historiographical debates: on the contrary, they have wide social ramifications in today's Spain in that they affect current political identities in the country, having recently influenced a number of significant debates and polemics (which will be discussed later in this chapter).

Franco's shadow looms large over all of these discussions. Perhaps the main question that remains to be fully answered is not so much what he did and to whom—on this there is widespread agreement among both historians and the general public—but rather how it was that such an ordinary individual could instil such devotion among millions of Spaniards for so long. In this regard, historians have abandoned simplistic explanations of Franco's political supremacy, a condition that was once thought to stem mainly (or even solely) from the terror the regime imposed and the interests it defended. Instead, many are exploring the path initiated in 1996 by Paloma Aguilar's seminal work on the role of the collective memory of political violence during and after the war; a memory of which the Caudillo was both the personification and main beneficiary.

For a minority of highly conservative historians, the response to the question of Franco's relationship with society remains very different from that of Aguilar and the majority of her colleagues. Ricardo de la Cierva, for example, continues to claim that all negative things we think we know about Franco are lies. Put differently, de la Cierva claims that people loved Franco because they lived in truth and happiness under his government, while Spaniards are now subjected to the falsehoods spread by academics and politicians. Superficially less crass historians have put forward more nuanced, though equally misleading, interpretations. In 1999, at Opus Dei's University of Navarra, Professor Gonzalo Redondo published an 1143-page study of the period 1939–1947. For all the book's length, the Franco regime was not called a "dictatorship" once, Redondo preferring instead to employ the term "organic democracy". He could not find space, either, to talk about the starvation that killed close to 200,000 people in the post-war period. Among other statements, some of which could be considered hilarious if they were not so insulting, the author refers to the exiled republicans (another 300,000 people) as "bad Spaniards" who "preferred" to emigrate in 1939.[10] For Redondo, Francoism was a period of prudent reform and steady progress.

Vicente Cárcel, a historian and a priest with a long career in the Vatican, concurred with Redondo's approach. For him, Franco was a moderate ruler, who allowed for enough diversity and guaranteed the stability needed to rebuild a country shattered by war. When Cárcel describes the Francoist period he makes plain his trust in both the legality and the fairness of the institutions. The following excerpt comes from a 1995 article on the attitude of Spanish bishops facing the 1947 Succession Law referendum that gave the Caudillo a "legal" mandate to continue his dictatorial rule as regent for life. Father Cárcel said that article 12 of the *Fuero de los Españoles*—the 1945 document that supposedly granted civil and political rights that the government could take away at any moment—"established in a determining way that all Spaniards could freely express their ideas". When the *Cortes* approved the law, after lengthy and expert analysis, "the Chief of State wanted the people to give their consent".[11] According to him, the opposition had "numerous opportunities" to distribute pamphlets with "propaganda" against the law in "working class neighbourhoods and some cinemas, but this was not followed by any detentions of those [subversive] elements". Furthermore, foreign radio stations, "daily and repeatedly", told "the Spanish people to show their repulsion towards Franco by not voting"; and while the government "did its propaganda, the enemies of the regime responded through foreign radios and passing from ear to ear among disaffected elements the instruction to abstain". Nevertheless, in spite of such propaganda—and the extremely high temperatures of July 6, 1947—Spaniards "delayed their holidays and went to vote".[12] Cárcel's conclusion: the *Cortes* were representative, Franco needed and sought his people's approval, the police were very lenient, both sides had the same opportunities to express their views, foreign forces once again interfered with Spain's affairs, and—with just a hint of class bias—people had enough income to go on holidays. This was Spain in 1947, as described several decades after Franco's death, to both colleagues and young students, and this in the name of moderation.

Common values, divided memories

In the twenty-first century, because of Spaniards' embrace of democracy and a concomitant improvement in historical knowledge, the figure of the Caudillo, for a majority at least, is no longer an object of debate. The overall social consensus, albeit filled with nuances and ambivalences, remains in place: in the eyes of most Spaniards Franco was a cruel dictator. Consensus remains, as well, around the fact that both the war and the dictatorship were the ultimate disgrace for Spain. However, one matter that still divides Spaniards is whether the July 1936 rebellion was avoidable. The answer to this depends on whether one blames the left or the right, or both, for the outbreak of the Civil War. Ideology affects the present debate over the failure of democracy in 1936, who was most responsible for the human rights abuses and atrocities that followed, and, ultimately, what to do with such an atrocious past. However, behind ideological differences lies a common element: a general embrace of humanistic values on the part of present-day Spanish society. Citizens may blame one side more than the other, or both, for the coming of the war, but they feel a general repugnance for the political violence that ensued.

The last available study on the memory of both the Civil War and the dictatorship was conducted by the CIS in 2008. When asked what they felt when they thought of the war, a majority of Spaniards, 55 per cent, said "sadness"; the feeling of "indignation" followed with almost 16 per cent of respondents. At the same time just 4.9 per cent of those polled were "indifferent", only 1.3 per cent claimed to feel "patriotism", and 0.2 per cent "pride". When asked what they felt for the dictatorship, positive feelings were in a clear minority: 3.2 per cent declared "patriotism", 2.5 per cent "nostalgia", and 1.2 per cent "pride". In total, less than 7 per cent of the population expressed clearly positive feelings towards the Franco period. When asked who killed more people in the war, 30 per cent declared, rightly, the "Nationals" (Francoists), while 35 per cent said (wrongly) "both equally", and 29 per cent had no idea; only 4 per cent pointed at the "republicans", as the official memory of Francoism has maintained for decades. When asked who caused the war, close to 40 per cent blamed "both sides", close to 30 per cent the right, and less than 7 per cent the left; 23 per cent did not know.

As evidenced by the data, Spaniards have clearly established a distance from the violence of the past, even if, in order to do so, many have adopted a middle-ground position, one that does not neces-sarily reflect the historical record (three-quarters of all executions, after all, were carried out by Franco's supporters). However, when so many of them said that both sides killed equally or both were responsible for the war, in reality they meant that both sides' killings were equally wrong. This distance from the horrors of the war and the dictatorship was also reflected in the claim, supported by 83 per cent of those asked, that victims from both sides deserve recognition and that the state should pay for the identification and recuperation of their remains. Moreover, almost 80 per cent of Spaniards declared that during the Franco dictatorship basic human rights were violated, with only 3.4 per cent in disagreement; 88 per cent said that people were afraid to give their opinions freely, while just 4.3 per cent disagreed. This overwhelmingly negative view of Francoism, and a support for human rights, obviously transcends the ideological divide between right and left. And yet, 58 per cent of Spaniards (2 per cent more than in 2000) still thought that the Franco regime had both good and bad aspects, while 35 per cent completely disagreed with this statement.[13]

In sum, Spaniards may still demonstrate ambiguities in their opinions of the regime's achievements, but they have certainly turned their backs on Franco's sectarian and manipulative interpretation of the past; even more on the intolerance and violence that many observers, local and foreign alike, described as natural, or intrinsic to the Spanish character. Yet, these shared political and cultural values do not imply a single, unified memory of the past. Since the late 1990s, a number of debates, at times extremely combative ones, have raged in the Spanish press, parliament, and even among historians. The context to those debates was initially a political confrontation between, mostly, social-democrats and conservatives, that then become a sort of historic-cultural conflict. During the twilight of Felipe González's social-democratic government (1982–1996) his administration was attacked by the extreme left for being corrupt and not sufficiently socialist; but attacks from the right were even more crippling. Both the Popular Party and conservative media used populist language and techniques very similar to the ones employed by the American right to erode the political legitimacy of the ruling party. This language included a vocabulary of religious and nationalistic symbolism (enemies of the family, destroyer of Spain's unity, etc.). This lurid and politically exclusive language—which the Popular Party maintained once in power in 1996—was seen by some sectors of left as a sign that the deep structures of Francoism, both economically and culturally, had remained intact during the transition to democracy, with the result that Spain's democracy was at best incomplete, if not a sham. These increasingly nasty political debates coincided with the new phenomenon regarding Historical Memory.

In the late 1990s, some of the relatives of missing victims of the Civil War and the dictatorship, relying on the knowledge provided by professional historians in the previous decades, started to ask where the remains of their loved ones were buried. They created associations for the recovery of Historical Memory. The international context provided inspiration, as this decade witnessed the establishment of several "Truth and Reconciliation Commissions" in newly-democratic countries that had experienced mass political crimes, such as Argentina, Chile, Guatemala, El Salvador, and South Africa. The mandate for these commissions often included discovering the fate of the victims and, sometimes, the exhumation of their bodies. Nothing like that had happened in post-Franco Spain, among other reasons because when the transition took place these types of commissions did not yet exist. This absence was used by some associations for the recovery of Historical Memory, groups of relatives, and by radical left-wing organizations to question whether the post-Franco governments in particular, and Spanish society in general, had any desire to deal with the unpleasant aspects of the past. The accusation was summarized in the claim that the political transition to democracy had implied a cynical or at least opportunist "pact to forget" and an immoral pardon of pro-Franco killers. This accusation ignored the work of historians and others to in carrying out accurate research on the past and the policies carried out by the different governments to compensate the victims of the dictatorship. Nonetheless, the critics had two unassailable points: no right-wing killer had ever been prosecuted, and tens of thousands of their victims were still unaccounted for.

The conservative José María Aznar government's (1996–2004) neo-nationalistic rhetoric lent credibility to the claims by the first associations for the recovery of Historical Memory. As the economy boomed in the late 1990s, Premier Aznar often said that things in Spain were "going well". The Memory associations did not question this, but they pointed out that under the soil of such a successful country remained the unidentified bodies of those murdered by Franco and his followers. With no public funding, except for some support offered by some left-wing mayors, they started to locate mass graves. The year 2000 proved to be a turning point, for two reasons. The associations for the recovery of Historical Memory merged into a national lobby group (*Asociación para la Recuperación de la Memoria Histórica*), and the first mass grave was opened. Victims' relatives, activists, volunteers, historians, anthropologists, and DNA specialists, among others, worked together in the excavation projects. The movement was now funded in some instances by provincial left-wing administrations. With public money coming, the opening of mass graves gained momentum, reaching a climax in 2009, right at the onset of the deep economic recession. That year some 43 mass graves containing the remains of 3239 individuals were unearthed. In spite of these efforts, the total number of people still missing is probably near 110,000. In the meantime, conservative administrations generally remained either indifferent or hostile to the opening of mass graves. Some argued that this was a re-opening of the wounds of the Civil War, which they claimed had healed after the transition to democracy. To this, activists responded that the only victims who were placed in cemeteries or were honoured by the state had been those of the right, and that all victims deserved the same treatment.

Having started as a small-scale grass roots movement, the issue of Historical Memory became a significant cultural and social phenomenon under the administration of the social-democrat José Luís Rodríguez Zapatero (2004–2011). Rodríguez Zapatero wholly supported the Historical Memory movement, with parliament declaring 2006 the "Year of Historical Memory". A commission was created to suggest changes that would attune public policies to new political and cultural sensitivities. At the end of 2007 a law (commonly but inaccurately) known as the Historical Memory Law was approved by parliament. This law guaranteed compensation to all victims of the war. It also required all public buildings to be cleared of any symbols that unilaterally exalted only one of the two sides in the war, or the Franco regime. More controversial was the ability granted to the relatives of the victims to apply for their pardon. As many have pointed out, these people had done nothing wrong: they had simply been victimised. The issue of the fate of the Valley of the Fallen, and of Franco's tomb, remained unresolved pending a special commission's careful study of this matter. However, all this time large parts of the right-wing media made it very clear that they were not happy with Zapatero's policies, denouncing both the law and the government as being partial and vengeful (Zapatero's grandfather, a police officer, was shot by the Francoists). There was more than a little posturing and politicking at play here: when the Popular Party formed a government after winning the November 2011 election, it did not scrap the Historical Memory Law.

At the same time that the Historical Memory movement was developing, a curious cultural and editorial phenomenon became obvious. Conservative opinion in Spain often considers professional historians to be mostly biased left-wingers, and claims that they have failed to give a balanced account of the war and the dictatorship. The fact that historians have devoted so much attention to the revelation of hidden truths and the debunking of Francoist myths and falsehoods may explain at least part of this criticism. In any case, in the late 1990s and early 2000s a number of conservative journalists and popular historians discovered that there was a sector of the public ready to buy books that, written in a light but polemic style, were sympathetic to Franco and highly hostile to traditional left-wing accounts of the past. The most well known among this group is Pío Moa, a former left-wing militant and convicted terrorist who later embraced populist and libertarian ideas, and who is highly critical of both the democratic system and left-wing parties. In 1999 he published a book that blamed the left for the war. This book became a best seller, perhaps helped by a long interview with the author on prime-time state television news (public television in Spain has a notorious and well-deserved reputation for catering to the interests of the party in power, in this case the conservatives). Similar books followed, each time making bolder claims. For example, in a 2005 publication Moa offered the following historical assessment of Franco: "Reality showed that there was no alternative to his rule" and "all accusations against him had to be put in the context of the times". His main achievements are: "(a) Franco defeated revolution three times [the last time in 1936]; (b) Spared Spain from World War II […]; (c) Left a prosperous, and even more important, politically moderate, country where the exaltations of the past were left behind. Thanks to this, it has been possible to have thirty years of democracy".[14] What is interesting about this book is not that it repeats so many of the old clichés, discredited by most historians, about the risk of revolution in 1936 or the role of Franco in World War II, but the third point: this pro-Franco author defends the Caudillo not for his Fascist/authoritarian ideas but for the opposite, for his contribution to democracy. In twenty-first century Spain, even apologists for Franco are, more often than not, defenders of democracy, regardless of whom they blame for the ills of the past. The Caudillo would not have been amused.

Unlike their forebears who went (or rather were led) to war in 1936, today most Spaniards embrace tolerance and liberty. However, their vision of the past, or if the reader prefers, their Historical Memory, continues to be contentious, and fractures have surfaced repeatedly. A good example of these not very hidden cleavages exploded in the press the year after Moa's 2005 apology for Franco was printed. On the morning of July 17, 2006, readers of *El País*, Spain's leading liberal newspaper, saw an unusually large (half page) death notice in the paper. Dated in Caracas, Venezuela, it was signed by the exiled daughter of an Army officer, Captain Virgilio Leret Ruiz. The author's intention was to recall the memory of her father. Leret, the commanding officer of the seaplane base at Melilla, in North Africa, had, along with two of his junior officers, remained loyal to the Republic in July 1936, and as a result their rebel comrades shot them. Melilla was the place where the rebellion started and these three men are considered to be among the first officers killed in the war. Leret's daughter, Carlota, wrote in the death notice that her father's body had yet to be found, and that his killers had not been punished. It was the beginning of that summer's short, intense and bitter "death notices war". Soon, other death notices for both republican and Francoist victims of the war appeared. The latter were published in right-leaning newspapers, such as *ABC*, *El Mundo* and *La Razón*, and they sometimes recycled the same old language ("Marxist hordes", "Chekists", etc.) once employed by the Francoist propaganda against the republicans. The family of Pablo Ruiz, for example, wrote he was killed in December 1936, aged 33, by the "red hordes" and asked for a prayer "for his soul and for Spain". However, not everyone employed the same confrontational language, and there were many nuances in their reasoning. Carmen Bonell, then an 85-year-old pensioner, paid for a death notice in *El Mundo* remembering her uncle, Father Jesús María Arroyo, killed in Madrid either on 19 or 20 September 1936 by left-wing militiamen, and whose body also remains missing. She asked for prayers "for all victims" but complained that all this pain was "now being unnecessarily remembered".[15] The polemic fizzled out over the following months, but Captain Leret's death notice continues to appear every July 17 in *El País*. This and other cases show that hundreds of thousands of Spaniards, from both sides of the Civil War, still feel pain for the terrible fate of their family members. Most Spaniards sympathize with them. But the personal opinions of the victims' relatives or their language are not necessarily shared by a majority.

One of the last initiatives of the Zapatero government before leaving office was to create a commission dealing with the future of the Valley of the Fallen, the monument that best represents the Caudillo's manipulation of the past and his appropriation, for his own political gains, of Spaniards' collective suffering. The commission recommended that Franco's body should be removed and, possibly in agreement with his family, buried elsewhere. It also proposed that the Valley should become a site of memory, a place where all Spaniards could remember their tragic past. However, both the unfolding economic crisis and the arrival of the new conservative government of Mariano Rajoy in late 2011 paralyzed those plans. The Valley is still open to the public, and it remains one of the most visited monuments in Spain. However, the majority of the people who go there are not Franco supporters; they are just ordinary citizens of a free country. Many are historical tourists— a task that can turn out to be rather frustrating, as there is scant information in the monument explaining the meaning of the stones, or of the memory of the people buried there. No guidebooks, plaques or guides are available to tell the visitor much of substance about the origins of the Valley or the horrors that it so consciously misrepresents. People avoid visiting the Valley on November 20, the anniversary of Franco's death, when a not very large crowd of the Caudillo's admirers gather there to honour their hero, whose body remains undisturbed to this day under the basilica's altar.

Notes

1 Félix Moral, *Opiniones y actitudes, 36, Veinticinco años después. La memoria del franquismo y de la transición en los españoles del año 2000*, Madrid, CIS, 2000, p. 12.
2 Ibid., p. 16
3 Fernando Arrabal, *Carta al general Franco*, París, Babilonia, 1976, p. 7.
4 See, for example, Ronald Fraser, *Blood of Spain: an Oral History of the Spanish Civil War*, New York, Pantheon, 1979.
5 Juan Alarcón Benito, *Resumen político de la Paz de Franco (1 de abril 1939–20 de noviembre 1975)*, Madrid, Vassallo de Numbert, 1977, p. 13
6 Ibid., pp. 14–16.
7 Ibid., p. 19.
8 José María Fontana, *Franco. Radiografía de un personaje para sus contemporáneos*, Barcelona, Ediciones Acervo, 1979, p. 8.
9 Fundación Nacional Francisco Franco, *El legado de Franco*, Madrid, Azor, 1993, p. 749.
10 Gonzalo Redondo, *Política, cultura y sociedad en la España de Franco, 1939–1975. Tomo I; La configuración del Estado español, nacional y católico (1939–1947)*, Pamplona, Ediciones de la Universidad de Navarra, 1999, pp. 87–88.
11 Vicente Cárcel Ortí, "Los obispos españoles tras la segunda Guerra Mundial: actitud ante el referéndum de 1945", *Anuario de Historia de la Iglesia*, 4 (1995): 39–77 (42).
12 Ibid., 43.
13 Centro de Investigaciones Sociológicas, *Estudio 2760 (April 2008), Memoria de la Guerra Civil y el franquismo*, Madrid, CIS, 2008, pp. 6, 13, 14, 16, 18.
14 Pío Moa, *Franco. Un balance histórico*, Barcelona, Planeta, 2005, pp. 188–189.
15 3-11-2006, "La Guerra civil de esquelas se dispara", *El Mundo*, digital edition, http://www.elmundo.es/suplementos/cronica/2006/566/1157234403.html

Bibliography

Acción Católica, *Los problemas sociales del campo andaluz*, Madrid, Acción Católica, 1953.

Actas de las Jornadas de Cultura Árabe e Islámica, Madrid, Instituto Hispano-Árabe de Cultura, 1981.

Adams, Mildred, "Twenty Years of Franco", *Foreign Affairs*, vol. 37, no. 2 (Jan. 1959): 257–268.

Aguilar Fernández, Paloma, *Memoria y olvido de la Guerra Civil española*, Madrid, Alianza Editorial, 1996.

Alarcón Benito, Juan, *Resumen político de la Paz de Franco (1 de abril 1939–20 de noviembre 1975)*, Madrid, Vassallo de Numbert, 1977.

Alcázar de Velasco, Ángel, *José Antonio, hacia el sepulcro de la fe*, Burgos, Cóndor, 1939.

Aldagate, Anthony, *Cinema and History. British Newsreels and the Spanish Civil War*, London, Scolar Press, 1979.

Alonso Baquer, Miguel, *Franco y sus generales*, Madrid, Taurus, 2005.

Alonso Ibáñez, Ana Isabel, *Las juntas de defensa militares (1917–1922)*, Madrid, Ministerio de Defensa, 2004.

Alper, Michael, *La Guerra Civil española en el mar*, Barcelona, Crítica, 2008.

Álvarez, Dolores, *Noticia, rumor, bulo: la muerte de Franco*, Madrid, Elías Querejeta ediciones, 1976.

Álvarez Junco, José, *El Emperador del Paralelo: Lerroux y la demagogia populista*, Madrid, Alianza, 1990.

Angosto Veléz, Predro Luis, *Alfonso XIII: un rey contra el pueblo: raíces de la Guerra Civil; una mirada a través de El Socialista*, Sevilla, Biblioteca Histórica, 2005.

Aróstegui, Julio, *Por qué el 18 de Julio ... y después*, Barcelona, Flor del viento, 2006.

Arrabal, Fernando, *Carta al general Franco*, París, Babilonia, 1976.

Arrarás, Joaquín, *Franco*, San Sebastián, Librería Internacional, 1937.

Arrarás, Joaquín, *Franco*, Burgos, Imprenta Aldecoa, 1938. Sixth edition.

Arrarás, Joaquín, *Historia de la Cruzada Española*, Madrid, Editora Nacional, 1939–1943, 8 vols.

Arrarás, Joaquín, *Memorias íntimas de Azaña (con ilustraciones de Kin)*, Madrid, Ediciones Españolas, 1939.

Artigas Arpón, Benito, *La epopeya de Alhucemas (Los alicates rotos)*, Madrid, J. Pérez Impresor, 1925.

Ashford Hodges, Gabrielle, *Franco: a Concise Biography*, London, Weidenfeld and Nicholson, 2000.

Así quiero ser (El niño en el Nuevo Estado), Burgos, Hijos de Santiago Rodríguez, 1940.

Atholl, Duchess of, *Searchlight on Spain*, Harmondsworth, Penguin, 1938.

Aznar, Manuel, *Franco*, Madrid, Prensa Española, 1975.

Bachoud, Andrée, *Los españoles ante las campañas de Marruecos*, Madrid, Espasa Calpe, 1988.

Bahamonde, Ángel and Cervera, Javier, *Así terminó la Guerra Civil*, Madrid, Marcial Pons, 2000.

Balfour, Sebastian, *Deadly Embrace. Morocco and the Road to the Spanish Civil War*, Oxford, Clarendon, 2002.

Balfour, Sebastian, *The End of the Spanish Empire*, Oxford, Clarendon Press, 1997.

Balfour, Sebastian and Preston, Paul (eds), *Spain and the Great Powers in the Twentieth Century*, London, Routledge-Cañada Blanch, 1999.

Bayod, Ángel (coord.), *Franco visto por sus ministros*, Barcelona, Planeta, 1981.

Ben Ami, Shlomó, *Fascism from Above: The Dictatorship of Primo de Rivera in Spain*, Oxford, Clarendon, 1983.

Bernanos, Georges, *Les grands cimetières sous la lune*, Paris, Plon, 1938.

Berthier, Nancy, *Le franquisme et son image. Cinéma et progagande*, Toulouse, Presses Universitaires du Mirail, 1998.

Blanco Escolá, Carlos, *La incompetencia militar de Franco*, Madrid, Alianza, 2000.

Bolín, Luis, *Spain: The Vital Years*, London, Cassell, 1967.

Box, Zira, *Espana, año cero. La construcción simbólica del franquismo*, Madrid, Alianza, 2010.

Boyd, Carolyn P., *Historia Patria. Politics, History, and National Identity in Spain, 1875–1975*, Princeton, Princeton University Press, 1997.

Brenan, Gerald, *The Spanish Labyrinth: an Account of the Social and Political Background of the Civil War*, Cambridge, Cambridge University Press, 1943.

Buchanan, Tom, *Britain and the Spanish Civil War*, Cambridge, Cambridge University Press, 1977.

Buchanan, Tom, *The Impact of the Spanish Civil War on Britain. War, Loss and Memory*, Brighton, Sussex Academic Press, 2007.

Buchanan, William and Cantril, Hadley, *How Nations See Each Other. A Study in Public Opinion*, Westport, Greenwood Press, 1953. Edition 1973.

Buffet, Cyril and Heuser, Beatrice (eds), *Haunted by History. Myths in International Relations*, Providence-Oxford, Berghahn Books, 1998.

Byrnes, Mark, "Unfinished Business: the United States and Franco's Spain, 1944–47", *Diplomacy & Statecraft*, 1 (March 2000): 129–162.

Cabanillas, Alfredo, *La epopeya del soldado*, Madrid, Imprenta Clásica Española, 1922.

Calle Velasco, María Dolores de la, "El Primero de Mayo y su transformación en San José Artesano", *Ayer*, 51 (2003): 87–113.

Canellas Romero, Juan, *El desembarco de Alhucemas. Crónicas periodísticas de Juan Luque, Diario de Barcelona, 1925*, Melilla, Comunidad Autónoma, 2007.

Cárcel Ortí, Vicente, "Los obispos españoles tras la segunda Guerra Mundial: actitud ante el referéndum de 1945", *Anuario de Historia de la Iglesia*, 4 (1995): 39–77.

Cardozo, Harold, *The March of a Nation*, London, The Right Book Club, 1937.

Carr, Raymond, *España, 1808–1939*, Barcelona, Ariel, 1969.

Carretero, José María [Caballero Audaz], *El general Sanjurjo*, Madrid, Ed. ECA, 1940.

Carretero, José María [Caballero Audaz], *Sanjurjo, Caudillo y víctima*, Madrid, Imp. Sáez Hernández, 1932.

Casares, Francisco, *Azaña y ellos. Cincuenta semblanzas rojas*, Granada, Prieto, 1938.

Cazorla Sánchez, Antonio, "Beyond They Shall Not Pass. How the Experience of Violence Reshaped Political Values in Franco's Spain", *Journal of Contemporary History*, 40, 3 (2005): 503–520.

Cazorla Sánchez, Antonio (ed.), *Cartas a Franco de los españoles de a pie*, Barcelona, RBA, 2013.

Cazorla Sánchez, Antonio, *Desarrollo sin reformistas. Dictadura y campesinado en el nacimiento de una nueva sociedad en Almería, 1939–1975*, Almería, IEA, 2000.

Cazorla Sánchez, Antonio, *Fear and Progress: Ordinary Lives in Franco's Spain, 1939–1975*, Oxford, Wiley-Blackwell, 2010.

Cazorla Sánchez, Antonio, *Las políticas de la Victoria: la consolidación del Nuevo Estado franquista (1938–1953)*, Madrid, Marcial Pons, 2000.

Cazorla Sánchez, Antonio, "Revisiting the Legacy of the Spanish Civil War", *International Journal of Iberian Studies*, 21, 3, 2008: 231–246.

Centro de Investigaciones Sociológicas, *Estudio 2760 (April 2008), Memoria de la Guerra Civil y el franquismo*, Madrid, CIS, 2008.

Cierva, Ricardo de la, *Francisco Franco. Un siglo de España. La España de 1892*, Madrid, Editora Nacional, 1972–1973, 2 vols.

Cierva, Ricardo de la, *Franco. La Historia. Después de la venganza, la mentira, la calumnia y la incompetencia*, Madrid, Editorial Fénix, 2000.

Cierva, Ricardo de la, *Historia de la Guerra Civil Española*, Madrid, San Martín, 1969.

Code, Joseph B., review of "Francisco Franco by Joaquin Arrarás; translated by J. Manuel Espinosa", *The Catholic Historical Review*, 24, 2 (Jul. 1938): 203.

Confederación Europea de Antiguos Combatientes, *Asamblea de la Confederación Europea de Antiguos Combatientes*, Madrid, Sección española en la Confederación Europea de Antiguos Combatientes, 1964.

Corona de Sonetos en honor de José Antonio Primo de Rivera, Barcelona, Edic. Jerarquía, 1939.

Costa Pinto, Antònio (ed.), *Ruling Elites and Decision-Making in Fascist-Era Dictatorships*, New York, SM-Columbia University Press, 2009.

Cox, Geoffrey, *Defense of Madrid*, London, Gollancz, 1937.

Crozier, Brian, *Franco: A Biographical History*, London, Eyre and Spottiswoode, 1967.

Cruz Martínez, Rafael, *En el nombre del pueblo. República, rebelión y guerra en la España de 1936*, Madrid, Siglo XXI, 2006.

Deacon, David, *British News Media and the Spanish Civil War: Tomorrow May Be Too Late*, Edinburgh, Edinburgh University Press, 2008.

Department of State, *Foreign Relations of the United States (FRUS)*, Washington, US Government Printing Office, 1946–1975.

Díaz Fernández, José, *Crónicas de la Guerra de Marruecos (1921–1922). Antología*, Gijón, Ateneo Obrero, 2004.

Dolor y memoria de España: En el segundo aniversario de la muerte de Jose Antonio, Barcelona, Ediciones Jerarquía, 1939.

Domínguez Arribas, Javier, "L'organisation de la presse et de la propagande dans la Espagne rebelle (1936–1939)", *El Argonauta Español*, 7 (2010) [electronic document].

Dumont, Jean, *Franco y los españoles*, Madrid, Círculo de Amigos de la Historia, 1975, 2 vols.

Echeandía, José, *La persecución roja en el País Vasco*, Fidel Rodríguez, Barcelona, 1945.

Edwards, Jill, *Anglo-American Relations and the Franco Question, 1945–1955*, New York, Clarendon Press, 1999.

Eiroa San Francisco, Matilde, *Política Internacional y Comunicación en España (1939–1975). Las cumbres de Franco con Jefes de Estado*, Madrid, Ministerio de Asuntos Exteriores y de Cooperación, 2009.

Emilio-Díez, José, *General Franco. Sus escritos y palabras*, Sevilla, Tip. M. Carmona, 1937.

Equipo Cinco, *Franco diferente. Diez perfiles históricos. Un álbum para el recuerdo*, Madrid, Sedmay, 1975.

España en sus Héroes. Historia Bélica del siglo XX, n. 14, Madrid, Ornigraph, 1969.

Espino, Juan del, *La espada de Franco*, Madrid, Imprenta Europa, 1966.

Espinosa Maestre, Francisco, *La columna de la muerte. El avance del ejército franquista de Sevilla a Badajoz*, Barcelona, Crítica, 2003.

Feis, Herbert, *The Spanish Story*, New York, Alfred A. Knopf, 1948.

Fernández Bastarreche, Fernando, *El Ejército Español en el siglo XIX*, Madrid, Siglo XXI, 1978.

Fernández Duro, Enrique, *Franco: una biografía psicológica*, Madrid, Temas de Hoy, 2000.

Fernández-Oxea, José Ramón [Ben-Cho-Shey], *Crónicas de Marruecos*, Ronsel, Santiago de Compostela, 1985.

Ferrer Guasp, Pere, *Juan March: el hombre más misterioso del mundo*, Barcelona, Ediciones B, 2008.

Fontana, José María, *Franco. Radiografía de un personaje para sus contemporáneos*, Barcelona, Ediciones Acervo, 1979.

Foss, William and Geraghty, Cecil, *Spanish Arena*, London, The Right Book Club, 1938.

Franco Bahamonde, Francisco, *Acto de conmemoración del XXXVIII aniversario de la fundación de Falange Española … . Discursos*, Madrid, Ediciones del Movimiento, 1971.

Franco Bahamonde, Francisco, *Alto de los Leones de Castilla. Concentración regional de excombatientes de las Dos Castillas*, Valladolid, Gerper, 1952.

Franco Bahamonde, Francisco, *Ante 1962. Mensaje de Franco al pueblo español*, Madrid, Ediciones del Movimiento, 1962.

Franco Bahamonde, Francisco, *Ante 1964. Mensaje de Franco al pueblo español*, Madrid, Ediciones del Movimiento, 1964.

Franco Bahamonde, Francisco, *Ante 1965. Mensaje de Franco al pueblo español*, Madrid, Ediciones del Movimiento, 1965.

Franco Bahamonde, Francisco, *Ante 1968. Mensaje de Franco al pueblo español*, Madrid, Ediciones del Movimiento, 1968.

Franco Bahamonde, Francisco, *Ante 1970. Mensaje de Franco al pueblo español*, Madrid, Ediciones del Movimiento, 1970.

Franco Bahamonde, Francisco, *Ante 1971. Mensaje de Franco al pueblo español*, Madrid, Ediciones del Movimiento, 1971.

Franco Bahamonde, Francisco, *Ante 1974. Mensaje de Franco al pueblo español*, Madrid, Ediciones del Movimiento, 1975.

Franco Bahamonde, Francisco, *The Caudillo's speech at the opening of the Spanish "Cortes"*, Madrid, Ediciones de la Vicesecretaría de Educación Popular, 1943.

Franco Bahamonde, Francisco, *Declaraciones de Franco a un periodista español*, Madrid, Publicaciones Españolas, 1946.

Franco Bahamonde, Francisco, *Declaraciones de S. E. El Jefe del Estado al "Sunday Times"*, Madrid, Publicaciones Españolas, 1947.

Franco Bahamonde, Francisco, *Declaraciones de su Excelencia el jefe del estado Español al periódico Norteamericano "The Evening Star"*, Madrid, Publicaciones Españolas, 1947.

Franco Bahamonde, Francisco, *Discurso de apertura de la VII etapa legislativa de las Cortes Españolas*, Madrid, Imprenta BOE, 1961.

Franco Bahamonde, Francisco, *Discurso de Franco en la Fiesta de la Unificación, 19 de abril de 1938*, Granada, Delegación Provincial de Prensa y Propaganda de FET de las JONS, 1938.

Franco Bahamonde, Francisco, *Discurso del Caudillo ante el III Consejo Nacional*, Madrid, Art. Graf. Larra, 1942.

Franco Bahamonde, Francisco, *Discurso pronunciado por S. E. el Jefe del Estado ante las Cortes Españolas al inaugurar la VI Legislatura y Promulgación de los Principios del Movimiento Nacional*, Madrid, Publicaciones Españolas, 1958.

Franco Bahamonde, Francisco, *Discursos y mensajes del Jefe del Estado, 1951–1954*, Madrid, Publicaciones Españolas, 1955

Franco Bahamonde, Francisco, *El Caudillo dice ... Discurso del Jefe del Estado en la inauguración de las Cortes Españolas. Año 1949*, Madrid, Hidalgo, 1949.

Franco Bahamonde, Francisco, *El Caudillo habla en Vizcaya*, Bilbao, Escuela Gráfica de la Santa Casa de Misericordia, 1950.

Franco Bahamonde, Francisco, *Habla el Caudillo*, Madrid, Editora Nacional, 1939.

Franco Bahamonde, Francisco, *Horizonte-73. Mensaje de Franco al pueblo español con motivo del nuevo año y comentarios editoriales de Prensa del Movimiento*, Madrid, Ediciones del Movimiento, 1973.

Franco Bahamonde, Francisco, *IX Consejo Nacional del Movimiento ... Discursos del Ministro Secretario General del Movimiento y del Caudillo de España y Jefe Nacional del Movimiento*, Madrid, Ediciones del Movimiento, 1964.

Franco Bahamonde, Francisco, *Marruecos. Diario de una bandera*, Madrid, Puedo, 1922.

Franco Bahamonde, Francisco [Jakin Boor], *Masonería. El libro secreto*, Barcelona, Ojeda, 2003. First edition 1952.

Franco Bahamonde, Francisco, *Mensaje de S.E. El Jefe del Estado a los españoles*, Madrid, Publicaciones Españolas, 1949.

Franco Bahamonde, Francisco, *Mensaje de Su Excelencia el Jefe del Estado Español en la Navidad de 1969*, Madrid, Ediciones del Movimiento, 1969.

Franco Bahamonde, Francisco, *Mensaje de Su Excelencia el Jefe del Estado Español en la Navidad de 1971*, Madrid, Ediciones del Movimiento, 1972.

Franco Bahamonde, Francisco, *Palabras del Caudillo 19 abril 1937–31 diciembre 1938*, Barcelona, Ediciones Fe, 1939.

Franco Bahamonde, Francisco, *Papeles de la Guerra de Marruecos*, Madrid, Fundación Nacional Francisco Franco, 1986.

Franco Bahamonde, Francisco *Pensamientos políticos de Francisco Franco*, Madrid, Delegación Nacional de Sindicatos, 1954.

Franco Bahamonde, Francisco [Jaime de Andrade], *Raza*, Barcelona, Planeta, 1997.

Franco Bahamonde, Francisco, *Texto del mensaje de S. E. el Jefe del Estado a los españoles al finalizar el año 1974*, Madrid, Ediciones del Movimiento, 1975.

Franco Bahamonde, Pilar, *Nosotros los Franco*, Barcelona, Planeta, 1980.

Franco Salgado-Araujo, Francisco, *Mis conversaciones privadas con Franco*, Barcelona, Planeta, 1976.

Franco. Dolor de España, Madrid, Publicaciones Españolas, 1975.

Fraser, Ronald, *Blood of Spain: an Oral History of the Spanish Civil War*, New York, Pantheon, 1979.

Fundación Nacional Francisco Franco, *Documentos Inéditos para una Historia del Generalísimo Franco*, Madrid, Azor, 1992–1994, 5 vols.

Fundación Nacional Francisco Franco, *El legado de Franco*, Madrid, Azor, 1993.

Fusi, Juan Pablo, *Franco: a Biography*, London/Sydney, U. Hyman, 1987.

Galinsoga, Luis de, with Franco Salgado, Teniente General, *Centinela de Occidente (Semblanza Biográfica de Francisco Franco)*, Barcelona, AHR, 1956.

Gallup, George H., *The Gallup Poll. Public Opinion 1935–1971. Volume One, 1935–1948*, New York, Random House, 1972.

Gamo Ortega, Pedro, *Coronas de laurel. a José Antonio, a España, mi Patria*, s.l., s.n., 1939.

García, Hugo, *The Truth about Spain! Mobilizing British Public Opinion, 1936–1939*, Brighton, Sussex Academic Press, 2010.

García, P., *Los chistes de Franco*, Madrid, Ediciones 99, 1977.

Garrido Bonaño, Manuel, O.S.B., *Francisco Franco. Cristiano ejemplar*, Madrid, Azor, 1985.

Giménez Caballero, Ernesto, *España y Franco*, s.l., Ediciones Los Combatientes, 1938 Moure-Mariño, Luis, *Perfil Humano de Franco*, s.l., Ediciones Libertad, 1938.

Giménez-Arnau, Joaquín, *Yo, Jimmy. Mi vida entre los Franco*, Barcelona, Planeta, 1981.

Gironella, José María, *100 españoles y Franco*, Barcelona, Planeta, 1979.

Goded, General, *Marruecos. Las etapas de la pacificación*, Madrid-Barcelona-Buenos Aires, Compañía Ibero-Americana de Publicaciones, 1932.

Goy de Silva, Ramón, *Borrón y cuenta nueva. Crónicas de Marruecos*, Alcoy, Imprenta de E. Insa, 1923.

Graham, Helen, *The Spanish Republic at War, 1936–1939*, Cambridge, Cambridge University Press, 2002.

Griffiths, Richard, *Patriotism Perverted: Captain Ramsay, the Right Club and British Anti-Semitism 1939–40*, London, Constable, 1998.

Gubern, Román, *Raza (Un ensueño del General Franco)*, Madrid, Ediciones 99, 1977.

Guerra Campos, Monseñor, *Ante el 1 de Octubre. La Iglesia y Francisco Franco*, Madrid, Artes Gráficas EMA, 1971.

Halcón, Manuel, *José Antonio (3 evocaciones)*, Madrid, Sucesores de Rivadeneyra, 1940.

Herce Vales, Fernando and Sanz Nogués, Manuel, *Franco el Reconquistador*, Madrid, Ediciones Sanz Nogués, 1938.

Hills, George, *Franco: The Man and His Nation*, New York, Macmillan, 1967.

Intituto Nacional de Industria, Secretaría del Plan Badajoz, *El Plan Badajoz*, Madrid, E. Casado, 1958.

Israel Garzón, Jacobo, "El Archivo Judaico del Franquismo", *Raíces*, 33 (1997): 57–60.

Jackson, Gabriel, *La República española y la Guerra Civil, 1931–1939*, México, Grijalbo, 1967.

Jaráiz Franco, Pilar, *Historia de una disidencia*, Barcelona, Planeta, 1981.

Jefatura del Movimiento de Melilla, *Veinte años de Paz en el Movimiento Nacional bajo el Mando de Franco*, Melilla, Jefatura del Movimiento, 1959.

Jefatura Provincial del Movimiento de Albacete, *Veinte años de Paz en el Movimiento Nacional bajo el Mando de Franco*, Albacete, Jefatura Provincial del Movimiento, 1959.

Jefatura Provincial del Movimiento de Guipúzcoa, *Veinte años de Paz en el Movimiento Nacional bajo el Mando de Franco*, Guipúzcoa, Jefatura Provincial del Movimiento, 1959.

Jefatura Provincial del Movimiento de Logroño, *20 años de Paz en el Movimiento Nacional bajo el Mando de Franco*, Logroño, Jefatura Provincial del Movimiento, 1959.

Jefatura Provincial del Movimiento de Murcia, *Veinte años de Paz en el Movimiento Nacional bajo el Mando de Franco*, Murcia, Jefatura Provincial del Movimiento, 1959.

Jefatura Provincial del Movimiento de Salamanca, *Veinte años de Paz en el Movimiento Nacional bajo el Mando de Franco*, Salamanca, Jefatura Provincial del Movimiento, 1959.

Jefatura Provincial del Movimiento de Segovia, *Veinte años de Paz en el Movimiento Nacional bajo el Mando de Franco*, Segovia, Jefatura Provincial del Movimiento, 1959.

Jensen, Geoffrey, *Irrational Triumph: Cultural Despair, Military Nationalism, and the Ideological Origins of Franco's Spain*, Reno, University of Nevada Press, 2002.

Juliá, Santos (ed.), *Víctimas de la Guerra Civil*, Madrid, Temas de Hoy, 1999.

Keene, Judith, *Fighting for Franco: International Volunteers in Nationalist Spain During the Spanish Civil War, 1936–39*, London and New York, Leicester University Press, 2001.

Kowalsky, Daniel, "The Soviet Union and the International Brigades", *Journal of Slavic Military Studies*, 19 (2006): 681–704.

Kowalsky, Daniel, *Stalin and the Spanish Civil War*, New York, Columbia University Press, 2004.

La Paz, patrimonio del pueblo español. Significación del 1 de abril en la obra histórica de Franco, Madrid, Ediciones del Movimiento, 1974.

Launay, Alain with Dumont, Jean, *Franco: España y los españoles*, Madrid, Círculo de Amigos de la Historia, 1975.

Liedtke, Boris N., *Embracing a Dictatorship. US Relations with Spain, 1945–53*, London, Macmillan, 1998.

Little, Douglas, *Malevolent Neutrality: The United States, Great Britain and the Origins of the Spanish Civil War*, Ithaca, Cornell University Press, 1985.

López Barranco, Juan José, *El Rif en armas. La narrativa española sobre la guerra de Marruecos (1859–2005)*, Madrid, Marenostrum, 2006.

López Rodó, Laureano, *La larga marcha hacia la monarquía*, Barcelona, Noguer, 1977.

Los últimos días de Franco vistos en TVE, Madrid, TVE, 1975.

Losada Malvárez, Juan Carlos, *Ideología del ejército franquista, 1939–1959*, Madrid, Itsmo, 1990.

Lowe, Sid, *Catholicism, War and the Foundation of Francoism. The Juventud de Acción Popular in Spain, 1931–1939*, Brighton, Sussex Academic Press-Cañada Blanch, 2010.

McGarry, Fearghal, *Irish Politics and the Spanish Civil War*, Cork, Cork University Press, 1999.

Madariaga, Maria Rosa de, *Los moros que trajo Franco ... La intervención de tropas coloniales en la Guerra Civil española*, Barcelona, Martinez Roca, 2002.

Maíz, Félix, *Mola frente a Franco. Guerra y muerte del general Mola*, Pamplona, Laaconte, 2007.

Martin, Claude, *Franco. Soldado y estadista*, Madrid, Fermín Uriarte, 1965.

Martínez de Baños Carrillo, Fernando, *Fermín Galán Rodríguez. El capitán que sublevó Jaca*, Zaragoza, Editorial Delsan Libros, 2005.

Martínez de Campos y Serrano, Carlos, *España bélica. El siglo XX. Marruecos*, Madrid, Aguilar, 1972.

Matthews, Herbert L., "Franco's Problems", *Foreign Affairs*, 17, 4 (July 1939): 723–731.

Meléndez de Arvas, Cecilia, *¿Franco predestinado?*, Madrid, Gráficas Lux, 1975.

Micó España, Carlos, *Los caballeros de la Legión (El libro del Tercio de Extranjeros)*, Madrid, Sucesores de Rivadeneyra, 1922.

Miguel, Amando de, *Franco, Franco, Franco*, Madrid, Ediciones 99, 1976.

Millán Astray, General, *Franco El Caudillo*, Salamanca, M. Quero y Simón Editor, 1939.

Ministerio de Agricultura, Servicio Nacional del Trigo, Delegación Nacional, *Viaje por Castilla de S.E. el Jefe del Estado, Señor Don Francisco Franco Bahamonde ...* , Madrid, Ministerio de Agricultura, 1959.

Ministerio de Información y Turismo, *Concierto de la Paz. XXV Aniversario*, Madrid, Ministerio de Información y Turismo, 1964.

Ministerio de Información y Turismo, *España cumple veinticinco años de Paz*, Madrid, Edicolor, 1964.

Ministerio de Información y Turismo, *Justas Poéticas de la Paz*, Madrid, Ministerio de Información y Turismo, 1964.

Ministerio de Información y Turismo, *Nota informativa sobre el Valle de los Caídos*, Madrid, Ministerio de Información y Turismo, 1959.

Ministerio de la Gobernación, *Dictamen de la Comisión sobre ilegitimidad de poderes actuantes en 18 de Julio de 1936*, Madrid, Editora Nacional, 1939.

Moa, Pío, *Franco. Un balance histórico*, Barcelona, Planeta, 2005.

Moa, Pío, *Los orígenes de la Guerra Civil española*, Madrid, Encuentro, 1999.

Moradiellos, Enrique, *Francisco Franco: crónica de un caudillo casi olvidado*, Madrid, Bilioteca Nueva, 2002.

Moradiellos, Enrique, "The Origins of British Non-Intervention in the Spanish Civil War: Anglo-Spanish relations in early 1936", *European History Quarterly*, 21 (1991): 339–364.

Moradiellos, Enrique, *Revisión histórica crítica y pseudo-revisionismo político presentista: el caso de la Guerra Civil española*, Madrid, Seminario de Historia de la Fundación Ortega y Gasset, 2009.

Moral, Félix, *Opiniones y actitudes, 36, Veinticinco años después. La memoria del franquismo y de la transición en los españoles del año 2000*, Madrid, CIS, 2000.

Moreno Luzón, Javier (ed.), *Construir España: Nacionalismo español y procesos de nacionalización*, Madrid, Centro de Estudios Políticos y Constitucionales, 2007.

Moreno Nieto, Luis, *Franco y Toledo*, Toledo, Diputación Provincial, 1972.

Muñiz Vigo, Acisclo, *El Generalísimo Franco en la escuela española. Bosquejo biográfico.-Efemérides. Lecturas.-Miscelánea*, Oviedo, Editorial F.E.T., 1939.

Musa Redimida. Poesías de los presos en la Nueva España, Madrid, Editorial Redención, 1940.

Nerín, Gustau, *La Guerra que vino de Africa*, Barcelona, Crítica, 2005.

Nourry, Philippe, *Francisco Franco: la conquista del poder*, Madrid, Ediciones Júcar, 1976.

Núñez Florencio, Rafael, *Sol y Sangre: La imagen de España en el mundo*, Madrid, Espasa Calpe, 2001.

Ortega Campos, Pedro, *Dieciséis años del "Plan Jaén". Evaluación Social*, Jaén, Cámara de Comercio, 1973.

Ortega y Gasset, Eduardo, *Annual. Relato de un soldado e impresiones de un cronista*, Madrid, Ediciones del Viento, 2008. First edition 1922.

Osuna Servent, Arturo, *Frente a Abd-El-Krim (Antes de la tragedia.- En el momento de la tragedia- Las "escurriduras" de la tragedia)*, Madrid, Imprenta de Felipe Samarán, 1922.

Oteyza, Luis de, *Abd-el-Krim y los prisioneros. (Una información periodística en el campo enemigo)*, Melilla, Ciudad Autónoma de Melilla, 2000. First edition c.1922.

Overy, Richard, "Parting with Pacifism", *History Today*, 59, 8 (2009): 23–29.

Palacios, Jesús, *Las cartas de Franco. La correspondencia desconocida que marcó el destino de España*, Madrid, La Esfera de los Libros, 2005.

Payne, Stanley, "Recent Historiography on the Spanish Republic and Civil War", *Journal of Modern History*, 60, 3 (1988): 540–556.

Payne, Stanley G., *The Collapse of the Spanish Republic, 1931–1936: Origins of the Civil War*, New Haven-London, Yale University Press, 2006.

Payne, Stanley G., *Franco y José Antonio: el extraño caso del fascismo español: historia de la Falange y del Movimiento Nacional (1923–1977)*, Barcelona, Planeta, 1997.

Payne, Stanley, *Spain: A Unique History*, Madison, University of Wisconsin Press, 2011.

Pérez de Urbel, Fray Justo, *El Monumento de Santa Cruz del Valle de los Caídos*, Madrid, Instituto de Estudios Madrileños, 1959.

Pérez del Pulgar, José A., *La solución que España da al problema de sus presos políticos*, Librería Santarén, Valladolid, 1939.

Pike, David Wingate, *Franco and the Axis Stigma*, Houndmills, Palmgrave, 2008.

Pilar Amador, María, *Análisis de los discursos de Franco. Una aplicación metodológica*, Cáceres, Universidad de Extremadura, 1987.

Porte, Pablo La, *La atracción del Imán. El desastre de Annual y sus repercusiones en la política europea (1921–1923)*, Madrid, Biblioteca Nueva, 2001.

Preston, Paul, *The Coming of the Spanish Civil War: Reform, Reaction and Revolution in the Second Spanish Republic 1931–1936*, London, Routledge, 1994.

Preston, Paul, *El gran manipulador. La mentira cotidiana de Franco*, Barcelona, Ediciones B, 2008.

Preston, Paul, *Franco. A Biography*, London, HarperCollins, 1993.

Preston, Paul, *The Spanish Holocaust: Inquisition and Extermination in Twentieth-Century Spain*, London, HarperCollins, 2012.

Prieto, Indalecio, *Con el rey o contra el rey. Guerra de Marruecos*, Madrid, Planeta, 1990, 2 vols.

Quintana, L., *Franco. Al muchacho español*, Barcelona, Librería Religiosa, 1940.

Radcliff, Pamela B., *Making Democratic Citizens in Spain: Civil Society and the Popular Origins of the Transition, 1960–78*, New York, Palgrave Macmillan, 2011.

Ramírez, Luís [Luciano Rincón], *Francisco Franco: historia de un mesianismo*, París, Ruedo Ibérico, 1964.

Redondo, Gonzalo, *Política, cultura y sociedad en la España de Franco, 1939–1975. Tomo I; La configuración del Estado español, nacional y católico (1939–1947)*, Pamplona, Ediciones de la Universidad de Navarra, 1999.

Reig Tapia, Alberto, *Franco "Caudillo": Mito y realidad*, Madrid, Tecnos, 1995.

Reig Tapia, Alberto, *Franco: el César superlativo*, Madrid, Tecnos, 2005.

Reig Tapia, Alberto, *Memoria de la Guerra Civil. Los mitos de la tribu*, Madrid, Alianza, 1999.

Rey Reguillo, Fernando del (ed.), *Palabras como puños: la intransigencia política en la Segunda República Española*, Madrid, Tecnos, 2011.

Ribeiro de Meneses, Filipe, *Salazar: A Political Biography*, New York, Enigma Books, 2009.

Riera, Augusto, *Crónica de la Guerra de Marruecos –Julio 1921-Enero 1922-*, Barcelona, [J. Sanxo], [1922].

Río Cisneros, Agustín del, *España, rumbo a la post-guerra. La paz Española de Franco*, Madrid, Afrodisio Aguado, 1947.

Rodríguez Jiménez, José Luis, *Franco, historia de un conspirador*, Madrid, Oberón, 2005.

Rodríguez Martínez, Saturnino, *NO-DO: catecismo social de una época*, Madrid, Universidad Complutense, 1999.

Ros Andreu, Juan B., *La conquista de Alhucemas o en el Tercio está el amor (Escenas "crudas" de la famosa retirada de Xauen y del glorioso desembarco de las tropas españolas en Alhucemas)*, Las Palmas, Topográfica La Provincia, 1932.

Rubio Alfaro, Plácido and Lacalle Alfaro, Miguel, *Alhucemas, 1925. Desembarco, asentamiento y evolución*, Málaga, Imprenta Carvajal, 1999.

Ruiz, Julius, "A Spanish Genocide? Reflections on the Francoist Repression after the Spanish Civil War", *Contemporary European History*, 14, 2 (2005): 171–191.

Ruiz Albéniz, Víctor [El Tebib Arrumi], *Así empezó el Movimiento salvador*, Madrid, Ed. España, 1940.

Ruiz Albéniz, Víctor [El Tebib Arrumi], *Biblioteca Infantil. La reconquista de España. La Historia de El Caudillo Salvador de España*, Madrid, Ediciones España, 1939.

Ruiz Albéniz, Víctor [El Tebib Arrumi], *Héroes de España. Siluetas biográficas de las figuras más destacadas del Movimiento Salvador: El Caudillo. S.E.D. Francisco Franco Bahamonde. Generalísimo del Ejército y Jefe del Estado Español*, Ávila, Imprenta Católica, 1937.

Ruiz Albéniz, Víctor [El Tebib Arrumi], *Las responsabilidades del desastre. Ecce Homo. Prueba documental y aportes inéditos sobre las causas del derrumbamiento y consecuencias de él*, Madrid, Biblioteca Nueva, 1922.

Sada Anguera, Javier, *Franco en San Sebastián a través de la prensa guipuzcoana*, Donostia, Xertoa, 2009.

Sáenz de Heredia, José Luis and Sánchez-Silva, José María, *"Franco … ese hombre" (1892–1965)*, Madrid, Difusión Librera, 1964.

Salas López, Fernando de, *El desembarco del Alhucemas (8 de Septiembre, 1925)*, Madrid, Guión, 1949.

Sánchez-Biosca, Vicente (coord.), *Materiales para una iconografía de Francisco Franco. Archivos de la Filmoteca*, 42–42 (2002–2003), 2 vols.

Sánchez-Silva, José María, *Cartas a un niño sobre Francisco Franco*, Madrid, Foresa, 1966.

Santiago Guerrero, M., Troncoso, J.M., and Quintana, B., *La Columna Saro en la Campaña de Alhucemas*, Barcelona, Tipografía La Académica, 1926.

Santoja, Gonzalo, *De un ayer no tan lejano: cultura y propaganda en la España de Franco durante la guerra y los primeros años del Nuevo Estado*, Madrid, Noesis, 1996.

Serrano Sanz, José María and Asensio Castillo, María Jesús, "El ingenierismo cambiario: la peseta en los años del cambio múltiple, 1948–1959", *Revista de Historia Económica*, XV, 3 (1997): 545–573.

Sevillano Calero, Francisco, *Franco. Caudillo por la gracia de Dios*, Madrid, Alianza, 2010.

Shubert, Adrian, *The Road to Revolution in Spain. The Coal Miners of Asturias, 1860–1934*, Urbana and Chicago, University of Illinois Press, 1987.

Solé i Sabaté, J.M. and Villarroya, J., *La represió a la retaguardia de Catalunya, 1936–1939*, Montserrat, Abdía de Monsterrat, 1989–1990, 2 vols.

Thomas, Hugh, *La Guerra Civil Española*, Paris, Ruedo Ibérico, 1967.

Thomas, Maria, "The front line of Albion's perfidy. Inputs into the making of British policy towards Spain: The racism and snobbery of Norman King", *International Journal of Iberian Studies*, 20, 2 (2007): 105–127.

Togores, Luis E., *Millán Astray. Legionario*, Barcelona, Planeta, 2003.

Torrent, Martín, *¿Qué me dice usted de los presos?*, Talleres Penitenciarios, Alcalá de Henares, 1942.

Townson, Nigel (ed.), *Spain Transformed: the Franco Dictatorship, 1959–1975*, Houndmills, Palgrave-Macmillan, 2007.

Tranche, Rafael R. and Sánchez-Biosca, Vicente, *NO-DO. El Tiempo y la Memoria*, Madrid, Cátedra, 2000.

Trythall, J.W.D., *El Caudillo. A Political Biography of Franco*, New York, MacGraw-Hill, 1970.

Tusell, Javier, *Franco en la Guerra civil: una biografía política*, Barcelona, Tusquets, 1992.

Ucelay-da Cal, Enrique, "Ideas preconcebidas y estereotipos en las interpretaciones de la Guerra Civil Española: el dorso de la solidariad", *Historia Social*, 6 (1990): 23–46.

Ullman, Joan Connelly, *The Tragic Week: A Study of Anticlericalism in Spain, 1875–1912*, Cambridge, Harvard University Press, 1968.

Useros, Manuel, *El hombre en el paredón*, Valencia, Editorial Bello, 1957.

Vaca de Osma, José Antonio, *La Larga Guerra de Francisco Franco*, Madrid, Rialp, 1991.

Vázquez Montalbán, Manuel, *Autobiografía del general Franco*, Barcelona, Planeta, 1992.

Vázquez Montalbán, Manuel, *Los demonios familares de Franco*, Barcelona, Dopesa, 1978.

Veatch, Richard, "The League of Nations and the Spanish Civil War, 1936–39", *European History Quarterly*, 20 (1990): 181–207.

Viñas, Ángel, *La conspiración del general Franco y otras revelaciones acerca de una guerra civil desfigurada*, Barcelona, Crítica, 2001.

Viscarri, Dionisio, *Nacionalismo autoritario y orientalismo. La narrativa prefascista de la guerra de Marruecos (1921–1927)*, Bologna, Il Capitello del Sole, 2004.

Viver Pi-Sunyer, Carles, *El personal político de Franco (1936–1975)*, Barcelona, Vicens Vives, 1978.

Vizcaíno Casas, Fernando, ¡Viva Franco! (con perdón), Barcelona, Planeta, 1980.

Watkins, K. W., *Britain Divided. The Effect of the Spanish Civil War on British Political Opinion*, Westport, Greenwood, 1976.

Wigg, Richard, *Churchill and Spain. The Survival of the Franco Regime, 1940–1945*, Brighton, Sussex UP, 2008.

Wright, Richard, *Pagan Spain*, New York, John Hawkins and Assocciates, 1957.

Zenobi, Laura, *La construcción del mito de Franco. De jefe de la Legión a Caudillo de España*, Madrid, Cátedra, 2011.

Zurita, Victor, *En Tenerife planeó Franco el Movimiento nacionalista (Anécdotas y escenas de la estancia del Generalísimo en Canarias y su salida para Tetuán)*, Santa Cruz de Tenerife, Imprenta El Productor, 1937.

Index